SERIOUS Training
for Endurance Athletes

Second Edition

Rob Sleamaker, MS

Ray Browning, MS
Seven-Time Ironman Series Triathlon Champion

Human Kinetics

Library of Congress Cataloging-in-Publication Data

Sleamaker, Rob, 1957-
  Serious training for endurance athletes / Rob Sleamaker and Ray
  Browning. -- 2nd ed.
    p. cm.
  Rev. ed. of: Serious training for serious athletes. c1989.
  Includes bibliographical references and index.
  ISBN 0-87322-644-5
  1. Endurance sports--Training. 2. Endurance sports--Physiological
aspects. I. Browning, Ray, 1961- . II. Sleamaker, Rob, 1957- .
Serious training for serious athletes. III. Title.
GV749.5.S53   1996
613.7'1--dc20   96-6729
                                                                   CIP

ISBN: 0-87322-644-5

Developmental Editor: Julie Rhoda; **Assistant Editor:** Sandra Merz Bott; **Editorial Assistant:** Jennifer J. Hemphill; **Copyeditor:** Bob Replinger; **Proofreader:** Jim Burns; **Indexer:** Craig Brown; **Graphic Artist:** Julie Overholt; **Graphic Designer:** Robert Reuther; **Photo Editor:** Boyd LaFoon; **Cover Designer:** Jack Davis; **Photographer (cover):** D. Graham/H. Armstrong Roberts; **Photographers (interior):** John Kelly, Anne Krause, Tim DeFrisco, Jero Honda, and Chris Brown; **Illustrator:** Mick Greenberg; **Printer:** Versa Press

Human Kinetics books are available at special discounts for bulk purchase. Special editions or book excerpts can also be created to specification. For details, contact the Special Sales Manager at Human Kinetics.

Printed in the United States of America   10 9 8 7 6

Human Kinetics
Web site: www.humankinetics.com

United States: Human Kinetics, P.O. Box 5076, Champaign, IL 61825-5076
800-747-4457
e-mail: humank@hkusa.com

Canada: Human Kinetics, 475 Devonshire Road, Unit 100, Windsor, ON N8Y 2L5
800-465-7301 (in Canada only)
e-mail: orders@hkcanada.com

Europe: Human Kinetics, Units C2/C3 Wira Business Park, West Park Ring Road
Leeds LS16 6EB, United Kingdom
+44 (0) 113 278 1708
e-mail: hk@hkeurope.com

Australia: Human Kinetics, 57A Price Avenue, Lower Mitcham, South Australia 5062
08 8277 1555
e-mail: liahka@senet.com.au

New Zealand: Human Kinetics, P.O. Box 105-231, Auckland Central
09-523-3462
e-mail: hkp@ihug.co.nz

Contents

Acknowledgments

When I first wrote *SERIOUS Training for Serious Athletes* in 1988, I acknowledged the help and encouragement of many people. This new edition is so heavily based on the earlier book that I again want to thank all those people who played a significant role in my writing it.

Specifically, I will always be grateful to Peter Hoag and my colleagues from the U.S. Biathlon Team of 1983 through 1988—coaches, athletes, and sports medicine specialists. I also thank the dozens of scientists, physicians, coaches, and trainers throughout the world who generously shared their information, experiences, and ideas.

This new edition would not have been possible without the efforts and support of several key people, and I thank them: Paige Erikson for some great graphics; John Kelly and the folks at Pearl Izumi for the use of John's world-class photography; Julie Rhoda, our developmental editor, and the great people at Human Kinetics.

Special thanks go to a group of dear friends who have created countless adventures with me in sports and have provided much inspiration: Don Kelley, Murray Banks, Bud Symmes, Bill Gerlack, and Mike Soules. Guys, let's meet next weekend at Murray's! Thanks to Bill, we all remember to "look for the entertainment value in life."

Once again, Bud Symmes, thanks for your mentoring, support, great sense of direction, and friendship—they've been profound. Many thanks go to my close friends and family who have showered me with love and support as I have sought my path in life. My gratitude extends to the athletes I have had the honor and pleasure to work with throughout my career: I wish you all the best of success and fun through a lifetime of sports.

Finally, I give sincere thanks to Ray Browning, dear friend and colleague. If not for you, this book would lack the knowledge, wisdom, inspiration, and sense of adventure that could only come from a true professional. Thanks for reminding me to "just say yes" to life!

Rob Sleamaker

Thank you to Peter and Karen Weiler, Stuart Rugg, Greg Melitus, and Brad Williams, whose persistence and encouragement began my triathlon career. Thank you also to Robert Gregor and Jeff Broker for teaching me the value of good science and critical thinking. And a special thank you to Jeff Simons for helping me in my quest to become a master craftsman and in finding the answers to the "why's."

Thanks to all of the athletes whom I have had the opportunity to train and race with: You have given me the gifts of experience, inspiration, and wisdom. Thank you, Scott Tinley, for showing me the lighter side of competition; Scott Molina and Erin Baker, for showing me what hard work really is; Mark Allen, for showing me how to focus; Dave Scott, for saying "yes"; and Davis Phinney, for always being in the right place at the right time. A very special thank you to my dear friend and playmate, Collen Cannon—your joyful spirit is such a positive part of my life.

Much gratitude goes to all the corporations whose support has allowed me to pursue my passion, especially to Pearl Izumi Technical Wear, World Triathlon Corporation, Saucony, and Oakley. Thank you to those whose talents made this book a reality: Julie Rhoda, our developmental editor, for your unending patience and support; John Kelly and Annie Krause, for your outstanding photographic contributions; and all the people at Human Kinetics.

To Shannon Eastman, a sincere thank you for your love, support, encouragement, and advice. To my family and close friends, thanks for reminding me that I can make a positive impact on the quality of people's lives. And abiding thanks to my father, Cliff Browning, whose pursuit of his dreams and whose untimely death taught me to live the attitude of *carpe diem*.

Had it not been for Rob Sleamaker's foresight, I would not have been a part of this book. Thanks, Rob, for including me and giving me a channel for my energies. Your creative talents are an inspiration. Thank you for being such a great teacher and friend.

Ray Browning

Introduction

I awoke this morning determined to finally write this introduction, my last assignment to complete this book. I began organizing my notes, but within moments, an amazing sight outside the window distracted me. Next to my wood pile, two white ermines with tail tips of jet black frolicked and chased each other in the newly fallen powder snow. Observing their play, I almost unconsciously gulped my coffee. Rays of early morning sun reached through the forest and licked at my face. The first snow decent enough for skiing sparkled in the sunlight, casting tiny rainbow prisms. Elsie Bubba, my black Labrador, glowered at me, wanting to go out to her frosty playground. Even my skis seemed to quiver impatiently in the corner rack.

It was all too much to bear. Drawn by the magnetic force of the snow-covered ski trails, I promptly pushed aside my notes and redirected my energies. In a hurried rush, I dressed and was out the door, gliding along through virgin powder. All forms of guilt, remorse, and "I-should-bes" vanished. I rationalized that skiing would clear the cobwebs and be a proactive approach to beating writer's block. It was a chance to walk my talk.

My skis felt reliable and sure as they guided me effortlessly along trails like elegant ribbons laid down thoughtfully amongst stately pines and sturdy sugar maples. Those trails weave through forests and meadows that have become beloved friends. Often I gain a sense of place and a feeling of warm gratitude when I venture out to ski, run, bike, or walk along them.

This morning was no different. As I skied, a full, satisfying feeling welled up and began to circulate through my entire being. At once I was transformed back into a 10-year-old, giddy with feeling, like being granted leave from morning chores or given a lifetime supply of Swiss chocolate!

Eventually, my body settled into a gentle rhythm that harmonized with the terrain, snow, and forest. Time ceased to exist: I was totally in the moment, with no other place to go and no other way to be. The trail turned southward, directly into the bright morning sun. It flashed in my eyes and drenched my body full force with golden streamers. I continued to ski into the blinding light, guided only by an invisible thread that connected my body, mind, and soul to trail, trees, forest, earth—to the universe. It was as if I could ski into that light forever, never wanting for anything else.

Eventually, the trail led me out of the sunlight, the silence ended by a passing skier's greeting. Yet, the experience reminded me of one of my life missions: I want to show others that getting outdoors in sport activities creates the space for them to experience an integration and balance of mind, body, and spirit.

Sports can present fulfilling and life-enhancing opportunities for self-expression. The human body needs regular, vigorous physical activity not only for physical health but also for emotional and spiritual well-being. We live in a hectic, stressful, man-made environment of countless distractions and meaningless expenditures of our life energies. Sport and fitness activities can help keep life in perspective and open spaces in time for us to connect with our true inner voices.

My goal or hope is not to help you live longer, win races, beat an arch rival, or impress your friends. Rather, my one wish for you is that, through sports participation you discover new forms of self-expression and energy to rekindle the passion for play that I believe is innate in all of us. That passion can fill the heart with joy, transforming your moments, your days, and your life.

Someone recently asked, "Rob, what one piece of advice would you give a person who wants to maintain a high-level fitness for life?" My advice is to find at least one sport activity that you are passionate about doing, one that makes you feel lost in the moment and like a little kid at play. Find a sport that elicits uncontrollable smiles, fits of laughter, and childlike behavior. Undertake a relentless search for that activity and persist until you find at least one sport. Surround yourself with opportunities to do the sport(s) regularly. If you can't do it every day, then do other activities that will prepare your body to do your sport better and with more fun and enjoyment. These preparations might include cross-training with several sports, joining a health club or team, setting up a home gym, finding great training partners, hiring a personal trainer or coach, or reading books and articles that inspire and motivate you.

A key to maintaining high-level fitness for life is to be clear about how fit you want to be and what you want to be able to do with your fitness. Stay focused on those goals and the payback you'll get by staying fit enough to achieve them. My *specific* goals, such as what races or active vacations I want to pursue, change every year. One standard I've set for myself, however, is to maintain a level of fitness and athleticism that will allow me to comfortably do my favorite outdoor sports for at least five hours on any given day. I reason that I can cover much ground and also have a lot of fun with my pals. Another standard is to maintain the strength, speed, and agility to play sports like soccer, tennis, or ice hockey anytime I want. These fundamental goals or standards motivate me to maintain my fitness because they keep the paybacks in my view.

Ray Browning shares my vision and mission. I am honored that he accepted my invitation to coauthor this second edition. His experiences as a professional athlete, coach, and exercise physiologist provide the pages ahead with an exciting and fortifying dimension. Coincidentally, it was the first edition of *Serious Training For Serious Athletes* that brought us together six years ago. He contacted me, asking that I help plan and guide his training and racing. Since the first meeting, our relationship has undergone a few transformations. At first I was the coach, and he was the athlete. Next we both coached and taught at camps and clinics, while he continued as a successful professional athlete. Then we worked together, training athletes through our company, *SportsAdvantage*. I introduced Ray to cross-country ski racing (now he kicks my butt!), and he got me excited about multisport training with mountain bikes, snowshoes, and a "just-say-yes" attitude toward new sport adventures. All the while, we've built a strong and powerful friendship that provides laughter, intellectual stimulation, and sheer joy. I am grateful to Ray for his involvement with this project. Once you've read this book, I believe that you will be, too.

It has been written, "If you meet the Buddha on the road, kill him." I feel the same way about anyone who claims there is only one way to train and race. However, since I am a nonviolent person, I hope you will just keep an open mind to any advice you hear or read—in lieu of the alternative. Ray and I don't claim to know it all or have all the answers. On the contrary, we want the information we've provided in the following chapters to challenge you to create your own training regimen, using your experience, intuition, and vision in concert with ours.

GUIDELINES TO CONSIDER

We've found a few concepts to be guiding lights in our work with athletes and in our own sport endeavors. Although these words of wisdom are not original, we've seen how they can help athletes stay the course and achieve the results they are after. We encourage you to consider them as you read along and map out your own plan.

Train and race smarter, not harder. Personal success in sport results from an integration of training, experience, technique, nutrition, mental ability, and equipment. We've known many athletes who were misled by the myth "If some is good, more must be better." In fact, many of the world's best athletes learned about the myth the hard way—by experiencing overtraining and burnout. We regard training harder, *not* smarter, as hitting your head against a wall: It feels good when you stop! Unfortunately, many endurance athletes think that mega-training hours alone will give them the results they need.

We adhere to the work-smarter philosophy of training and racing. This is not to say you won't have challenging training sessions. Indeed, you'll have many. However, they will be part of a thorough, well-conceived plan based on systematic progressions that challenge your body's physiology and mental ability to adapt and grow gradually stronger.

Every training session should have purpose. Working smarter affords you maximal benefit from your training sessions and the ability to tune into your body's inner wisdom.

Plan your play, play your plan. In business, failure to create a sensible business plan very often leads to failure. The same can be said for sports training. Failing to plan your training and racing program can undermine your potential results. Some athletes start with a solid plan only to jump ship midseason and choose another plan or abandon a plan altogether. We've seen athletes choke in the big events or get overtrained, sick, injured, frustrated, unhappy, and burned out—all attributable to their failure to create and follow a sensible plan.

Careful planning need not be a chore. It's an incredible opportunity to create whatever you want and to maximize your enjoyment in sports. Remember, everyone follows a plan. It's just that some do their homework and others make up their plan five minutes before running out the door! Usually people with the solid plans are the ones who have clear directions. It's as if they have a good road map—they get to their destinations more easily and with fewer frustrations and pit stops to ask for directions.

Discover the entertainment value in every training session and race. Once I asked my friend Bill Gerlack to tell me his secret of life. His reply was so simple that it shocked me. He said that he looks for the entertainment value in everything he does, including work, marriage, community affairs, and fitness. In an instant I understood why he has a smile on his face and a lighthearted attitude most of the time. Remember that around every corner, down a new trail, or over the next hill awaits the possibility for greater entertainment! Challenge yourself to keep an open mind, look for new adventures in training, and "just say yes" to new and exciting experiences.

Set goals not as expectations but as possibilities. Anytime you set goals with strong expectations, you also risk disappointment if you don't achieve the desired result. If you view goals as possibilities, however, they remain possibilities regardless of the result. You will automatically use your creativity to overcome the obstacle, rather than be defeated. It's like stepping back from a locked door only to discover an open window!

SERIOUS TRAINING: THE ACRONYM DEFINED

In the first edition of *SERIOUS Training For Serious Athletes*, I used the acronym S.E.R.I.O.U.S. to convey the seven essential components of successful systematic training plans for endurance sports. This system can be a useful teaching tool and method for standardizing training with regard to purpose and physiological effect. The acronym stands for

Speed training and drills,
Endurance/easy distance,
Race/pace training,
Intervals,
Overdistance/long, slow distance,
Uphill intervals/vertical training, and
Strength/resistance training.

Each component has an ideal intensity range, frequency, duration, and technical aspect within the overall training plan. For example, the off-season is a good time to build endurance and strength. Therefore, the total time you spend conditioning each week would consist of a high percentage of Endurance and Overdistance, interspersed with three sessions of Strength training and one or two short, low-intensity Speed drills. The makeup of the training shifts to include more of the other SERIOUS components as the competition season is near.

HOW TO USE THIS BOOK

We've written the book so you may use the information in each chapter independently or utilize the entire book to create a complete training system. Either way, we believe that reading every chapter will give you the best foundation for creating your own winning training plan. Through chapters 1 and 2, you can determine your objectives and gain an understanding of systematic training that will help you achieve those objectives. You'll learn the whys and whens to shape your body's physiology for endurance sports. Chapter 2 provides specifics for determining correct training intensity zones and using heart monitors. Chapter 3 outlines in detail how to create a day-by-day training program. Be prepared to use a pencil, paper, and calculator (or a computer spreadsheet program)! In chapter 4 you'll learn how to do each SERIOUS training component specifically for your sport: Ray is a master at doing fun, creative workouts, and you'll benefit from his vast experience.

In chapter 5, you'll discover the best methods for warming up, cooling down, and gaining flexibility—all key ingredients to preventing injury and maximizing performance. Chapter 6 is a practical guide to nutrition and fluid intake for training and performance. We adhere to a no-nonsense approach! Chapters 7, 8, and 9 provide methods for recovering from and managing the stress of daily training, as well as for tracking your efforts with an effective log and journal.

Chapter 10 gives an insider's view to optimizing training for racing, with techniques for tapering, race preparation, and postrace recovery. Finally, in chapter 11 you'll learn how to stay motivated to train and race. We explain how motivation works and provide some mental conditioning techniques that can truly give you an edge.

Each chapter (except chapter 7) concludes with a section called, "From Experience." Ray has interviewed elite athletes and experts in several sports who provide practical, sage, and entertaining advice. We hope you find this addition useful and fun to read.

REACHING YOUR POTENTIAL

The first edition, which was translated into several languages, has been used by athletes and coaches of all abilities from points around the world. It has been an honor and pleasure to talk with people who have benefited from reading the book. At the 1995 Ironman Triathlon in Hawaii I met the national team coaches from Germany and was delighted to learn that they used the first edition of the book to train their elite athletes. However, what means the most to us is that all readers, in some way, are using this book to reach for their own potential. Sport can be a beautiful form of self-expression, with a tremendous potential for learning about oneself. Training and racing can provide metaphors for living, as long as we take time to listen and notice. We wish you many hours of enjoyment in sports—and may you always find happy trails!

Determining Your Training and Competition Needs

It has been our experience, as athletes for over 20 years and from training and racing as well as coaching and advising thousands of athletes for the past 16 years, that there are as many paths to athletic success as there are participants. Of course, what makes each path unique is the athlete and a multitude of variables converging to allow the athlete to perform to his or her potential. There is not a "one and only one way" that will guarantee your success. Don't believe anyone who tells you that following his or her method is the only way to achieve success. We have found, however, that there are fundamental tenets of successful training. The secrets of athletic success are revealed as a synergy of these tenets and the athlete's experiences combined with time and practice.

Let's use the analogy that planning a training program is like preparing a pot of homemade chili to enter in the annual chili cook-off at the county fair. There are any number of combinations of ingredients one could use in making the recipe. Each time you taste a new batch you've created, it would be ideal to

1

know how much of each ingredient you used, how long you let it simmer, and so on. This would certainly help you make informed decisions about changing the recipe next time. However, like many wanna-be chili champions, most people just add a bit of this and a pinch of that, and the chili comes out tasting good sometimes and terrible other times.

Like chili chefs, nearly every athlete and coach follows some kind of recipe for training and competition. Many just add a bit of this and a pinch of that, with little regard for long-term success or reproducible results. Many recreational athletes strictly adhere to the "UDU IDU" training program; loosely translated that means "I'm doing whatever you're doing today," even if it means that the athlete chooses the day's training session five minutes before running out the door. Of course, this approach may get you fit, but will it deliver your best potential and the most satisfaction and fun?

There are pros and cons to every method of training. After studying numerous approaches to training, and developing and implementing our systems, we believe that some methods are more effective in producing desired results, can more easily track progress and spot potential setbacks, and are more enjoyable to use on a daily basis. We're referring to the SERIOUS systematic method of training mentioned in the introduction to this book. SERIOUS is the acronym used to describe the seven types of training (more details later). It's a useful way of sorting through all the information about training, putting it in a logical, step-by-step plan, and ultimately discovering the recipe that works best for you.

Regardless of the path we take when planning training programs or the objectives we've made for ourselves, the planning process will ultimately be the basis that determines our success in achieving our objectives (fig. 1.1). To borrow a favorite expression from successful athlete-businessman John Schweizer, "Plan your play, play your plan."

Training may be regarded as a tool that when used correctly elicits specific physiological and psychological responses. Endurance athletes, in contrast to team sport athletes, need individualized training plans to meet specific goals within the general guidelines for success in a given sport. The object is to improve the body's ability to supply oxygen and energy to the muscles, increase energy reserves, strengthen the sport-specific muscles, remove metabolic waste from the muscle tissues, and become more efficient in the specific neuromuscular functions required for the

Fig. 1.1. A training plan is like a map. It's a good idea to discuss your planned route with someone who has "been there."

sport. Systematic planning provides an effective, objective method to incorporate a wealth of personal experiences, scientific research findings, current coaching practices, and innovative ideas into a thorough, structured plan. Once such a plan is created, the athlete knows in advance what is to be accomplished in any given week. This allows for planning logistics and flexibility to incorporate one's training into the other aspects of life, like work, family, social, and civic commitments.

It is important to maintain accurate training logs and journals to compare actual training with the plan. This allows the athlete to monitor progress, track recovery signals, and adjust for special needs along the way. Planning the next competitive cycle becomes easier and more accurate. Changes from month to month and year to year can be made with informed reference to the original plan, with those components that worked well and those that need improvement. A systematic plan may cover a full year or simply one competitive cycle between 12 and 24 weeks.

CONSIDER YOUR OBJECTIVES

To be effective at any task, it is essential to be very clear why we are going to do it. This applies to planning a training program. If you are not sure why you want to train and race, it becomes difficult to make a plan that will deliver the physical and mental readiness required to reach personal potential. Perhaps as important, knowing why we undertake formidable tasks helps us stay motivated during the inevitable low moods that we will encounter during the process.

We encourage you to establish clarity about your goals and objectives for fitness, health, training, and racing. Depending on your sport and level of commitment, the objectives of your plan may be to prepare you for your first sprint triathlon in six months or to prepare you to contend at the world championships or Olympics four years in the future.

Consider that there are goals that have a specific outcome, such as winning or placing in a specific race, and goals that do not have a specific outcome, like improving your swim technique or increasing leg strength. It's likely that you'll have both types of goals. We find it helpful to put less emphasis on the outcome goals, because there are so many variables that will affect your place on the results sheet. Besides the finite outcome goals, be sure to pay much attention to the nonoutcome goals (fig. 1.2). There is an old saying, "You walk a mile one step at a time." The message applies to training and racing; complete each aspect of the workout or race to your best ability, and the result will take care of itself.

Chapter 3 will help you outline the objectives of a long-term plan and learn the fundamental structure for creating a systematic training plan in a worksheet format.

While most of the material in this book pertains to the physical preparation of the body for competition, you will discover that following a thorough, systematic training plan will allow you to use every training session to make small, but cumulative, improvements in nutrition, technique, mental skills, and equipment. Regard the physical preparation as the main ingredients in your chili recipe. These other avenues are the spices that make a winning pot of chili.

OVERVIEW OF THE TRAINING YEAR

In systematic training, we consider the year a series of 52 training weeks in which every week is related to the others. There are 13 four-week cycles comprising the 52-week year. The type of training that you plan for each of these cycles depends on the number of competitive seasons or sports for which you will need to prepare. For example, most triathletes in North America plan to compete

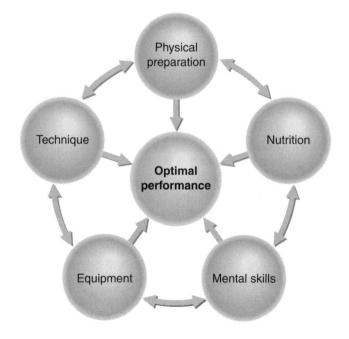

Fig. 1.2. Include physical preparation as well as proper technique, equipment, mental skills, and nutrition in your recipe for optimal performance.

between May and October. Cross-country ski racers typically compete from November through April. Cyclists may compete from April until November, depending on locale.

At the elite level, most athletes carefully choose the races that are most important to their goals, and many will refrain from racing in other sports at a serious competitive level during the off-season months. This allows their mind and body some down-time that affords maximal recovery and a gradual base-building period for the next competition period. Recently, however, some multisport athletes, like seven-time Ironman champion Ray Browning and former pro cyclist Davis Phinney, have mastered cross-country skiing and successfully compete at the elite level. At the 1995 American Birkebeiner, the largest cross-country ski race in the U.S., Ray placed 11th, only seconds behind the leaders. This was quite an accomplishment considering Ray had learned to ski only four years earlier and was competing against world-class contenders who had been skiing over 20 years!

In comparison, nonprofessional athletes may compete success-fully in several sports throughout the year, using their fitness level and cross-training benefits to provide maximum sport en-joyment. Once you've identified your goals and objectives, you'll be on your way to planning the training route that will prepare you best. Regardless of how often and in which sports you wish to compete, you can plan each week of the training year according to available training time and facilities to prepare you effectively for meeting your goals.

FIVE TRAINING STAGES

Ideally, preparation for competitive endurance sports includes five stages for each competition season: *base, intensity, peak, racing,* and *recovery.* The number of weeks given each stage depends on the number of competitive seasons planned per year, your experience, and your physical condition. Figure 1.3 illus-trates the five training stages for an athlete participating in one competition season per year. In planning, it is helpful to consider actual dates for competitions, training camps, clinics, and any medical or physiological testing desired during the year.

We have chosen to segment the systematic training plan into five stages for each competitive season for several reasons. First, there are essential physiological developments that take place

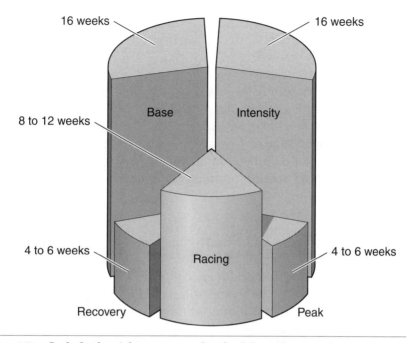

16 weeks

16 weeks

8 to 12 weeks

Base

Intensity

4 to 6 weeks

Racing

4 to 6 weeks

Recovery

Peak

Fig. 1.3. Include the right amounts of each of these five training stages in your training plan.

by stages in a progressive fashion during the weeks and months preceding competition. Second, the recipe of each stage changes in total training time, intensity, and SERIOUS components. Third, the systematic approach allows you to project precisely the percentage of total time you'll spend in each mode of training, thus allowing you to measure what you actually complete. Finally, by thinking in terms of progressive stages, the athlete is able to stay motivated toward building a foundation of strength and endurance that will support much more difficult training and competition later in the plan. This helps to keep his or her sights on long-term goals instead of prematurely reaching a plateau that is lower than the athlete's potential. The concept of using five training stages applies well if you are planning one or two competitive seasons per year, such as a six-month buildup toward certain events. However, if you are planning a shorter training season leading up to a competition phase, adapt the concept of using five stages and apply this to your plans. Chapter 3 will provide more on specific planning.

Each stage represents distinct physiological, neuromuscular, and psychological developmental phases necessary for system-

atically developing your conditioning. The graph in figure 1.4 illustrates the characteristics of each stage with percentages of
each training component. Ideally, there will be a subtle distinc-
tion between successive stages as training volume and emphasis
change appropriately from one training cycle to the next.

The following is a summary of the five stages of training. Understanding them will help you decide the necessary training components for each stage of your plan. Using the terminology we've
presented will build your training vocabulary and help you orga-
nize your thoughts about planning your winning training program.

Base

The primary objective during the base stage is to construct an
intricate and effective aerobic foundation and "plumbing system."
Doing overdistance and endurance training a high percentage of
the time will create the system foundation. When constructed
carefully, the aerobic plumbing system—the cardiovascular system and lung capacity—will be able to support high-intensity
training and racing that will occur in later stages of your plan. The
base stage also emphasizes muscular strength, developed through
weight lifting or resistance training, both nonspecific and sport
specific. High-intensity training, such as race/pace, intervals,
uphill intervals, and speed, will represent only a small portion of
the total training done during this stage. Gradually, during the
next stages, a greater proportion of the program is devoted to the
high-intensity components.

Aerobic Conditioning

The primary reasons for establishing a sound aerobic base during
this stage are related to the body's energy and oxygen transport
mechanisms. To build a strong oxygen transport system that can
support high-level aerobic exercise, we recommend that a high
percentage (60 to 70 percent) of the total training volume (hours
of exercise per week) during the base stage be devoted to
overdistance and endurance/easy distance training, which will be
described in detail in chapter 4. To produce optimal training
effect, do this exercise at relatively low intensity. Koivisto, Hendler,
and Nadel (1982) demonstrated that improvements in fat oxidation occur with regular training at intensities of 55 percent to 60
percent of $\dot{V}O^2$max. Training at this intensity and duration also
improves the muscles' blood capillary density and mitochondrion

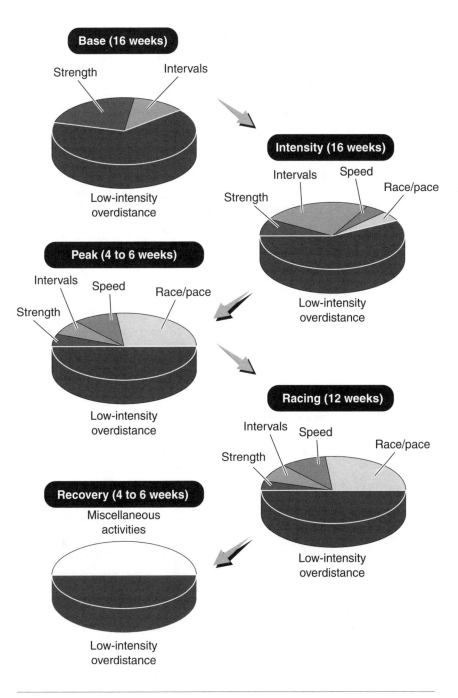

Fig. 1.4. Each of the five training stages can be further broken into the SERIOUS training components.

numbers and efficiency, all of which contribute to improved oxygen transport and energy use at the cellular level. Chapter 2 will describe these adaptations in detail.

Strength Conditioning

The base stage emphasizes strength training for improving general muscle strength as well as sport-specific strength. The important reasons for strength training during the base stage are to increase the force per contraction of the primary movers that propel the body during a race and to strengthen the musculoskeletal system sufficiently to prevent injury, either from chronic use or from an acute trauma, such as a fall or crash. What must be determined is the amount and type of strength training to be employed in the overall plan.

As the muscles are placed under sufficient loads during strength training, they adapt or accommodate to the loads and grow stronger, as long as this is followed by 24 to 48 hours of no strength training. Only after adaptation has occurred may the loads be increased. Typically, muscles improve in strength when placed under loads of greater than two-thirds of maximum strength and repeated in sets in which the muscles fatigue in fewer than 25 repetitions per set.

There are many methods for increasing strength. Sport-specific strength-training machines like the Vasa Trainer, or weight machines, free weights, calisthenics, plyometrics, and rubber tubing all work well when used correctly (fig. 1.5). In general, most strength exercises should simulate the motions used in competition, thereby strengthening sport-specific muscles and connective tissue. During the base stage, however, it is less critical to be completely sport-specific in strength exercises. The physiological details of strength training are discussed in chapter 2. Actual strength workouts and recommendations for each sport are outlined in chapter 4. Please refer to these for specific guidance in doing sport-specific strength routines. During the base stage, approximately 10 percent to 20 percent of total training time will be devoted to strength exercises, depending on your goals, areas that need improvement, and abilities.

Intensity

One of the most important goals of any competitor training program is to improve the body's ability to sustain high-intensity

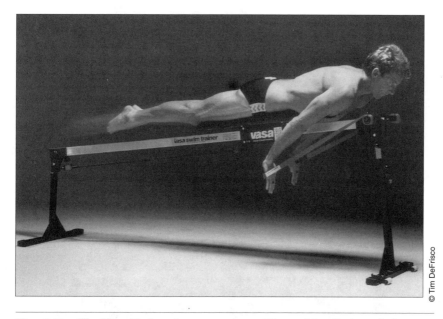

© Tim DeFrisco

Fig. 1.5. The Vasa Trainer is one sport-specific machine that can help you increase your strength. Ironman legend Dave Scott demonstrates good form.

effort for longer periods of time. Therefore, our training plan recipe must change a bit, with the addition of some new ingredients, such as higher intensity interval, speed, and race/pace exercises. The intensity stage increases overall training stress by increasing exercise volume (hours) and intensity. The amount of these higher intensity components must be increased gradually throughout this stage so the body can adapt adequately. We recommend that a high percentage of this stage's total training volume (50 to 60 percent) still be planned as low-intensity aerobic training. Overdistance and endurance/easy distance exercise will maintain the aerobic base established during previous weeks. Below and in figure 1.6 is a brief summary of these training components, which will be discussed in greater detail in chapter 4.

Speed training increases efficiency by teaching the body to learn about pace and to coordinate movement patterns. Intervals on flat and hilly terrain improve the ability of your heart and lungs to transport oxygen and blood, and to use heart rate, pace, and perceived exertion to develop a subjective sense of anaerobic threshold and racing intensity (described in detail in chapter 2). As the stage progresses, designated race/pace workouts, such as time trials and early season races, will be introduced to the pro-

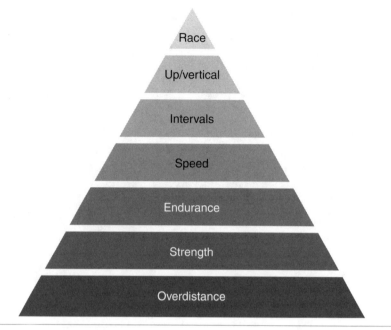

Fig. 1.6.   The SERIOUS training pyramid relies on a solid overdistance base.

gram. These will provide benchmarks for measuring progress and for working out any technical and psychological bugs well before the competition season arrives.

The important factor in workouts during the intensity stage is that you carefully control your efforts with respect to your level of fitness. It's best to do these workouts staying under control with heart rate intensity, as well as psychological and emotional investment. Too much high-intensity racing early in the season may lead to premature peaking or burnout. Race simulations, doing a designated course and simulating a real race, can be incredible confidence builders and learning sessions. Establishing a specific purpose for every race or pace workout during this stage, such as trying a new energy drink, using a specific warm-up routine, or testing a different position on your bike, will enhance the learning and preparation for the upcoming competition season. Early races can be useful learning experiences if approached with a productive attitude.

Peak

Many coaches and athletes refer to tapering as peaking or sharpening—the terms are synonymous. The main purpose for the peak stage is to get ready for "show time." You'll want to arrive at the competition stage race ready, with all the kinks and bugs worked out of your system. This stage is characterized by a decrease in training volume from the intensity stage. However, the intensity of certain training components, such as speed, intervals, and race/pace workouts, will typically be very high to refine technique and energy systems at race speeds. This is a good time to enter races or do some race simulations on your own or with friends. We still recommend that 40 to 60 percent of the training volume be low-intensity aerobic training. Overdistance and endurance/easy distance activities will maintain the aerobic base and create easy days between high-intensity efforts, thus encouraging full recovery. The taper stage is a great time to emphasize restoration and recovery from training so that the body may become fully rested and energy stores completely replenished before intense competition. Restoration will be discussed in detail in chapter 7.

Racing

Ideally, the previous three stages of your plan will have been productive and you will be in optimal racing condition at this stage. Depending on you and the design of your training plan, peak racing form and top racing will last between 8 and 20 or more weeks. Some sports, such as cycling, may involve slightly longer competition stages, which you must consider in the overall plan. We recommend that a fairly stable training volume be maintained throughout this stage and that about 40 to 50 percent of the total training time be overdistance or endurance/easy distance to maintain the aerobic base and provide active recovery training. Intervals, speed, and racing will constitute the remaining time. Frequent racing can be very demanding physiologically and mentally. Coupled with the stress of travel, change of diet, and psychological adjustment, racing a lot may wear you down. Restoration methods, such as massage, relaxation, proper nutrition and hydration, and consistent rest, are as important as each training session during this stage. (See chapter 7 for specific guidelines on proper recovery methods.)

Recovery

Many weeks of training and racing will leave even the most experienced athlete weary, a bit stale, and unmotivated. This is why we advocate a two-to-four-week period of active recovery between seasons. Just as the farmer's field must lie fallow every winter, so does the human body, mind, and spirit need a rest, with time to reflect, recover, and rejuvenate. This stage is characterized by a reduced training volume, low-intensity exercise, and alternative activities. While you may want to keep doing some unstructured exercise in your primary sport activities, we recommend alternative exercises or sports, done in a variety of terrain or conditions. Break your routine, use different routes, tackle the jungle gym with your kids at the playground, try a mountain bike, dust off the tennis racquet, jump into a pickup soccer game. You get the idea. The key to all exercise in this stage is that it be less structured and have variety.

TRAINING SESSION

The next steps for completing the training plan involve the selection of the activity and intensity level for each training session. Consider the following variables:

• Your training philosophy. Systematic training allows you the opportunity to be creative within a framework. This accommodates your personal philosophy and ideas about the overall and specific aspects of the plan. You may choose to follow your plan exactly or use it as a general guideline for your training.

• Your experiences, including successes and mistakes. For example, if you have had good results using a certain strength routine with key exercises, then this will play an important role in determining what strength workouts to schedule into the plan.

• Training facilities that are available. You might not have easy access to optimal sport-specific strength-training equipment and, therefore, may need to improvise. Weather may prohibit you from taking a long bike ride, so using the stationary bike at the local health club may be your best solution.

• Injuries or handicaps. These may dictate the activity you should use for a given training session. A runner with a strained hamstring muscle would be well advised to train in the water, using a flotation vest designed for water running. A swimmer with an ear infection can use the Vasa Swim Ergometer as a sport-specific alternative.

• Your present state of mind (attitude, stress levels, etc.). Using a variety of activities can help prevent boredom and psychological burnout during training. For example, after a particularly difficult week of training, go for a mountain bike ride, swim in a scenic lake instead of going to the masters workout, go for a hike, or strap on the backcountry skis and tour a new area. You'll prevent mental burnout if you plan more variety and fun diversions.

• Your level of recovery from previous workouts. Another consideration in planning each workout is your level of recovery from previous training sessions. Occasionally it may be necessary to plan a non-sport-specific activity between two hard sport-specific sessions to encourage full recovery. Multisport athletes, like triathletes, have already discovered this benefit.

• The specificity and technical requirements for the training session. The need for specificity of training for a sport must be reflected by the workouts. A cross-country skier may need to use roller skis and trail running with poles for summer workouts. It is best to designate a specific activity or type of movement for each workout; you should record deviations from the original plan for future reference and study.

There are many ways to accomplish a training objective, and therein lies the opportunity to be creative and to use new information. Remember, your training plan is a recipe. You need to know which ingredients you put into the pot before you can improve the recipe next time.

PUTTING IT TOGETHER

It is necessary to view the training year with goals and objectives such as performance, physical preparation, technical preparation, tactics, psychological preparation, and any tests or standards. The steps outlined in this chapter will serve as the fundamental structure for any systematic training plan you might wish to create. The chapters that follow will help you fill in the gaps by presenting information regarding physiological principles and ways to monitor the training plans you have created. Chapter 3 uses a workbook approach so that you can design your training plans using these guidelines.

FROM EXPERIENCE

RAY BROWNING, MS

The importance of setting clear objectives and goals cannot be overstated, since this provides your overall direction for the program. I always begin by asking myself "what do I want to achieve with this part of my lifestyle?" It is difficult to be motivated to do something I really don't want to do, so I plan my training objectives and goals with this in mind.

If you're not sure about setting realistic goals, begin by looking at how much time you have available. Most athletes with a full-time commitment to work, family, and other duties will have between 6 and 12 hours per week (300 to 600 hours per year) available to train. This volume is adequate for most endurance activities but may not be enough for you to race well in an Ironman. Establishing a realistic training volume will help you set obtainable goals.

Put faith in the training program you develop. Adhering to the concepts outlined in this book will put you on the right course. In 1994, my second year as a competitive cross-country skier, I did six weeks of base skiing, followed by four weeks of intensity training, and then began to race. I got faster in every race for eight weeks! This progress was so motivating that I couldn't wait until the weekends so I could race again.

Many of you, like me, will be competing in long seasons of up to six months. It is unrealistic to try to maintain top form for 24 weeks, since a peak during a season will typically last between 6 and 12 weeks. If your season is longer than 12 weeks, there are two options to consider: (1) Plan your early races in the intensity and taper stages of the year, but remember to refrain from all-out racing efforts. If you know you won't be able to control yourself on the race course, avoid doing many early races so that you can adequately prepare for your most important races. (2) If your early season races are important qualifier events, you can split the season into two shorter seasons and plan to rebuild in midseason for your later races. This will mean putting less importance on or avoiding midseason races. I have tried both approaches and found them to be equally effective. Since I have started ski racing in the winter, I don't race early in the summer triathlon season. This allows me to prepare adequately for the later races in the triathlon season, such as the Ironman.

Foundations of Systematic Training

*L*ife was so simple in the '70s. Concepts of heart rate, anaerobic threshold, perceived exertion, pace, and intervals were about as unfamiliar to us as life on other planets. As cross-country ski racers, my high school team buddies and I did a lot more playing than training. I don't mean to imply that we were lazy. On the contrary, our "play" consisted of many games and challenges on our skis. One of our favorites was ski jumping on a hill in my family's back pasture, using our skinny racing skis. We would spend hours shoveling snow to build up the jump and hauling water from a brook in a sprinkler can so we could create an icy glaze over the runway tracks. Once the tracks were set, we'd put on our skis and take off down the runway. Score was carefully judged by distance, style, and landing without falling or breaking the skis. In the waning light of a December afternoon in New England, we were forced to be expeditious if we wanted to get in much jumping. So up and down that hill we would ski until dusk turned to night and our tongues dragged from delighted exhaustion. It never occurred to us that we were actually "training" during these winter romps. We were just boys doing what we knew best—having fun!

Now that I've studied the science of exercise physiology, I understand that the boyhood ski-jumping escapades were nothing but high-intensity hill intervals as we climbed the slope after each jump. Our "recovery" took place while gliding down the icy tracks of the runway. It's no wonder our team eventually won the state championships. We knew how to ski fast up the hills—and smiling to boot!

I've since learned that an essential ingredient of the systematic approach to training is intensity. Every training session has a distinct physiological purpose, and the intensity and duration of each will determine the conditioning benefit. If you want to get optimal training effect, you must exercise at the right intensity level for each type of training. This allows you to control precisely the physiological stress of each workout in the entire training plan. Accurate monitoring of intensity, coupled with workout duration and purpose, creates the foundation of systematic training.—Rob

In this chapter we describe the basic principles of training and the following components of intensity with the systematic approach:

- Physiology of intensity
- Intensity level for each SERIOUS component
- How to measure intensity levels
- Determining the right intensity levels for you

PRINCIPLES OF TRAINING

Systematic training is most effective if key physiological principles are understood and followed. Chapter 1 outlined the basic structure of a systematic training plan. The following will help you understand the relationship of several key factors used when considering the overall plan.

Overload

One of the fundamental purposes of training for endurance sports is to give the body a tough workout followed by just the right amount of rest. Theoretically, you'll get stronger and more fit. Without an overload, there is little stimulation for your body to improve its ability to handle higher levels of training stress. Or, as Kenny Souza, world champion duathlete, would say: "You gotta break it down and build it up." Using our chili analogy, it would be like bringing the pot to a vigorous boil and then turning down the flame, covering the pot and letting it simmer and mellow for a while, allowing all the seasonings to do their magic.

Endurance, power, and strength will improve if an appropriate load imposes a demand on the body's systems. As the body adapts to training, usually with the correct mix of stress and rest, an increased workload stimulates further improvements in conditioning. This relates to the gradual increases in time and intensity throughout the base and intensity stages, which are intended to impose enough demand on the body to stimulate growth. Endurance overload will allow the energy systems and the oxygen transport systems to adapt. The contractile proteins in muscles will increase if there is a strength overload.

Adaptation

Ten years ago at a sports medicine conference, Frank Shorter was discussing his "two-week, two-month" rule. The essence of his message was that when you make a significant change in your training, be it an increase in hours, mileage, intensity, or altitude, you can count on it taking your mind and body two weeks to adjust to the new stress, but about two months before you fully adapt to the changes. Since then, we've put that theory to the test with athletes we coach and with our own training. All the evidence we've accumulated shows that Shorter's observation is astute and full of wisdom that applies well beyond athletics.

Physiologically, stressing the body in training will bring subtle changes as the body adjusts and finally adapts to these imposed demands. Improved circulation, respiratory function, and heart function; increased muscle endurance, strength, and power; and sturdier connective tissue, tendons, ligaments, and bones are all part of the body's adaptation to appropriate training stress. Athletes who train too much or too fast too soon are likely candidates for illness or injury, having overstressed the body so it could not adapt. Psychologically, an adjustment and adaptation process also happens with an increase in training loads. If the fitness plan is just right, one's confidence, attitude, and motivation may ebb and flow, but the overall trend will be steady growth toward greater success.

Progression and Periodization

I remember my first tastes of authentic salsa when I was in graduate school in Tucson, Arizona. The first few times I tasted the hot stuff, it made me guzzle lots of water and reach for the Pepto Bismol. I learned that it was easier to start out with the mild salsa and gradually try spicier versions until my taste for the three-alarm salsa came around. It was a reasonably sane and safe progression.—Rob

The endurance athlete's body will adapt well to increasing training overloads only if there is a proper progression. We recommend considering several factors when formulating the correct progression for a training plan. These include the weekly pattern, the number of sessions per week, the percentage of the total year's training volume used in each four-week cycle, the stage of the competitive season, the percentage of low- versus high-intensity training each week, and the periodization pattern for a given training cycle (fig. 2.1). Each of these factors will influence the body's ability to adapt.

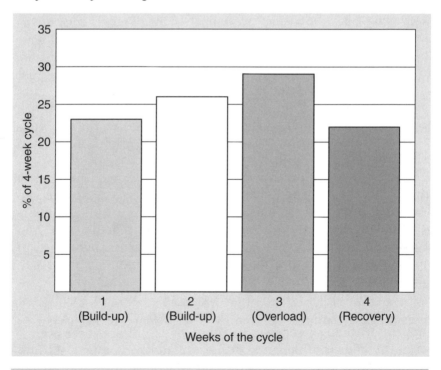

Fig. 2.1. A periodization pattern of buildup, overload, and recovery during a 4-week training cycle.

The progression from week to week and cycle to cycle needs not be a steady increase in training time and intensity. A periodization pattern for each training cycle should allow a staircase progression that overloads the body for the first three weeks, followed by a week of decreased training volume and intensity. In a taper for a race, the periodization pattern for the four-week training cycle could be a descending staircase, with the first week of the cycle providing the most stress and the fourth week having the least volume and intensity, thus allowing the body to rest up fully for a race at the end of the cycle.

A progression in training volume and intensity should take place from cycle to cycle, thereby gradually overloading the system. Using progression, rather than an excessively aggressive approach, means taking a bit more time to gradually build up conditioning but is easier on the body.

If you're an athlete with a limited or fixed training time per week, you will need to modify the periodization patterns within a four-week training cycle. You might end up training the same amount of time each week, but the intensity and duration of workouts would vary from hard week to easy week to promote adequate recovery.

Rome was not built in a day, as the saying goes. We live in a sensation-seeking society that is shy of patience and plagued by unrealistic goals and dreams. Fortunately, the human body hasn't caught up with the 20th century mind-set. Our bodies have amazing abilities to tell us how to train properly, if only our minds would listen! It's been our experience that long-term training progressions from year to year will lead to long-term, sustainable improvements. Most of the best endurance athletes reach their highest performance potentials only after many years of training and competition. Gradual physiological development, refinement of technical skills, education about strategy, and personal development and maturation all lead to steady improvements over the years. Today's top endurance athletes did not begin their careers training 25 hours per week. (If anyone did, they burned out fast and either quit or had to go back to square one!) Instead, they started as young athletes and progressively increased their training volume by 5 to 10 percent each year to allow growth and adaptation to take place gradually and positively.

Countries such as Norway, Finland, and Italy, which consistently produce the most successful cross-country skiers in the world, have highly organized training systems guiding steady and consistent progression in young skiers. Young skiers focus on technique and gradually increase their training volume and intensity through the years to continue to improve their performances. These athletes become students of athletic performance and work with coaches to guide their success. One prodigy of the Norwegian system, Björn Daehlie, a world and Olympic champion, reduced his training volume in 1994 to focus his attention on the technique and intensity required to increase his racing speeds. This strategy paid off with a victory in the overall World Cup title in 1995. Perhaps we can learn something from these examples.

Specificity of Training

To our taste buds, chili just wouldn't be chili without the beans, tomato sauce, and spices. In sports, the best way to improve your performance in a given sport is to practice that sport often. Every sport places unique physiological, biomechanical, and psychological demands on the body. Endurance sports such as triathlon, duathlon, running, cycling, mountain biking, rowing, swimming, cross-country skiing, and in-line skating all require efficient aerobic metabolism, anaerobic metabolism, strength, power, and neuromuscular coordination for efficient technique. Each sport has a different technical or biomechanical requirement that must be met to develop efficient, energy-saving movements that propel you from start to finish.

When deciding which sport activity to use for training workouts, consider several factors simultaneously: technique, conditioning, recovery, injury prevention, and psychological freshness. The type of training you use should relate closely to the specific action that you will use in competition. In this way the intensity, duration, tempo, and speed of the training session will lead to improved sport-specific results in the metabolic pathways and energy systems used, the muscle fiber types recruited, and the various organs and systems used during that session. For example, if you want to become a top triathlete but you never practice swimming fast, on race day you'll likely be caught up in the excitement at the start and attempt to swim faster than you ever have in training. We can guarantee that you'll become tired in a hurry, your stroke will fall apart, and you'll start your race *after* you get out of the water.

It is important to remember that all work and no play will make Joe Athlete a dull boy (and probably a bit bored, burned out, and possibly injured). Look to achieve balance in your training between sport-specific conditioning and variety that promotes proper recovery, injury prevention, and psychological freshness. For example, many triathletes become caught up in a "gotta do my swim, bike, run routine" mentality, using the same pool, the same bike, and the same running loops every week. We think it's great to do a variety of activities that complement the sports you'll race in. Instead of swimming, try some cross-country ski skating; in place of riding your road bike with aero-bars, try some exciting mountain biking on trails; do a little running in the water or on trails instead of pavement. If you do this occasionally, aerobic conditioning will not suffer, but the muscles and connective tissue will get a break, and the you'll gain a refreshing perspective on your overall training plan. Cross-training, which is the use of a variety of aerobic activities for training, has become very popular among endurance athletes. Cross-country skiers have long used a variety of activities to cross-train during the dryland season (fig. 2.2). Many top runners use cycling, water running, swimming, and cross-country skiing during the base stage to allow full recovery of the running muscles, enhance endurance and strength, and avoid psychological burnout.

These factors considered, it is still essential that a certain percentage of the training be completely specific to the requirements of competition in the chosen sport. As a guideline, the nearer your competition stage, the more your training must become sport-specific. By the time you reach the end of the intensity stage, most of your training should be specific, provided weather and other conditions cooperate. Aerobic conditioning in the sport-specific muscles will become sharpened. Perhaps most important, the neuromuscular coordination for sport-specific technique will be refined. In all endurance sports, efficient technique and form are critical for improvements in performance. Cross-country skiers need to ski, ski, ski. Triathletes need to do more open-water swimming and bike rides in the aerodynamic riding position. Cyclists must ride a lot, particularly with a group to refine bike handling, get mentally tougher, and to brush up on the technical aspects of riding in a pack. The key is to cross-train wisely, keeping the sport-specific goals in mind and practicing the sport as much as is appropriate, given the variables described above.

© John Kelly

Fig. 2.2.   Roller-skiing is the next best thing to being on snow for sport-specific training. Davis Phinney demonstrates good form.

Now that you have an understanding of the basic principles of training that make the SERIOUS system effective, let's discuss another fundamental aspect of training, exercise intensity.

PHYSIOLOGY OF INTENSITY

If you've ever driven a car with a stick shift, a tachometer, and a speedometer, then you know what it is like to accelerate, to hear the engine noise reach a whine that speaks "shift gears!" and then to shift gears to reach a new speed and level of engine noise. Well, exercise intensity is a little like this. Your heart pumps a certain volume of blood with every beat. Like a tachometer, which measures revolutions per minute, your heart rate is simply the number of times the heart beats per minute. As your effort and speed increase, so will your heart rate and all the "engine noise" of your body, like breathing and throbbing sounds in your ears. Hopefully, you'll also hear the gasping of your competitors as you leave them in the dust! In short, intensity is how hard your body is working to propel you along.

Physiologically, intensity may be described in terms of heart rate level, energy expended (kilocalories burned per minute), and the percentage of your maximal oxygen uptake capacity ($\dot{V}O_2$max). In the scientific community, oxygen consumption is considered the standard for measuring the physiological intensity of exercise. If heart rate is the tachometer, then oxygen consumption is how much gas per mile you're burning to achieve a certain speed. In endurance sports, success is largely dependent on the body's oxygen uptake ability. The more oxygen that can be delivered to the working muscles, the greater the energy supply, and the faster the body can travel over distance. You've probably heard that elite cross-country skiers are considered the most powerful in oxygen uptake capacity. This is partly due to genetics, but those genes are the foundation on which the athlete builds an aerobic powerhouse over many years of training in a sport that demands the highest aerobic output.

Exercise science has determined that you achieve specific training adaptations by exercising at various intensities or percentages of $\dot{V}O_2$max. Oxygen uptake capacity is measured directly, however, only in the sports physiology laboratory with expensive equipment by qualified professionals to which few of us have ready access. Fortunately, research has shown a reliable relationship between oxygen consumption and heart rate (beats per minute) for monitoring intensity during training. The methods for calculating intensity levels by heart rate, described later in this chapter, produce results that accurately correspond with relative percentages of $\dot{V}O_2$max.

Remember that in each stage of the training plan, the amount and type of exercise you do will determine how fit and race ready your body will become. The physiological effects of each training intensity will dictate the amount of each SERIOUS training component scheduled during a given training cycle. For example, low-intensity overdistance training sessions are most effective if the intensity is between 55 and 65 percent of $\dot{V}O_2$max. This develops aerobic energy pathways and improves capillary density in muscle tissue, proliferation of muscle cell mitochondria, oxidative enzyme activity, and fat substrate mobilization and utilization in the muscle cells. Concurrently, intervals and race/pace sessions, when planned appropriately, are best accomplished at an intensity at or slightly below the anaerobic threshold (AT), discussed in detail later in this chapter.

FIVE INTENSITY LEVELS

To achieve maximal training effect, the athlete must perform each component of SERIOUS systematic training at a predetermined intensity level. Changing the intensity specified for a given workout will alter the purpose of the session and will profoundly affect the overall pattern of the training plan. Many endurance athletes tend to train at medium intensity, medium speed, and medium duration for a large percentage of the training volume. We've never seen an athlete win a race doing medium intensity and speed! This type of training occurs because the athlete does not understand the specific purposes of training components and their appropriate intensities.

We've used five levels of intensity for generating the desired training effects from SERIOUS training workouts. It's been our experience that simultaneous monitoring of three variables—heart rate, pace, and perceived exertion (how hard you feel you are exercising)—will provide biofeedback that integrates proper training effect and balances one with the others. Since each SERIOUS workout maintains its personality, the level of intensity will be an integral factor in determining the training effect. Table 2.1 illustrates these three variables and the physiological adaptations that occur at each intensity. Of course, your pace and perceived exertion at each level of intensity will depend on many factors, including your fitness level, the stage of training, terrain, environmental conditions, and fatigue. Please use the following descriptions of the five levels of intensity as guidelines for application to your training situation.

Level One

All overdistance workouts will be done at level one. Although the effort may seem ridiculously easy at first, it is essential to maintain close control and complete this training within the zone. In the end, the effort, because it is longer than other types of training, will be quite fatiguing due to energy and fluid depletion. For these reasons, overdistance workouts lasting over 75 minutes should be considered moderate- to high-stress sessions, despite the low intensity. Most strength workouts will elicit heart rates at this level as well, depending on the exercises and the tempo at which the athlete performs them.

Table 2.1

Physiological Adaptations to Various Training Intensities

Level	% V̇O₂max	% Maximum heart rate	Physiological adaptations (↑ = improves or increases)	SERIOUS components or workouts used at intensity levels
I	55-65	60-70	↑ Aerobic energy sources ↑ Aerobic energy pathways ↑ Capillary density ↑ Mitochondria proliferation ↑ Free fatty acid mobilization	Overdistance, Strength
II	66-75	71-75	↑ Aerobic energy sources ↑ Aerobic energy pathways	Endurance, Strength, Body Speeds
III	76-80	76-80	↑ Aerobic energy pathways ↑ Recruitment of FOG fibers ↑ Aerobic glycolysis ↑ Oxygen transport system	Endurance, Strength
IV	81-90	81-90	↑ Aerobic energy pathways ↑ Anaerobic energy pathways ↑ Recruitment of FOG fibers ↑ Anaerobic threshold (AT) ↑ Oxygen transport system ↑ Lactic acid clearance	Intervals, Up/vertical, Race/pace
V	91-100	91-100	↑ Anaerobic energy sources ↑ Fast-twitch FG fiber recruitment ↑ Speed and neuromuscular coordination	Racing, Peaking Speeds

Level Two

Endurance, body speed (except during peak and racing stages), and some strength workouts (typically those with a faster tempo, such as plyometric routines) will be done at level two intensity. The feeling is slightly harder than overdistance but must not exceed the limits. Level two intensity is probably the level at which the vast majority of people train day in and day out. This certainly has a positive aerobic training effect, especially with untrained or beginning exercisers, but we find that for serious endurance athletes, too much training at this intensity precludes the more optimal adaptations that occur with level one intensity.

Level Three

Typically, very little training should take place in this intensity zone. Sometimes during endurance workouts, your intensity may bump up to this level on hills. In longer races, such as an Ironman triathlon, a cross-country ski marathon, or a running marathon, you'll probably be in this intensity zone, depending on your fitness and the terrain of the course. Much depends on your anaerobic threshold as expressed as a percentage of $\dot{V}O_2$max. If your threshold is low and falls in this range, then you should perform interval, vertical, and race/pace work at this level until the AT occurs at higher heart rates—a training effect you can expect over time.

Level Four

Most intervals, uphill training, and race/pace sessions need to be done at level four intensity. This is sometimes referred to as anaerobic threshold (AT) training. Training at this intensity will improve the body's ability to transport oxygen, increase the recruitment of fast oxidative glycolytic (FOG) muscle fibers, remove metabolic waste products, shorten lactic acid clearance time, and improve both aerobic and anaerobic energy pathways.

Level four training is perfect for simultaneously monitoring the three variables of heart rate, pace, and perceived exertion. These workouts require you to tune in to the physiological cues that indicate the level of work at the threshold between aerobic and anaerobic effort. As your fitness improves after weeks of interval training, you'll find that your pace will be faster and your perception of effort will seem easier at a set heart rate. You'll be able to do your favorite loops faster at the same intensity level.

Anyone who has run hill intervals probably has experienced the "rubbery legs" syndrome. Scientists are still arguing about what to call this physiological state. The popular expression used over the last decade has been "crossing the anaerobic threshold." Anaerobic threshold is the point at which lactic acid accumulation reaches concentrations where it limits performance and is fatiguing.

All skeletal muscles have a lactic acid accumulation threshold—a point beyond which the muscle cells can no longer effectively process and clear the lactate being produced. Generally, this point occurs at high percentages of $\dot{V}O_2$max for well-trained endurance athletes and at lower percentages of $\dot{V}O_2$max for less fit individuals. The lactate, or metabolic waste, quickly accumulates in the muscle cells and then enters the bloodstream. If the accumulation becomes too great and cannot be cleared on a timely basis, the muscles will fail to contract efficiently, and exercise will slow considerably until recovery is allowed.

As I go over the AT in my training and racing, I feel as if a bear has climbed on my back for a ride—it's heavy, it's disconcerting, and it growls!—Rob

Training at or slightly below the AT will result in the ability of the body to buffer, recycle, and clear waste from lactic acid production during high-intensity exercise. Endurance athletes need to have high ATs if they are to sustain high-intensity exercise for a long time before fatiguing; you must have a high AT to race your fastest. Later in this chapter, we will discuss the AT in greater detail, including some of the methods currently used to determine when it occurs for you.

Level Five

The best time to include some level five intensity training is during the taper and competition stages of the training program. This type of training stimulates anaerobic energy pathways and fast-twitch muscle fibers, and improves anaerobic energy supplies and speed. If you think of your body's energy systems as a fuel tank, then the energy you'll need to do level five intensity exercise will be like a reserve tank of super-duper high test that burns out in less than 60 seconds of all-out effort. Doing some level five training will "top off" this reserve tank so you have it when you need it during races. During a taper stage, you will use it only in peaking speed sessions. These workouts are very difficult, but they will sharpen muscle efficiency and neuromuscular coordination at maximum speed and will boost the anaerobic and aerobic energy systems. When the first race arrives, your body will be in top condition. During races, you'll be able to rely on this speed for starting out fast in a mass start to get the best position in a pack, passing surges, breakaways, or all-out sprints for the last 200 meters of the race.

DETERMINING INTENSITY LEVELS

I've always driven a car with a manual transmission and a tachometer. It's become automatic for me to shift gears at the appropriate time by the sound of the engine, the vibrations of the car, and tachometer needle. I don't even think about it anymore. The same thing happened to me when I began using heart monitors 10 years ago. Now I can go out for a run with my heart monitor strapped on and at any given time, I can accurately tell you my heart rate without looking at my monitor. My subjective feel for each heart rate zone has become refined through years of simultaneously measuring pace, perceived exertion, and heart rate.—Rob

Most successful athletes are extraordinary when it comes to listening to their bodies' intensity cues. Years of trial and error have enabled them to fine-tune their response to each intensity level. However, the majority of endurance athletes have not learned how to distinguish the levels of intensity required for each component of SERIOUS training, especially athletes with the "no pain, no gain" approach to training. As with any refined craft, this takes either a very special talent or a dedication to shaping a rough concept into a fine work of art. Therefore, monitoring heart rate can be an effective tool for refining your ability to feel each level of intensity. It takes practice, and you may learn faster than others. The key is that eventually you will possess an entire repertoire of cues for detecting the intensity level of every training session. As top masters athlete Skip Hamilton once remarked, "I never realized that overdistance level one intensity training should be so low. It's become guilt-producingly easy, even though I get tired enough over the long run."

Heart Rate: The Foundation of Measuring Intensity

Consider your heart for a moment. It's the hub of most circulatory functions at rest and during exercise. It gets messages from the control center in your brain telling it to speed up or slow down its pumping action. If your muscles need more fuel and oxygen, the heart is stimulated to pump more blood to the needy muscle tissues. When it's time to rest or recover, the messages tell it to slow down. The process is an autonomic response—in other words, the body will do this automatically without us thinking about it.

When conditioning the body, coaxing it into a higher level of fitness, you can use heart rate as a monitor of the intensity you are asking your body to perform. Consider the components of your training. Each objective—speed, endurance, race/pace, and so on—needs to be performed at the right intensity to achieve maximum benefit from the workout. Therefore, measuring heart rate will quantify and ultimately optimize the conditioning response of your training sessions. You'll maximize the effectiveness of your training time. In the past, intensity levels were considered to be the same for everyone. If your coach or the latest magazine training program instructed you to do a six-mile run at a six-minutes-per-mile pace, that's what you did, regardless of the intensity for you personally. Now we know better. Each of us has different abilities and corresponding intensity levels.

The least expensive way to check heart rate is by feeling the pulse in an artery on your wrist, throat, or under the left breast (fig. 2.3). The only thing you need is a watch with the seconds indicated. Digital sport watches work well and are fairly inexpensive. Manual pulse measuring, however, can be subject to significant errors. You may have trouble feeling your pulse or being able to count the beats at high heart rates. It takes practice before you gain a good feel for pulse taking. If you are counting heart rate by feeling an artery, it is most accurate to count the beats for only 10 seconds and multiply the 10-second value by 6. The reason for this is that your body will recover very rapidly when you stop to count your heart rate, and your pulse will drop significantly within one minute. Therefore, you will not obtain a true representation of exercise heart rate if you count for more than 10 seconds. If you count your pulse for 6 seconds and multiply that number by 10, realize that an error in counting a single beat will mean a 10-beat error in calculating heart rate. It's just more accurate to count your pulse for a full 10 seconds. At rest, it is better to count the beats for a full minute.

Since the development of sophisticated wireless heart monitors, such as the model shown in figure 2.4, many top endurance athletes are using heart rate monitoring in conjunction with subjective feelings to judge intensity levels in training. Once you have determined the actual heart rates for each level or training zone (either with direct measurement of $\dot{V}O_2$max or by estimating the percentages), you can use the heart rate levels in training and measuring your effort precisely with the heart monitor. This method eliminates much guesswork. These monitors also offer fantastic opportunities for biofeedback when training in different sports, terrain, and environmental conditions.

Variation in the Training Heart Rate With Different Sports

Heart rate is not always the best measure of oxygen uptake and training effect. There can be significant differences in the pulse rate response to a given workload or oxygen consumption relative to $\dot{V}O_2$max. It has been shown that with arm work alone, such as

© Anne Krause

Fig. 2.3.   To check your pulse manually, count the beats for 10 seconds and multiply this number by 6.

© Anne Krause

Fig. 2.4. Wireless heart rate monitors are easy to use and offer a more accurate means of determining heart rate than the manual method.

with double-poling in cross-country skiing, you cannot obtain the same $\dot{V}O_2$max that you can reach with running, although your pulse can reach the maximum in both cases. The probable reason for this is that less muscle mass is engaged in arm work than in leg work, so the oxygen demand is less as well. Thus, the cross-

Tips for Choosing a
Heart Rate (HR) Monitor

- Select a model that uses a wireless chest strap and receiver (watch).
- Choose a model that allows you to record exercise time and time spent in your set HR range. Alarms that indicate being out of your range are helpful but not necessary.
- Choose a model that is water-resistant.
- Very sophisticated models are great if you have experience with HR monitors but are not necessary for most athletes.
- A model that you can easily mount on either bike handlebars or your wrist is a plus.

country skier will gain greater training effect by running, diagonal, or freestyle skiing, which engages more muscle mass and creates a greater load on the system than double-poling at the same heart rate.

Additionally, it is thought that $\dot{V}O_2$max values vary according to training specificity. Tests have shown that trained triathletes achieve their highest $\dot{V}O_2$max scores while running, with $\dot{V}O_2$max scores for cycling and swimming at 95.7 percent and 86.8 percent of the running $\dot{V}O_2$max, respectively. Other tests have shown that untrained subjects also achieve their highest $\dot{V}O_2$max values in running, with cycling $\dot{V}O_2$max typically 8 to 12 percent lower and swimming $\dot{V}O_2$max 18 to 22 percent lower. Conversely, highly trained cyclists' cycling $\dot{V}O_2$max values have tested approximately equal to their running scores, and highly trained swimmers achieved 94 percent of their running $\dot{V}O_2$max scores while swimming.

Training heart rate levels relative to percentages of $\dot{V}O_2$max as calculated with the Karvonen method (determined later in the chapter) seem to be most accurate for running and may need adjustment depending on the level of training, the sport, or the training method. We recommend that you adjust your heart rate zones by subtracting 10 beats per minute for cycling and 10 to 15 beats per minute for swimming. Unfortunately, it is unclear exactly how much adjustment is necessary. Experimentation using heart rate, perceived exertion, and pace will help you determine training zone adjustments for various activities.

Adaptation of Heart Rate

As your body adapts to training, your heart rate response for a given workout will change. For example, during week 1 of your program, you may run three miles in 21 minutes at a level one heart rate. Twelve weeks later, you probably will be able to run the same three-mile course in less time at the same heart rate. Also, your perceived exertion for the effort may be lower (easier). Your body will have adjusted to the demands of your training program. We think it's a good idea to have specific training sessions every month when you do a set distance using the same course at a set heart rate. Measure your pace and heart rate, and note your subjective feeling. Theoretically, each month you'll do the set distance a bit faster at the set heart rate.

Monitoring your training heart rate levels regularly will lead to a finely tuned sense of your body and its response to various exercise demands. It does not take long before you will gain a fairly accurate feel for the various levels of exertion. The more you know about your body, the better you'll be able to deal with the stresses of training.

Resting Heart Rate

Resting heart rate, or morning pulse, serves as a good indicator of your state of training. Typically, morning pulse will decrease as your level of fitness increases. One Olympic biathlete reported that he has recorded his at 29 beats per minute! Resting pulse is not the only indicator of fitness—there are too many other variables affecting it. However, monitoring morning pulse on a daily basis can be very useful. We recommend that you record it in your training log so that you can refer to it later.

A morning pulse 10 percent above average can mean one of several things regarding your training. You may be coming down with a cold, the flu, or another ailment. Other times it may mean that your hard, level four workout the previous day was a bit too much. Emotional stress, low hydration, lack of sleep, or jet lag can all elevate the morning pulse. In each case, the body is responding to the demand by requiring more rest. The best remedy for elevated morning pulse is lots of water and rest, rest, and more rest. You needn't fear losing a conditioning benefit by modifying or missing the workout scheduled for the day. You'll do much better to make it an easy workout or take the day off and pick up the training plan on the next scheduled workout. Chapter 8 describes the SERIOUS training log and journal system, including a complete description of monitoring stress factors that affect training and recovery.

Environmental Factors and Heart Rate

Some environmental conditions will affect both morning and training pulse. Training in the heat puts a greater stress on the cardiovascular system as the body struggles to keep the cooling mechanism working properly. Therefore, training in the heat reduces the value of heart rate as a good training monitor. Your body will adapt to training in the heat with 7 to 12 days of exposure, and HR levels will return to near normal levels. If you live in an environment that is hot in the summer, monitor your level of hydration carefully and use an elevated HR during a workout as a cue to the onset of dehydration.

Hypohydration, dehydration, or lack of adequate fluids will cause the heart rate to soar above normal. Your perspiration system is the body's cooling mechanism. As sweat evaporates, the skin is cooled and blood flowing near the skin is cooled. This blood circulates to cool the vital organs at your body's core. If your total body water content drops, your heart has to beat more often to maintain a constant temperature at the core. Be sure to stay well hydrated before, during, and after training.

Altitude also affects heart rate. During the first two or three weeks of training at high altitude, you will have higher heart rates for given workout intensities. Later this effect on the body usually goes away. Whenever you go to high altitude, we recommend that you back off on training times and intensities, get plenty of rest, and consume plenty of fluids.

Using Perceived Exertion to Monitor Intensity

Perceived exertion, sometimes measured on a scale of 1 to 10 (10 being maximal effort), includes such cues as ventilatory (breathing) rate, force of inhalation and exhalation, and other bodily cues such as the feel of the muscles, the throbbing of blood in the ears, coordination, and the level of fatigue. Perceived exertion has a direct relationship with intensity—the harder it feels, the greater the intensity. Overdistance workouts, done at level one intensity, have a low perceived exertion and seem easy, although the perceived exertion will be higher at the end of an overdistance session than at the beginning, due to fatigue. You will need to pay attention to the physical cues at each level of intensity to learn the feeling associated with different intensities. Once perceived exertion levels are learned for each intensity level, they become a valuable tool in monitoring intensity.

Using Pace to Monitor Intensity

Often, elite athletes will systematically do race simulations to measure improvements in pace over a set distance at a set heart rate. Each intensity level will correspond to a given speed or pace, whether cycling, running, skiing, or swimming. For example, your level four intensity may correspond to a six-minutes-per-mile pace running, and therefore that is the pace you should use for your running interval training. Keep in mind that environmental factors such as wind and temperature can affect the pace/intensity relationship.

The following sections will give you a system for calculating training heart rate (THR) levels of your own. Pace and perceived exertion will be measurements that you'll observe as you exercise at each heart rate level.

Calculating Intensity Levels

There are several methods for calculating THR intensity levels. Some are more accurate than others, and some are more convenient than others. The following methods are the most widely accepted by sport scientists and coaches.

Exercise Stress Test

The best way to determine training levels is to have a maximal stress test administered by a qualified professional such as a sport physiologist, sports medicine physician, or cardiologist. An exercise stress test determines maximal oxygen uptake capacity ($\dot{V}O_2max$), maximum heart rate, and training heart rate zones. Most elite endurance athletes take this test at least once per year to help determine some training intensity benchmarks. It's a good idea for all athletes who are over 35 years old or have a family history of heart disease to take such a test annually, especially before participating in strenuous exercise or before beginning to exercise after a layoff from regular physical activity.

Typically, two physiological measurements will be taken. First, your heart rate will be measured, including your maximum heart rate (MHR), which is the maximum number of beats your heart can make in one minute (fig. 2.5). Along with the MHR, the health status of your heart will be monitored and assessed for signs of heart disease with an electrocardiogram (EKG). This is a valuable preventive health measure. Many stress tests are administered with consideration only to maximum heart rate and heart health status. While this is useful, it does not tell the entire story, which can be discovered with the second measurement, $\dot{V}O_2$max.

It is ideal to have $\dot{V}O_2$max and heart rate measured simultaneously. This way, you'll be able to determine training heart rate levels as a function of a percentage of $\dot{V}O_2$max for each of the five levels. After all, the main goal of systematic training for endurance sports is to raise your oxygen uptake capacity. Given that each training component in the SERIOUS model has a specific

Fig. 2.5.   The maximal oxygen uptake test determines one's $\dot{V}O_2$max.

physiological purpose, it is useful to know the relative percentage of $\dot{V}O_2$max and corresponding heart rate for each component. If you do have a stress test to measure $\dot{V}O_2$max directly, use the steps in worksheet 2.1 to determine training heart rate levels.

One bit of caution regarding $\dot{V}O_2$max tests. There are many types of oxygen uptake analyzing systems as well as other variables that can affect the results of a $\dot{V}O_2$max test. If you use this method, try to compare your results over time if you can be tested two to four times (or at least once) per year. Comparing your test results to those of people who are tested on other equipment by different professionals can be misleading.

Calculating Training Heart Rate by the Karvonen Method

Calculation of the five training heart rate levels using the Karvonen method is one of the most common approaches used today. It was developed by taking real test data from many $\dot{V}O_2$max tests done with runners and cross-country skiers and creating a formula that produced heart rate levels that accurately matched the real data. Worksheet 2.2 provides a summary worksheet approach to calculating the five levels of intensity with the Karvonen method.

Step 1. Determine maximum heart rate (MHR). The Karvonen method is dependent upon knowing your true MHR. There are a couple of ways to find your true MHR:

1. The best way to find true MHR is to take an exercise stress test on a treadmill or bicycle ergometer while being monitored with an electrocardiogram as described above. This is also the safest way. You'll also benefit by learning about the health status of your heart. If you do not have VO_2max measured, then at least you can get your true MHR.
2. If you are positive that you are in good condition, you can do one of the following sport-specific tests. Warm up for at least 20 minutes and stretch well before the test. Good pacing and motivation are necessary for you to do well. A helpful tool for these tests is a good heart monitor, which affords you accuracy and ease of measurement. If you use a heart monitor, you may be able to estimate your AT during this test by noting your heart rate when you feel that you've begun to get very anaerobic. (*Note: Do not attempt these if you are over 35 and have not had a thorough physical exam with a stress test, or if you are in poor condition.*)

┌───┐
│ **Worksheet 2.1**   │
│ **Determining Training Zones From a Stress Test** │
└───┘

Step 1. Determine $\dot{V}O_2$max value.

_____ Your $\dot{V}O_2$max value (ml/kg/min)

Step 2. Multiply your $\dot{V}O_2$max by the percentages given for each level as follows (Example: 55% = .55 x $\dot{V}O_2$max):

Level one: 55%–65%   _____ (55%) – _____ (65%) $\dot{V}O_2$ max

Level two: 66%–75%   _____ (66%) – _____ (75%) $\dot{V}O_2$ max

Level three: 76%–80%   _____ (76%) – _____ (80%) $\dot{V}O_2$ max

Level four: 81%–90%   _____ (81%) – _____ (90%) $\dot{V}O_2$ max

Level five: 91%–100%   _____ (91%) – _____ (100%) $\dot{V}O_2$ max

For example, if your $\dot{V}O_2$max is 66 ml/kg/min, then level one $\dot{V}O_2$ value will range between 36.3 ml/kg/min (55%) and 42.9 ml/kg/min (65%).

Step 3. For each $\dot{V}O_2$ level, look at the test data for the heart rate values you had during the test and determine the actual heart rate values you experienced at each $\dot{V}O_2$ level. For example, if at 55% $\dot{V}O_2$max (36.3 ml/kg/min in the example in Step 2) the heart rate was 136 beats per minute (bpm), then 136 bpm will serve as the lower limit for level one training.

Percent of $\dot{V}O_2$max	_Corresponding Heart Rate Value_
Level one: 55%–65%	_____ (55%) – _____ (65%)
Level two: 66%–75%	_____ (66%) – _____ (75%)
Level three: 76%–80%	_____ (76%) – _____ (80%)
Level four: 81%–90%	_____ (81%) – _____ (90%)
Level five: 91%–100%	_____ (91%) – _____ (100%)

Calculating Intensity Levels Using the Karvonen Method

Measured maximum heart rate (MMHR): _____

Measured resting heart rate (MRHR): _____

Estimated maximum heart rate (EMHR): _____
(220 − Your Age = EMHR)

Heart rate reserve (HRR): MMHR or EMHR − MRHR = HRR: _____

Level	Formula for HR values	Calculated HRs *Lower − Upper*	SERIOUS workouts
One	Lower limit = HRR × .60 + MRHR	_____ − _____	Overdistance, Strength
	Upper limit = HRR × .70 + MRHR	_____ − _____	
Two	Lower limit = HRR × .71 + MRHR	_____ − _____	Endurance, Strength, Speed
	Upper limit = HRR × .75 + MRHR	_____ − _____	
Three	Lower limit = HRR × .76 + MRHR	_____ − _____	Endurance, Strength,
	Upper limit = HRR × .80 + MRHR	_____ − _____	
Four	Lower limit = HRR × .81 + MRHR	_____ − _____	Intervals, Up, Race/pace
	Upper limit = HRR × .90 + MRHR	_____ − _____	
Five	Lower limit = HRR × .91 + MRHR	_____ − _____	Racing, Speed
	Upper limit = HRR × 1.0 + MRHR	_____ − _____	(peaking sprints)

Running and cross-country skiing: This running test involves running one mile as fast as you can over a fairly level course (a running track works well). During the last quarter mile of the run, go all out. Time your run and use it as a reference later in your program. At the finish, stop and count your heart rate immediately. This will be your MHR.

Cycling: The cycling test involves cycling on a bike trainer or cycle ergometer (preferably using your bike) as fast as you can for five minutes. Cycle all out for the last 30 seconds and when finished count your heart rate immediately. This will be your MHR.

Swimming: The swimming test involves swimming 400 meters as fast as possible. Swim the last 50 meters all out and record your HR immediately after finishing.

3. Probably the easiest method of calculating MHR is simply subtracting your age from 220 for men or from 226 for women:

- Men: 220 − age = estimated MHR
- Women: 226 − age = estimated MHR

Although we have seen variations between a person's true MHR and the estimated MHR (sometimes as great as 20 beats per minute), this method is still useful. Minor adjustments in the five calculated levels of training heart rate will help compensate for error. If the training level seems too hard or too easy, make the appropriate adjustments.

Step 2. The next measure you'll need before calculating the five training levels is your true resting heart rate (RHR). Do this by counting your pulse for a full minute, first thing in the morning, preferably *before* you get out of bed. Do this for three mornings and take an average. (*Note: You may need to use the bathroom and void before taking a morning pulse. A full bladder can slightly elevate heart rate. If you do this, go back to bed and rest for a few minutes before measuring RHR.*)

Step 3. Now you're ready to calculate the five levels of training heart rate. Use the formula in worksheet 2.2 for figuring each level. Figure 2.6 illustrates the various training zones calculated by the Karvonen method. You can use this graph to determine your heart rate zones.

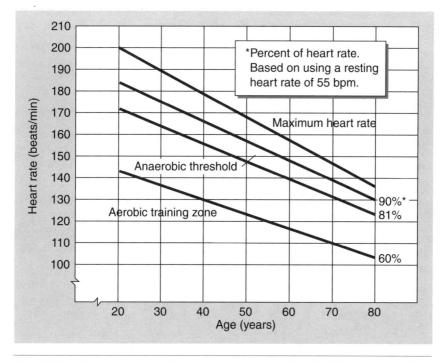

Fig. 2.6.   Heart rate training zones calculated using the Karvonen method.

Determining Anaerobic Threshold Intensity

Ultimately, the endurance athlete who competes needs to train the body to sustain the highest possible intensity level and speed for the race distance, to do the distance as hard and as fast as he or she can. Why can you sustain a faster pace in a short race than in a longer event?

Much of the answer has to do with anaerobic threshold, or AT. Exercise scientists have defined AT as the point at which blood lactate levels exceed four millimoles per liter. At rest, lactate levels are about one millimole per liter and gradually increase as exercise intensity increases. Our bodies can sustain paces above our AT for about one hour or less before the cumulative effects of high lactate levels begin to impair performance. The shorter the event, the higher the lactate levels that can be tolerated. So, for endurance events, especially those lasting over one hour, a high AT (meaning AT occurs at a high percentage of $\dot{V}O_2max$) is essential for fast race paces. And remember, you improve your AT by training at or slightly below the AT heart rate (see figure 2.7).

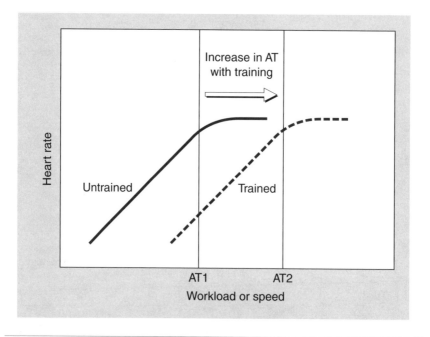

Fig. 2.7. You can increase your anaerobic threshold (AT) by training at or slightly below your AT heart rate.

Some controversy exists concerning the value of and the methods for determining the anaerobic threshold (AT). One way to measure the AT is in a physiology laboratory, with blood lactate tests taken at frequent intervals during ever-increasing work intensity. The sports scientists of the former Soviet Union and some Western European countries have been using the blood lactate test for years to determine ATs for their athletes and to adjust training according to these values. In the United States, blood lactate testing was not widely used until the last five years; it is now used to monitor and train athletes on a daily basis. Blood lactate testing is available primarily to elite athletes. We feel that the recreational athlete can do very well without blood lactate tests.

Conconi, Ferrari, Ziglio, Droghetti, and Codeca (1982) indicate that there are easy-to-do, noninvasive (no blood samples) field tests to determine the AT and the heart rate at which the AT occurs. Dr. Conconi developed what is now referred to as the test Conconi for cyclists, runners, cross-country skiers, and swimmers. The test involves a series of repeated intervals of gradually increasing intensity over a set distance and course. Heart rate for the last quarter of the interval and the speed of the interval are recorded and plotted. The AT is said to exist at that point where the line between speed and heart rate deflects, creating a "knee" in the graph. By performing this test periodically, say, every two to three weeks, one can determine the heart rate at AT. Once AT is determined, all interval, vertical, and race/pace training should take place within a range from 10 percent below to the AT heart rate.

Cyclists have used the test Conconi with great success over the last two decades. In January 1984, Francesco Moser broke the world hour cycling record twice in one week. He had trained using the test Conconi. The Italian foursome who won the 1984 Olympic 100-kilometer time trial, setting Olympic and world records, used the test Conconi to prepare for the race. Runners and cross-country skiers are beginning to use the method in the field. We think that it has merit but must be applied with prudence and with a scientific approach that considers environmental factors such as wind, temperature, humidity, and surface used, all of which must be exactly the same for each test. We have modified the test Conconi and have used it successfully with many athletes. Refer to appendix C for detailed instructions on how to perform this test.

Besides the test Conconi, we have created another simple test to estimate AT, which you may find beneficial (see pages 46-48). Either test may be used to determine your AT level.

Another way to detect the AT is with cues from the muscles. Reduction in coordination, rubbery feelings, or burning are all signs of working above the AT. Again, tune in to this feeling and the heart rate associated with it and reduce the intensity accordingly. However, reliability of these cues is questionable, and we're sure there is considerable variation among athletes. Remember to use pace and perceived exertion with heart rate to get the best results in monitoring your training levels.

Since endurance athletes traditionally train too much volume at or above the AT, we recommend conservatism be exercised with all level four training. It is best to train about 5 to 10 heartbeats per minute below the AT heart rate for most level four training. When the taper stage comes, it will not take long to fine-tune your body for racing. Premature high-intensity training will likely lead to an early peak, if you achieve one at all.

Anaerobic Threshold Estimation Test

Purpose. To estimate the anaerobic threshold and adjust and use this level of intensity, perceived exertion, and pace in training.

Equipment. Reliable heart monitor; a stop watch; a performance log in which you record date, distance, time, average heart rate during the effort; and subjective feeling (1 to 10, 10 is hardest effort). *Optional: a friend or training partner to monitor your progress and provide support.*

Protocol.

1. Choose a certain location that will be reliable and repeatable. This could be a favorite stretch of road, a running track, your local swimming pool, et cetera. The distances can vary for each athlete, but once you settle on a distance, stick with that exact course and distance for each trial you perform over the months. It's ideal if you can mark your courses with one-kilometer markings. Choose a distance that takes you about 30 to 60 minutes to complete.

Suggested distances are the following:

Running—5 to 10 kilometers

Cycling—25 to 40 kilometers

Swimming—1,500 to 2,000 meters

Cross-country skiing—10 to 15 kilometers

Rowing—2,500 to 5,000 meters

2. Warm up for 15 minutes at low to medium intensity before starting.

3. Perform the distance at a pace that is the fastest you feel you can sustain at a steady effort with no loss of pace (tricky part). If you find yourself slowing down, you started at a pace that was above your AT. Stop the test and repeat it the following week starting with a slower pace. Start your stopwatch as you begin and record your time for the distance when you finish. Heart rate should stabilize in about 5 minutes. The heart rate you achieved and sustained is an

estimate of your AT heart rate. Also, record your subjective feelings.

4. Do a 15-minute warm-down and some stretching after the workout.

Frequency. Ideally, do this or the test Conconi once each month for each sport you are competing in (once every eight weeks is OK, too). If you are a triathlete, do the trial for cycling the first week, running the next week, and swimming the third week. It is important to substitute this workout for a scheduled interval, hill interval, or race/pace workout.

Special considerations. After each determination, take some time to make a relationship between the heart rate, subjective feeling, and pace per kilometer you sustained during the test. Use these three variables to fine-tune your AT heart rate and pace. Then, for the coming four weeks, do your intervals, hill intervals, and race/pace workouts between 0 and 10 heartbeats per minute lower than your AT heart rate.

You'll probably adjust this after the next month's test. Eventually, you'll fine-tune these three variables so that you'll have as much confidence in subjective feeling and pace per kilometer as you do in heart rate.

Now you have determined your five intensity levels and an estimate of your AT. Remember that you should perform your high-intensity training at or slightly below your AT, which may not be within your calculated level four intensity range. For example, you may have determined your level four intensity range to be a heart rate of 150 to 160 beats per minute, while your AT estimate is 148 beats per minute. Use the estimate of AT in your training, not your level four values. Soon enough your fitness will improve so that your AT falls within your level four range. By training above your AT for all high-intensity training you will not elicit the improvement in AT that comes with training at or below AT.

You may choose to rely on other means to estimate your AT intensity level. Your perceived exertion, rated on a scale of 1 to 10, with 10 as exhaustion, would rank between a 7 and 9 at the AT. Although not conclusively documented, ventilation, which is your rate and depth of breathing, can be an effective cue for AT. Generally, when you are at the AT, breathing will become markedly more rapid. This is associated with increased anaerobic energy metabolism. The by-product of this increase is greater lactic acid production. The body tries to clear lactic acid, and one result is an increase in carbon dioxide production. The system does not tolerate carbon dioxide, so the body does everything it can to eliminate it. Your breathing increases to "blow off" CO_2 as fast as possible (it is the increased CO_2 production that causes the breathing changes, not a need to get more oxygen into the system). When you feel your breathing change from deep and rhythmical to a significantly increased frequency, ease off on the throttle and try to maintain an effort slightly below the one that caused the change in ventilation. Figure 2.8 illustrates this phenomenon.

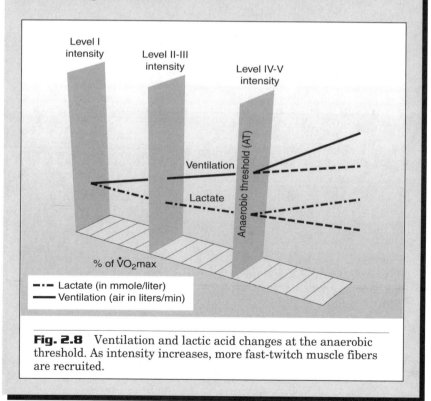

Fig. 2.8 Ventilation and lactic acid changes at the anaerobic threshold. As intensity increases, more fast-twitch muscle fibers are recruited.

FROM EXPERIENCE

RAY BROWNING, MS

If you are going to invest in the concept of systematic training, you're relying on the training effects of different intensities to guide you to optimum performance. The success or failure of the training hinges on adhering to the proper intensity. Therefore the single most important tool for measuring intensity is the heart rate monitor. Heart rate monitors are inexpensive, accurate, and easy to use. They will take the guesswork out of your estimates of training intensity and allow you to focus on the feelings and paces associated with each intensity level. I have been using a heart rate monitor for 13 years and I have learned the feelings of the different efforts, thus allowing me to leave it at home occasionally with the confidence that I will train properly based on subjective feeling.

As valuable as it is, the HR monitor does have a few limitations. My experience has been that they can be a bit fickle when used around electrical equipment such as large treadmills and cycle ergometers. If you use a treadmill or ergometer for determining AT or maximum HR, have an assistant stand one meter behind you away from the electronic display to record your HR, pace, and time. The monitors can also be upset outside by power lines or other electrical apparatus, so check around before you assume your monitor is out of order.

It has been my personal experience that HR levels will vary depending on the activity and primary sport background of the individual. If you have a running background, your running MHR and AT HR will usually be higher than for other activities. I come from a cycling background. As a result my MHR and AT HR are similar for running and cycling. The truth is that to accurately determine your training intensity levels, you must do an MHR and AT HR determination for each of your primary sports. This is especially important for the older athlete who has been active for a number of years, as MHR will not decline as rapidly as the 220-minus-age calculation will predict. I have friends in their mid-40s who still have MHRs above 200.

If you train in a group and several members of the group use HR monitors, remember that the monitors can interfere with each other, so you may be getting a friend's HR rather than your own. Occasionally I play a little trick on Mark Allen. When he is hammering in a group ride, I'll ride up close to his side and let his HR monitor pick up my heart rate from the transmitter on my chest. Since my heart rate zones are higher than his, he thinks that he is going too hard, slows down, and we all get a break!

Scheduling Your Training

Now the real fun of planning your day-by-day training schedule begins. This chapter will guide you as you create your training recipe. When we finish, you will have designed your own systematic training plan, using the easy-to-follow, step-by-step process outlined on the following pages. Chapters 1 and 2 provided the foundation for the planning phase presented here. In this chapter, you will

- review and outline the objectives of your training plan,
- learn about training cycles,
- determine how much time you will train each month,
- create the character of each training cycle,
- create a systematic training plan using a simple format, and
- learn about adjusting your plan.

DETERMINE YOUR SYSTEMATIC TRAINING OBJECTIVES

If you are like most athletes, you're juggling several life commitments along with your sports training and racing. This makes it all the more useful to outline your goals and objectives before you begin the process of planning your program. Table 3.1 provides an outline that we use with every athlete we coach. Take a moment

Table 3.1

Outline of Goals and Objectives

1. List 10 nonoutcome goals for training that you'd like to accomplish.
2. List three specific outcome goals you have for the coming season.
3. List 10 of your specific strengths in your sport.
4. List five specific areas that you need to improve in your sport.
5. Describe five things you did that helped you during the past season.
6. Describe five things you did during the past season that didn't help you and what you'd like to change about each.
7. Review your past season as follows:

Race	Distance	Original goals	Actual result	Comments

8. List below the races and goals for your upcoming competition season.

(Rate on a scale of 1-5, 5 being highest)

Date	Race	Distance	Goals	Importance	Fun Factor	Difficulty

to complete this outline now, since it will help you determine the most important aspects of your plan.

If you're interested in projecting your performance goals over a longer time, as many elite and Olympic athletes must do, there are six basic categories to consider for the overall outline. Along with table 3.1, refer to table 3.2 as an example for organizing these objectives.

The first category is *performance*. Identify actual race times and ranking classifications for the events in which you will compete. These are specific outcome goals. It is important to be realistic about these goals.

The second category is *physical training preparation*. Make a clear assessment of your current physical strengths and weaknesses. A knowledge of proper physiological progressions is necessary for correctly mapping the objectives for this category. For example, as an endurance athlete, you will need to develop an outstanding aerobic endurance capacity over a base period of several months. This will provide the foundation for optimally effective (and safe) anaerobic activity.

Psychological preparation is the third category. Make an assessment of your mental skills and the areas needing improvement. Then outline the objectives for improving these areas and for sharpening mental skills.

Fourth is *technical preparation*. This includes learning correct stroke technique, aerodynamic body position, efficient stride, and so on, according to the requirements of the sport. For example, you may elect to swim with a masters swim program to get instruction on proper swim mechanics.

The fifth category is *tactical preparation*. This involves developing your race strategies, race day preparation protocol, equipment choices for various courses and conditions, nutritional strategies, and so forth. Your race strategies will depend on the time of year. Early races will serve as a test of your fitness while later races are your chance to go all out.

Finally, objectives for *tests and standards* will be outlined. Throughout the training year, various performance objectives will serve as benchmarks for comparison to actual performance, thereby letting you check the effectiveness of the training plan on a periodic basis.

Most of the material in this book pertains primarily to the physical preparation of the body for competition. However, when you follow a thorough systematic training plan, you'll

Table 3.2
Planning Four-Year Training Objectives

ATHLETE: __RHS__ EVENT: __10K__

Performance (time)	Objectives	
	Year 1 35:20	Year 2 35:00
Physical preparation	Develop general physical preparation Develop aerobic endurance	Improve general physical preparation Develop muscular endurance Improve aerobic endurance Develop anaerobic endurance
Psychological preparation	Develop mental awareness and the resulting consequences Attempt to modify the above	Develop mental awareness Develop self-concept
Technical preparation	Correct arm carriage Correct position of head	Efficient stride length Minimum vertical bouncing
Tactical preparation	Steady pace throughout the race	Fast start in the first 400 meters Steady pace in the body of the race
Test and standards	$\dot{V}O_2max = 3.7$ liters	$\dot{V}O_2max = 3.7$ liters

be able to use every training session as an opportunity to make small improvements in each of the other areas mentioned here.

Now that you've determined your training and competition objectives you can start planning training cycles.

Table 3.2

(continued)

	Objectives	
Year 3 **34:30**		**Year 4** **34:00**
Improve specific physical preparation Improve muscular endurance Perfect aerobic endurance Improve anaerobic endurance		Perfect specific physical preparation Perfect aerobic endurance Perfect anaerobic endurance
Identify anxieties and stressors and how to handle them Relaxation techniques		Identify anxieties and stressors and how to handle them Relaxation techniques
Relaxed running Efficient technical movement		Relaxed running Efficient technical movement
Take a good position before the finish Perfect the start		Cope with various strategies Perfect the finish
$\dot{V}O_2max = 4.1$ liters		$\dot{V}O_2max = 4.1$ liters

USE THE FOUR-WEEK TRAINING CYCLE

To make planning more organized and sensible, we like to divide all the weeks of a competitive season into smaller four-week increments or cycles. We then apply our chili recipe analogy to each cycle, carefully creating just the right flavor by varying the percentages of SERIOUS components. We've found that using four-week cycles works well, but some athletes and coaches use cycles of different lengths. Depending on the stage of the year, each of these cycles is planned to elicit the proper training response for that part of the year.

The basis of systematic training rests with a term we call *year hours*. This represents the total amount of time you'll devote to training and racing over a 52-week period. Every training plan accounts for 100 percent of the year's training time, regardless of your experience, the number of competition seasons you do per year, or your total amount of training time (year hours). Therefore, the amount of training you will do in each four-week cycle will represent a percentage of the total year hours. Table 3.3 illustrates this point. For simplicity, let's consider this four-week cycle percentage as the cooking pot in which you'll put the ingredients for each four-week cycle. You'll eventually select how much of each SERIOUS training component you'll want to use in each four-week cycle recipe.

Several factors dictate the percentage of the total year hours assigned to each four-week cycle. First, the training stage must be

Table 3.3

4-Week Training Cycles as Percentages of Yearly Training Volume

Cycle	Stage	% Year hours
1	Base	6
2	Base	7
3	Base	8
4	Base	9
5	Intensity	9
6	Intensity	10
7	Intensity	11
8	Intensity	9
9	Peak	8
10	Race	7
11	Race	7
12	Race	6
13	Regeneration	3
	Total	100

considered. Typically, training during the base stage is low in intensity and low-to-moderate in volume. As the weeks progress, you introduce a greater volume of training, and increase the number of high-intensity workouts per week. The intensity stage is marked by a progressive increase in both intensity and volume. Typically, this stage has the highest volume per four-week cycle of any stage during the year. The taper stage is characterized by less total training volume, but by high-intensity and "sharpening" workouts. The competition stage typically has high intensity, yet markedly reduced volume per cycle. The restoration stage is always characterized by alternative activities and unstructured exercise.

Use caution and foresight when deciding the volume increase from one four-week cycle to the next, especially during the intensity stage. Too much training too soon may result in overtraining. You must allow the body to adapt gradually to increases in volume and intensity.

As mentioned earlier, each four-week cycle will have a distinct flavor or format for eliciting the desired physiological training response. Planning this aspect of the cycle is critical because each cycle must prepare you for the next. Some experience with successfully planning training is helpful in designing each cycle's format. If all this is new to you, we'll help you with this process in the worksheets later in the chapter.

This first part of the process involves deciding which training components to use in each four-week cycle. Though you may use different names for each component, we use the SERIOUS training components. SERIOUS is the acronym for the seven training components in our system: speed, endurance, race/pace, interval, overdistance, up/vertical, and strength. Next, the percentage of each four-week cycle is divided into the SERIOUS components that will be used during that cycle. You'll want to consider your strengths and areas needing improvement. For example, if you are lacking in strength, then you must allocate more of the total training volume for that four-week cycle to improving strength. Figure 3.1 illustrates a typical division of the percentages of each training component per four-week cycle.

Weekly Patterns

You could say that the recipe you use for each four-week cycle will have a special flavor, but the difference in taste from one cycle to the next should be subtle, rather than distinct. This will allow

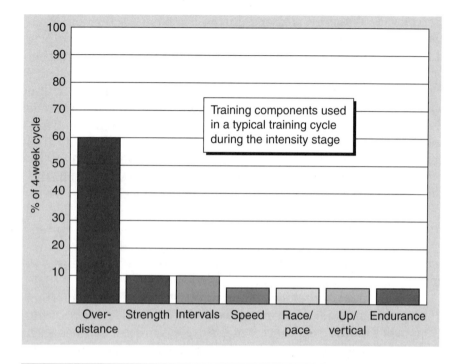

Fig. 3.1. Determine what percentage of training components you will use during each stage of your training cycle.

your body to adjust and adapt without causing too much stress to your system. Physiologically, the optimal training response is derived through training cycles that have weekly patterns designed around the following considerations:

Sensible and Predictable Weekly Pattern

First, it's ideal if the training pattern is similar from week to week and therefore predictable. For example, overdistance (long, slow distance) workouts might fit in best on Saturdays or Sundays if you have more time to train or your friends can join you on those days. Strength training on Monday, Wednesday, and Friday may fit your schedule best. Creating the weekly pattern depends on the logistics of life's other commitments, best time of day for workouts, days of the week when a certain facility is available, days when your friends are available, number of workouts that can be done per day, team workout schedule, and competition schedule. You may need to try several weekly patterns to find the best one. It is wise to remain flexible about the weekly pattern so that you can make necessary changes according to other changes in your schedule that might occur with family, work, and school. Also, the pattern you use during the few days before a competition (race week pattern) is important and must be designed appropriately.

Intensity

You must consider the intensity of each workout when creating the weekly pattern. Typically, you'll get the most benefit from a hard workout when it is followed by an easy workout, either that day or the next day. The hard day-easy day routine has been popular with athletes and coaches for some time. However, many athletes require two easy days following a hard day. Experience in understanding your body's recovery cues will help you determine the best routine for your body.

Multisport athletes, such as triathletes, duathletes, and cross-country skiers have entered a new dimension of training regarding hard-easy weekly patterns. Many athletes cross-train, using a high-intensity session in one sport followed by moderate-to-hard sessions in another sport, yet do not feel the debilitating fatigue that might result from back-to-back hard workouts using the same muscles. You won't see many successful runners doing high-intensity interval sessions followed by a hard race the next day.

Recovery

The weekly pattern should allow proper recovery between workouts. Some types of training actually promote restoration following high-intensity exercise. Low-intensity, short-to-moderate duration exercise serves to promote circulation and speed removal of metabolic waste from, and transport of nutrients to, damaged tissue. For example, many top runners rely on water running once per week as a specific restoration workout. For many athletes, one day off (no training) per week is an excellent method for promoting recovery. A detailed discussion of restorative theories and methods is presented in chapter 7.

Available Time

Since you'll be using some or all seven SERIOUS training components (speed, endurance, race/pace, intervals, overdistance, up/vertical, and strength) in a given week, you must schedule these into the available training sessions of the week. Depending on the athlete and the amount of time he or she is training, we may plan more than one workout per day. Athletes training at extremely high volumes (greater than 750 hours per year) may need to schedule three or four training sessions per day to fit in all the necessary types of training.

As a professional triathlete, I will sometimes swim, bike, run, cross-country ski, and do some strength training all in the same day (but that's my full-time job!)—Ray

However, most of us "desk jockeys" and developing younger athletes will be limited by work, school, family, and other commitments. Many will be able to train once per day during the week and possibly twice each day on the weekend. You need to be realistic when planning each week.

Figure 3.2 illustrates three different weekly training patterns. There is much room for variation here, depending on the time of year and what seems to work best for you. In general, we recommend that the weekly training pattern be consistent for each week of a four-week cycle and fairly consistent from cycle to cycle. Of course, you will need to make subtle changes in the patterns as you progress through the stages of the training year toward the competition stage. The basic framework of the weekly pattern, however, can remain much the same. Your body, your friends,

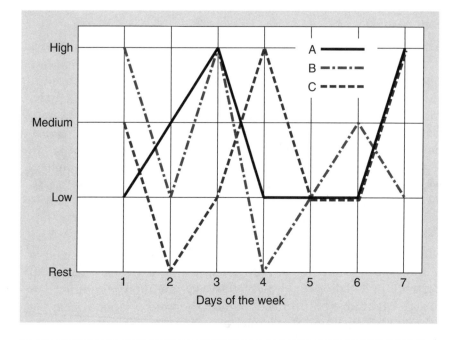

Fig. 3.2. Different weeks of training will have different stress loads.

and your family will adapt to it, too. For example, overdistance days can remain on Sundays throughout the year, strength days can remain on the days when facilities are available, and days that will be designated race/pace days during the peak and competition stages can be high-intensity interval days or pace days during the intensity stage.

Consistent weekly patterns will promote recovery between workouts, reduce mental stress caused by constantly changing schedules, and very gradually tune the body for the competition stage. Predetermined weekly training patterns promote an organized, sensible, and fluid progression of the training stimuli. While variety is the spice of life, unnecessarily changing the pattern each week is like changing your chili recipe—you might not like the taste very well.

Remember that you must occasionally toss aside even the best-laid plans to accommodate changes because of work, illness, family, or other factors. In such cases, there are several strategies recommended in chapter 9.

Periodization

If the percentage of your year hours you'll do in each four-week cycle is your pot of chili for the month, then how much of that chili you consume each week is referred to as the *periodization*. It is the structuring of the training hours for a given cycle to produce a progressive increase of training stress (volume and intensity). We like to use a staircase format for the first three weeks of the cycle, followed by steeply reduced hours (and sometimes intensity) during the fourth week of the cycle to allow for adequate recovery, restoration, and adaptation from the three buildup weeks. Figure 3.3 illustrates this staircase effect. Some athletes, in preparation for a major competition, might choose a descending periodization pattern, with the first week of the cycle being the hardest, the second week next hardest, the third week next in difficulty, and the fourth week the easiest. It is reasonable for a four-week cycle to have a different periodization pattern than those described above. For example, one might plan the first week as a hard week with higher volume, the second week as an easy week with lower volume, the third week like the first, and the last week of the cycle like the second week. A clever way to manage a vacation week away from your regular routine is to plan the easy week of the four-week cycle during your holiday. The options are many. The key is to experi-

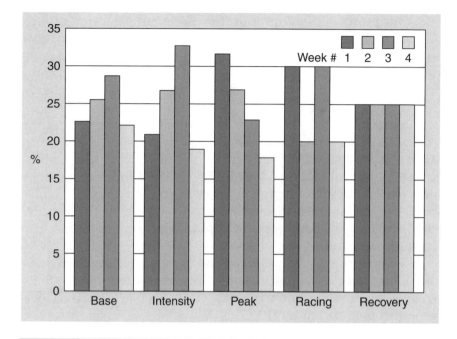

Fig. 3.3. Experiment with differing periodization patterns to select the right increase in training load from week to week.

ment with the periodization patterns and to consider the stage of training. Also, in structuring the periodization, select the correct increase in training load from week to week and insert low-volume rest weeks at the appropriate times.

The four-week cycle seems to be the most common length used by top athletes and coaches. It is not uncommon for elite competitors to plan the last week of each cycle to include different training activities, games, a change in training environments, or special treats such as extra massages. We learned that one European Olympic cross-country ski team, after a particularly difficult three-week training buildup, took a trip to the French Riviera for some warm sun, beaches, and easier training. We'll bet the coaches were popular that week!

Periodization will also take place from cycle to cycle, and stage to stage. In other words, the volume of training in the first cycle of the year may be slightly less than in the second cycle, and so on until you reach the highest volume during the last cycle of the intensity stage. Figure 3.4 illustrates periodization from cycle to cycle during a yearlong training program.

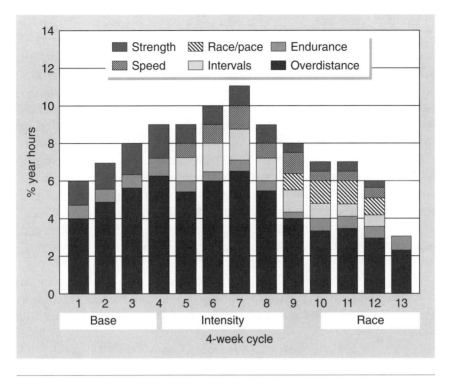

Fig. 3.4. Periodization distribution among training cycles.

The structure of periodization within each four-week cycle is subject to your individual experiences, proven methods used by top athletes and coaches, and the stage of the year. For example, during the base stage, a 23, 26, 29, 22 percent periodization might be best. However, during the intensity stage, a 21, 27, 33, 19 percent periodization might allow a more effective stress and recovery pattern. A taper cycle before a race could have a descending 32, 27, 23, 18 percent periodization, with the race planned for the fourth week of the cycle.

PLAN THE TRAINING YEAR

If you would like to learn thoroughly the process of creating your systematic training program from scratch, then this is the approach for you. Even though the process is fairly simple and easy to follow, it will take some perseverance and patience on your part.

You'll need some tools to make your job a bit easier (fig. 3.5). First, you will need a calculator. (A scientific calculator is best because it reads minutes, but you can use a standard calculator and work to fractions of an hour, finally converting fractions of an hour to minutes by multiplying the fraction by 60. For example: 1.25 hours = 75 minutes.) Second, you will need a pencil with an eraser. If you try to use a pen, you may find it frustrating when you make mistakes!

You'll need to photocopy the blank worksheets from appendix A that correspond to the sample worksheets used in this chapter. We strongly advise that you make several copies of each of the blank worksheets before you begin. It will be valuable and useful to copy all of your master worksheets after you have finished your planning so that you can refer to them later or in case of loss.

If you are accustomed to using a computer and know how to use spreadsheets, we recommend that you set up each of the blank worksheets on your computer as you read through the steps that follow.

© Anne Krause

Fig. 3.5. Take the time to carefully map out and document your training plan.

1: Determining Your Systematic Training Plan Objectives

It's useful to take some time to establish your goals and objectives for training and racing. Depending on your sport and level of commitment, the objectives of your plan may be to prepare you for your first sprint triathlon in six months or you may wish to design a four-year plan that will have you in your best shape ever to contend in your age group at the nationals.

Consider that there are goals that have a specific outcome, such as winning or placing in a specific race, and goals that are nonoutcome in nature, like improving your swim technique or increasing leg strength. It's likely that you'll have both types of goals. Since there are so many variables that will affect your place on the results sheet, we recommend that you pay a lot of attention to the nonoutcome goals. The old saying, "You walk a mile one step at a time," applies to training and racing. If you complete each aspect of the workout or race to your best ability, the result will take care of itself. If you have not done so yet, take some time to complete tables 3.1 and 3.2 to clarify your objectives for this program.

2: Competitions and Events

In table 3.1, you listed the races and events you are planning to do for the coming competition season. It is not critical that you know exact dates of races that are as much as 48 weeks away. The important part of this step is for you to decide which are the key events and to be clear about why they are most important to you.

3: Number of Weeks for This Plan—24 or 48 Weeks?

To simplify the planning process, we've designed the sample worksheets to incorporate 24 weeks of training and competition. This includes 8 weeks of base, 8 weeks of intensity and taper, and an 8-week competition phase. However, we recommend variations on this, depending on your time frame for the events you wish to complete.

If you are planning to compete in events that will occur in less than 16 weeks, then use the 24-week format for planning and start your training plan so that the competition phase of your plan matches your racing schedule. For example, if your competitions begin in 12 weeks you would begin your training plan with week 5, which would allow you to complete 4 weeks of base training, and 8 weeks of intensity and taper before the start of your season. If your events begin later than 16 weeks from your start date, then you can repeat one or more of the training cycles. For example, if your events are 24 weeks from your training start date, you would do 12 weeks of base training and 12 weeks of intensity and taper training before your events. If your events occur in 33 to 48 weeks, then you'll need to plan your training by repeating each of the 4-week cycles presented in the examples (you'll be using a 48-week program). A 48-week program includes four base cycles (16 weeks), four intensity cycles (16 weeks), a taper cycle (4 weeks), and three competition cycles (12 weeks).

4: Determining Your Level of Fitness and the Correct Year Hours

This is the most important step of the process, so pay close attention! Just how much chili do you want to make? Is your body ready to put away all that spicy stuff? Is your pot big enough to hold it all once it begins to simmer? Are you clear about this consuming a lot of time in your life?

Selecting the correct amount of training time that you'll use for your new training plan is probably the most critical, if not the most fundamental, decision you will make during this process. The reason is that the body can accommodate increases in training volume and intensity provided you apply these gradually. Too much too soon, and the body will beg for merciful rest. Or worse, it may betray your ambitious mind by plaguing you with injuries, fatigue, performance plateaus and staleness, or general lethargy. Overtraining is a phenomenon usually associated with too much training before the body is prepared to adapt.

How much training is enough? This is the critical question we must answer with every athlete we coach. History has shown some interesting approaches to answering it. The most common method for measuring training volume has been by measuring distance in miles, kilometers, or meters run, biked, swam, skied, rowed, and so forth. Rarely has the intensity of these distances been specified beyond hard, medium, or easy. Much emphasis is usually placed on pace, resulting in the compulsive use of stopwatches and chronometers. Every workout has the potential to become a time trial. Obviously, we have sincere reservations about this approach. We find that measuring distance/pace alone makes it difficult to determine the quality of a workout in terms of overall stress on the body. Instead, we've found it very useful to incorporate distance/pace information with other means of measuring workout stress and cumulative stress from, and adaptation to, the training plan. We also want to know how intense the workout was in terms of percentage of maximal aerobic capacity (percentage of $\dot{V}O_2max$). How much time did it take to cover the distance? Did you adhere to a predetermined time for completion of the distance, despite environmental conditions and how you were feeling? What was the physiological objective of the workout?

For example, let's say your magazine article "12 Weeks to a 10K PR" directs you to do an "easy" six-mile run at an eight-minutes-per-mile pace. If you are capable of a 36-minute 10K, this will be an "easy" run. However, if you're a 45-minute 10K runner and you run in a stiff headwind and 90 percent humidity, you'll struggle to complete the workout. The entire personality of the run changes, and the physiological stress of the workout is completely different from what was originally intended. There are many such examples, some of which you may have already experienced.

We have a more effective and complete way to calculate the training hours required for you to meet your goals. It begins by expressing your training loads in terms of time (volume) and intensity (heart rate as a percentage of $\dot{V}O_2max$). The expression of training volume that we advocate is year hours—the total amount of time spent training per year. After designing the structure of the training program, determining the correct volume of training in year hours is probably the most important decision you or your coach will make. There are several guidelines that will help you understand and select the right amount of time to train to meet your athletic goals and still live within your body's "workout budget."

Experience

The number of years you have been training and racing is an important consideration. An athlete with 12 years of training and competition most likely will be able to handle a higher volume as well as a larger increase in volume from year to year. Conversely, it would be out of line for a beginner athlete to start training at high volumes.

Your Present Fitness Level

Your present level of fitness will influence your training volume. If you were inactive through the winter, it would be asking for trouble to pick up the training where you left off in the fall when you were at peak fitness after a solid racing season. It's funny how the mind works—it expects one thing, but the body will deliver something completely different. Table 3.4 guides you in selecting a reasonable increase in training volume, if desired, based on your training history and your present level of fitness. First, estimate your present level of fitness by rating yourself on a scale of 1 to 10, with 1 being totally unfit and 10 being your best-ever fitness level. Then, using table 3.4, cross-reference your year hours last year with your present level of fitness to determine the recommended percentage increase in year hours for your new plan. Add this increase to last year's hours to obtain the new year hours.

If, for example, you spent 300 hours conditioning last year (including all types of aerobic training, racing, and strength exercises) and you rate your present level of fitness a 7, then this year you would increase your year hours by 10 percent (you do not calculate this number; find it in table 3.4) to obtain the new figure: 330 year hours.

Table 3.4

Recommended Percent Increase in Year Hours This Year

Year hours last year	Present level of fitness									
	1	2	3	4	5	6	7	8	9	10
<200	5	5	5	5	10	10	10	15	15	20
210-300	5	5	5	5	10	10	10	15	15	20
301-400	–	5	5	10	10	10	10	15	20	20
401-500	–	–	–	–	10	10	10	10	15	15
501-600	–	–	–	–	–	10	10	10	10	15
601-700	–	–	–	–	–	10	10	10	10	10
701-800	–	–	–	–	–	–	10	10	10	10
801-900	–	–	–	–	–	–	–	5	5	5
901-1000	–	–	–	–	–	–	–	–	–	–
>1000	–	–	–	–	–	–	–	–	–	–

Note. 1 = poor fitness level; 10 = best fitness level.

Another way of looking at this potential increase in year hours is to consider as a guideline an increase of 5 to 20 percent per year. This works well for experienced athletes who have not trained much recently but know it is possible for their bodies to safely handle such increases. However, we do not recommend that anyone training over 600 hours per year increase volume by more than 10 percent per year.

Available Training Time and Other Life Commitments

How much time do you have available each week, based on your commitments, such as work (or school), family, social, or civic activities, and so forth? It's a good idea to determine a list of priorities for these commitments and see where training fits in. Striving for balance in life, we believe, enhances training and competition.

If you are bound to a fixed amount of available training time per week, an easy way to calculate your year hours is to multiply your available weekly training time by 50 weeks. Because you have to abide by time guidelines, there will be no need to increase training time. *Caution: This method works well only if your available training time does not exceed the amount you trained last year by more than 20 percent.*

Training Volumes Determined by Event Goals

Another consideration in determining the correct amount of training is the standard volume used by elite athletes in your sport to train for the distances you wish to race. If professional and elite amateur triathletes are training 700 to 800 hours per year to prepare for an Ironman event, then it would probably be inappropriate and counterproductive for an inexperienced athlete to train more than that (unless training was the primary objective and competition was secondary).

Training volumes for various levels of commitment and experience in each endurance sport are presented in table 3.5 so that you can set an appropriate ceiling on year hours to train. In endurance sports, athletes who have trained for 10 or more years and who have developed the necessary physiological adaptations may be able to train fewer year hours with a slightly higher percentage of high-intensity work. This might not work for every experienced athlete; each will have to determine this individually.

Table 3.5

**Year Hours for Endurance
Events and Ability Level**

Event	Beginner	Average competitor	Age-group contender	Elite	World-class professional
			Ability		
Running 10K	100-200	150-250	200-350	300-400	400-600
Running marathon	200-250	250-300	300-400	350-500	500-800
Cycling road race	150-250	250-350	300-500	500-800	800-1200
Cycling century	150-250	200-300	250-400	350-500	500-800
Mountain bike race	150-250	200-300	300-350	400-700	650-1000
Triathlon/ duathlon sprint	200-300	250-350	300-400	350-500	500-700
Tri/Du Olympic	250-350	300-400	400-500	500-700	600-1000
Tri/Du ultra (Ironman)	NA	400-500	500-600	600-800	800-1200
Nordic ski race	150-250	200-350	250-500	400-700	700-1000
Rowing	150-250	250-350	300-450	400-600	600-1000
In-line skating	100-200	150-250	200-350	300-500	400-800

If you are a coach, the information presented here can form the basis of any training plan you might wish to design. One advantage of planning this way is that any of the variables—workout objective, percentage of year hours per workout, weekly patterns, periodization within a cycle, or total year hours—can be changed at any time for different athletes or training goals, and you can see clearly how the changes affect the overall program. For example, if an athlete starts a training program at 550 hours per year and after two months decides that family commitments make this goal unrealistic, the year hours can be reduced without undermining the integrity of the total program.

USE THE MASTER TRAINING TEMPLATES

We've created a series of master training templates like sample worksheets 3.1-3.6 and placed them in appendix A (A.1-A.6). These will serve either as guides or as gospel for your particular situation. All you'll have to do is determine your year hours and plug in the appropriate percentage of your total year hours as indicated in the template. We have created these plans based on our experiences successfully training many top athletes. We have developed these master template programs to suit typical situations, such as training for a 10K road race, a middle-distance triathlon, or a cross-country ski marathon. However, we encourage you to go through the planning process outlined in this chapter, even if you use one of the master templates, so that you will gain a solid understanding of the physiological principles of systematic training. If you use a template from appendix A, most of the work in worksheets 3.2 and 3.3 will have been done for you. You will still need to determine

- your objectives for the overall plan;
- your year hours (sample worksheet 3.1), actual dates of the four-week cycles, and the training stage and emphasis of each cycle (steps 1, 2, and 3 of worksheet 3.2);
- the percentage of SERIOUS components for each cycle (worksheet 3.3); and
- your weekly pattern and daily workouts for each four-week cycle (worksheet 3.6).

Let's get started! *Note: As you work through the planning process, remember to refer to the sample worksheets provided to give you ideas for your plan.*

Worksheet 3.1: Your Year Hours

If you have not already determined your year hours, worksheet 3.1 offers a step-by-step approach that will guide you in selecting an appropriate amount of training volume, based on past training and present level of fitness.

The number of year hours you select for your plan is based on several important factors. If you have accurate records, you can compare your year hours to those listed in table 3.5. If you would like to add more volume to this year's program, you can typically be safe with a 5 percent to 10 percent increase over last year. Otherwise, refer to table 3.5 to determine the correct percentage increase in training volume.

However, make increases in your yearly volume only up to the highest levels for top athletes in your sport. If you trained less than 400 hours last year and feel confident that you can handle an increase greater than 10 percent, you may select as much as a 20 percent increase in this year's volume. Do this with extreme caution, however, and be sure to follow many of the restoration principles described in chapter 7. Increasing your training volume too much can result in overtraining and illness and will adversely affect your racing.

If you are like many working professionals, you may have a limited, set amount of time you can devote to training each week. In this case, determine your total year hours by multiplying your available training time per week by 50. (We subtract two weeks of the year for no training due to illness, travel, etc.) For example, if you can devote 5 hours per week maximum to training, then your total year hours will be about 250 hours. You'll also need to keep this in mind when planning the percentage of total year hours per cycle and the periodization per cycle so there is not undue variation from your schedule.

Another factor that needs consideration is the amount of time you will spend warming up and cooling down at level one and two intensities. Typically, you might spend as much as 40 to 75 hours on warm-up and cool-down during the year. You do not specifically plan this into the total time allotments for speed, interval, up/vertical, race/pace, and strength workouts as presented in the master templates in appendix A. You can approach this problem in one of two ways. First, and perhaps most desirable, keep year hours as planned and use part of the overdistance and endurance training time allotments as warm-up and cool-down time for the other training components during the week. This approach works best if you have limited training time per week and probably can fit only one workout per day into the schedule. For example, plan a short, 30- to 45-minute endurance workout on a day you are planning a strength workout; use the endurance time as warm-up and cool-down for the strength session. A moderate-

Determining Your Year Hours

1. Rate your present level of fitness on a scale of 1 to 10, with 1 being totally unfit and 10 being your best fitness level ever.

   Your rating ___7___

2. How much aerobic exercise have you done in the last six months? Use an average number of hours per week. ___6-8___

3. Of the average number of hours per week determined in question #2, what percentage of those hours were done in each activity?

Activity/Sport	Percentage of average training hours/week
Example: Cycling	30%
1. Swimming	20%
2. Cycling	50%
3. Running	15%
4. In-Line Skating	5%
5. Weights	10%
6.	

4. How much time do you have available per week for training?

   ___15___ hours

5. Have you successfully trained more hours than your current average in past years? If yes, how much more?

   ___10___ hours per week

6. Do you want to decrease, maintain, or increase the amount of training in your new program?

   Decrease ____%   Maintain ____   Increase _5_ %

7. Your planned year hours _400_

length overdistance workout of 60 minutes may enhance recovery if you use 30 minutes of it as a warm-up before a stressful interval or race/pace session and 30 minutes of it directly after the session.

If you are training seriously year-round, use the second approach for integrating warm-up and cool-down time into your schedule: Add warm-up and cool-down time to the year hours planned earlier. We suggest that you adjust your selected total year hours by the amount of time you plan for warm-up and cool-down (usually 15 to 30 minutes each for workouts of intensity higher than overdistance or endurance).

Worksheet 3.2: Character of the Four-Week Cycle

This worksheet will help you make informed decisions about the character or personality of each four-week training cycle. It will be helpful if you have previous log records for reference. If not, do your best to remember how you have trained in the past. Then fill out the worksheet in these steps.

1: Total Year Hours

Copy your total year hours figured in worksheet 3.1 onto worksheet 3.2.

2: Actual Dates of Four-Week Cycles

Determine the actual date you will begin training with your plan. Then, using a calendar, count off four-week blocks and list the dates next to each training cycle (see sample worksheet 3.2.).

The year can be divided into 13 distinct four-week cycles totaling 52 weeks. You may wish to rearrange this format to include 17 three-week cycles or 10 five-week cycles, depending on your experience about what works best for you. In general, four-week repetitions are the most popular, and perhaps most natural, length for these cycles. If, as illustrated in sample worksheet 3.2, you are planning a program of 24 weeks, it is still necessary to use the same format for planning the training cycles as you would if planning for an entire year. You'll just need to abbreviate the length of the training stages and carefully select the emphasis of each cycle (see worksheet 3.2).

3: Training Stage and Emphasis of Each Cycle

You must designate each training cycle by stage and emphasis to clarify the physiological and psychological goals of that cycle. It is especially important to identify actual dates of your racing season(s) to designate the appropriate cycles. Refer to chapter 1 for a detailed explanation of each of the training stages. Also, you may want to emphasize particular technical aspects of training at certain times of the year.

4: Percentage of Total Year Volume per Cycle

This is the percentage of the total year hours included in each cycle. Determining this value for each cycle is critical to the effectiveness of the overall plan. If you are planning for two 24-week competitive seasons per year, then use 50 percent for each 24-week planning phase. In general, there is about a 5 percent to 10 percent increase per month, starting with the base stage and ending at the end of the intensity stage (see sample worksheet 3.2). The taper/peak stage usually is about a 20 percent decrease from the previous intensity cycle. Competition cycles typically contain 5 percent to 10 percent less volume than peaking stage cycles. This format holds true for 24-week plans, though the increases and decreases might be slightly less steep. Refer to appendix B master plan templates for your sport if you need more ideas on determining the percentage of total yearly volume per cycle.

5: Determination of the Periodization per Four-Week Cycle

A gradual increase in training volume per week for the first three weeks of the cycle followed by one week of decreased volume for the last week of the cycle will positively stress the body and allow recovery and adaptation to the imposed physiological demands. This will improve both the overall conditioning of your body and your confidence. Typically, the base stage requires gradual increases and decreases within its cycles, whereas the intensity, peak, and race stages require somewhat more drastic increases and decreases within cycles. However, you may wish to experiment with the periodization in your program. For example, we've used a 30, 20, 30, 20 format for a competition cycle, planning the races to occur at the end of the light-volume weeks. Sample worksheet 3.2 together with the master plan templates in appendix B will help you determine the periodization percentages for each week of the cycle.

Determination of Each 4-Week Cycle's Character

Training plan for March 1st – August 15th

Name Rob Sleamaker

[1] Year hours to train 400

4-week cycle	**[2]** Date	**[3]** Stage	**[3]** Emphasis	**[4]** % year hours	**[5]** Periodization %			
					Week			
					1	2	3	4
1	3/1 – 3/28	Base	Aerobic build-up; improve general strength	7	23	26	29	22
2	3/29 – 4/25	Base	Aerobic build-up; improve specific strength	8	23	26	29	22
3	4/26 – 5/23	Intensity	Aerobic base, intervals, hills, and specific strength	9	23	26	29	22
4	5/24 – 6/20	Intensity	Intervals, hills, speed, technique, and specific strength	9.5	20	30	20	30
5	6/21 – 7/18	Peak/race	Intervals, anaerobic speed, and race-pace	8.5	20	30	20	30
6	7/19 – 8/15	Race	Racing, maintain aerobic base and recovery	8	20	30	20	30

Worksheet 3.3: The Percentage of Training Components per Four-Week Cycle

In this worksheet you will need to make decisions about which SERIOUS training components you will use for your plan as well as the percentage of each within each training cycle. For simplicity, worksheet A.3 from appendix A and sample worksheet 3.3 use the components from the SERIOUS system, explained in chapter 4. You may wish to change the names of these components to fit your style, or you may end up using only some of the components—that's up to you. We must emphasize the importance of using common terminology when planning and discussing training. If you use terminology other than that presented with the SERIOUS acronym, be sure to include a description of the intensity and physiological purpose of each training component. Speaking the same language with other athletes or coaches will save much time and frustration. Follow these steps:

1: Stage

Copy the stage for each cycle as determined in worksheet 3.2.

2: Percentage of Hours

Copy the percentages of total training volume per cycle as determined in worksheet 3.2.

3: Percentage of Training Component per Cycle

Each training stage will emphasize a gradual increase in some components but decreases in others. Typically, 60 percent to 70 percent of a training cycle during the base stage will be overdistance, while 15 percent to 20 percent may be strength. The discussion of training stages in chapter 1 will be useful for deciding these percentages. Also, look back at tables 3.1 and 3.2 to review strengths and weaknesses so that you can incorporate these into your plan at this step. Sample worksheet 3.3 and the master template plans in appendix B offer guidance as well.

Worksheet 3.4: Training Plan for the Year—Spreadsheet Calculations

Now you're ready to create your training plan! Use worksheets 3.1, 3.2, and 3.3, along with your calculator and sharp pencil (or

Sample Worksheet 3.3

Determinination of the Percentage of Training Components Per 4-Week Cycle

Training plan for March 1st – August 15th

Name Rob Sleamaker

Year hours to train 400

4-week cycle	Date	**[1]** Stage	**[2]** % of hours	**[3]** Percentage per 4-week cycle						
				Speed	Endurance	Race/pace	Interval	Over-distance	Up/vertical	Strength
1	3/1 – 3/28	Base	7	0	15	0	0	60	5	20
2	3/29 – 4/25	Base	8	0	15	0	5	55	5	20
3	4/26 – 5/23	Intensity	9	5	15	0	10	50	10	10
4	5/24 – 6/20	Intensity	9.5	5	15	5	10	45	10	10
5	6/21 – 7/18	Peak/Race	8.5	5	15	10	10	50	0	10
6	7/19 – 8/15	Race	8	5	10	15	10	50	0	10

computer spreadsheet). Sample worksheet 3.4 will help you gain a clear picture of this process.

1: Projected Year Hours to Train

Copy this value from worksheet 3.2. Remember, you can set up your entire plan, and then easily decide to train more or fewer hours per year than originally planned. The integrity of your overall plan will stay intact, though the actual volume will change.

2: Training Stage

Copy these from worksheet 3.2.

3: Actual Dates of Each Cycle

Copy these from worksheet 3.2.

4: Percentage of Year Hours per Cycle

Copy these from worksheet 3.2.

5: Actual Hours per Cycle

Multiply your projected total year hours from step 1 by the percentage of year hours per cycle listed in step 4. Enter these values on worksheet 3.4.

6: Periodization Pattern

Copy this from worksheet 3.2.

7: Actual Hours per Week

Multiply actual hours per cycle calculated in step 5 by the periodization value in step 6. For example, if cycle 1 actual hours are 25 and week 1 periodization is 23 percent, then actual hours for week 1 will be 5.75 hours (.23 × 25 hours).

8: Determining Actual Hours of Each Training Component per Week

Multiply actual hours per week calculated in step 7 by the percentage of training components per four-week cycle you determined in worksheet 3.3. For example, taking the value of 5.75 hours for week 1 from the example in step 7, multiply 5.75 by 70 percent (or .70) if you want to train 70 percent overdistance in cycle 1. Be sure to double-check your calculations of each of these entries as you complete this step.

Worksheet 3.5: Spreadsheet Calculations With Percentages for Each Sport

In worksheet 3.4 you've created most of the training plan. The next step is determining how many minutes per week you'll do each SERIOUS component for every sport activity. This step applies primarily to multisport athletes, but single-sport athletes who like to do some cross-training will want to complete this step.

1: Expand Worksheet 3.4

Use the calculations for total minutes per week of each SERIOUS component from worksheet 3.4, step 8.

2: Percentage of Total Time per Sport for Each SERIOUS Component

We find that the best way to determine how much to train in each sport rests in actual race results. For example, of the total race time in a typical triathlon, you'll probably spend 20% swimming, 50% cycling, and 30% running. These will vary depending on each race course and your strengths.

Look at your last few race results and determine your time splits for each sport leg of the race in proportion to the total time. Calculate the average and this will give you the best breakdown to use in training.

3: Actual Minutes per Week for SERIOUS Components

Multiply the time for each SERIOUS component from step 8 in worksheet 3.4 by the percentage for each sport from step 2 above. Now you have an idea of how much time to train in each sport for each SERIOUS training type.

4: Sport

Single sports: Decide which sport activity you will use for the workout. This does not mean that your decision will be cast in stone. You may want to run one week and ride your mountain bike the next. As a rule, use sport-specific activities as you approach the competition stage.

Multisports (triathlon, duathlon, etc.): Since these sports require training in two or more sport disciplines, it's a good idea to divide your training time, by SERIOUS component, according to sound judgment. For example, in triathlon, if we analyze the total time to complete the race by reviewing the time splits for each sport, we would learn how to emphasize our training. A typical triathlon is 18 percent swimming, 55 percent biking, and 27 percent running, give or take a few percentage points depending on the race and the athlete's strengths and weaknesses.

Therefore, we believe it is a good idea to analyze your sport, the percentage splits you will experience in racing, and then determine your training pattern according to that formula. This rule applies for each SERIOUS component. For example, if you are a triathlete planning two hours of intervals this week, then you'll do 22 minutes of swimming intervals, 66 minutes of bike intervals, and 32 minutes of running intervals.

Duathletes might use a 60/40 split between biking and running. Mountain bike racers may use a 60/40 split between road biking and mountain biking.

Worksheet 3.6: The Weekly Pattern for Each Four-Week Cycle

Now you have created the actual yearly plan and calculated to the minute the amount of training for each component in each week of the year. This will create a balanced weekly training pattern that will indicate which training component to work on, which sport activity to use, intensity, and the actual time in minutes for each workout. Worksheet 3.6 allows you to plan one training cycle at a time. Use the calculations from worksheet 3.5 to create the weekly pattern for each cycle.

It is usually best to maintain the same weekly pattern for every week of a given cycle. However, you may need to alter this slightly in some cases. For example, during the competition stage you may want to race only twice per month. Therefore on two of the weeks you will use up the cycle's total time allotment for racing. During the other two weeks you will not race but instead do an overdistance or endurance session. Another variation you may want to try occasionally will be extra-long overdistance workouts, such as five-hour bike rides or daylong hikes during one week of the cycle. Therefore, you must change the other overdistance workouts of the cycle to accommodate the time taken from the cycle's overdistance time allotment. You may decide to take two or three days off one week, depending on schedule, need for rest, illness, and so on. You should be prepared to vary from your plan. The worst habit many athletes have is slavishly observing their original plans, neglecting to listen to their bodies and their inner voices, and therefore becoming overtrained or ill. Stay flexible!

Sample weekly patterns for each stage are outlined in sample worksheet 3.6. Typically, you'll want to follow some basic rules in creating your weekly patterns. Here are some ideas you may want to use:

• If you typically have more time available to train on weekends, then plan a long overdistance day on a Sunday or Saturday. This workout can be as much as 50 percent of the overdistance time allotment for the week. It's also a great way to get in some long sessions with friends or do some distance progressions if you are training toward an Ironman, marathon, century ride, or other long-duration event.

• Plan strength-training sessions to occur every other day or every third day to allow recovery to take place.

• Plan interval, up/vertical, race/pace days with at least one day of lower-intensity training between these high-intensity days for a given activity. Another way of thinking about this is to create a pattern that allows one or two easy days to follow hard days. For example, you may do biking intervals on Tuesday, running intervals on Wednesday, swim intervals on Thursday, and then a race/pace bike/run combination on Saturday.

• Follow all interval, up/vertical, race/pace, and hard speed workouts with an easy cool-down of 20 to 30 minutes. This promotes recovery from the high-intensity workouts. If possible, the next day should include an overdistance or endurance/easy distance workout in that activity.

• Maintain the same weekly patterns for several cycles in a row. The body becomes accustomed to consistency. This is particularly important during the peaking and competition stages, when recovery from stressful racing is essential. For example, during the competition stage, you may find that planning intervals on Wednesday, easy overdistance and easy speed on Thursday, and a short endurance workout on Friday will help you prepare best for a Saturday race. However, you will find that on some weeks, you'll want to change this pattern slightly to accommodate a very long overdistance workout or to make things fit with the logistics of travel, work and family, or the availability of facilities.

1: Training Cycle Number

Copy the training cycle number from worksheet 3.5 to worksheet 3.6.

2: Actual Dates of Training Cycle and of Each Week

Copy the actual dates from worksheet 3.5 to worksheet 3.6.

3: Objective

This describes the training component for each workout of the cycle's weekly pattern. Refer to the sample at the bottom of worksheet 3.6.

4: Intensity

Each workout has a specific physiological purpose, which is monitored by the intensity. Chapter 2 described five levels of intensity by heart rate and subjective feelings. Also, each SERIOUS training component has been assigned a relative intensity. The calculation for determining correct heart rate intensity ranges for each of the five levels is described in chapter 2. Turn to worksheet 2.1 now and calculate your heart rate intensity values. Then return to worksheet 3.6 and enter these values in the appropriate space.

5: Time in Minutes per Workout

Refer to worksheet 3.4 for this step. You've already calculated actual time per week for each training component, and you've chosen a weekly pattern for training with those components. Now you need to decide how much of each component you will use on each day. The sample at the bottom of worksheet 3.6 identifies the associated percentage of training component time allotment during the week. Generally, you'll find that you'll need to divide overdistance and strength time allotments between two or three days during the week. The other components, because of the relatively small total time for each, will easily be planned into one workout each per week.

PLAN WITH FLEXIBILITY

Training plans can be modified. You are in control of your plan, and it's a good idea to remain in control rather than become a slave to it. The planning you have done in this chapter has

Training Plan for a 24-Week Cycle—Spreadsheet Calculations

Training plan for March 1st – August 15th

Name Rob Sleamaker

Projected year hours to train 400

Objective Olympic distance triathlon and multisport preparation

1	**Four-week cycle**	**1**				**2**				**3**			
2	**Training stage**	BASE				BASE				INTENSITY			
	Week numbers	1 – 4				5 – 8				9 – 12			
3	**Actual dates**	3/1 – 3/28				3/29 – 4/25				4/26 – 5/23			
4	**% of year hours**	7				8				9			
5	**Hours/cycle**	28				32				36			
	Week number	1	2	3	4	5	6	7	8	9	10	11	12
6	**Periodization**	23	26	29	22	23	26	29	22	23	26	29	22
7	**Hours/week**	6.44	7.28	8.12	6.16	7.36	8.32	9.28	7.04	8.28	9.36	10.44	7.92
8	**Below: Total minutes per week of each SERIOUS component**												
	Speed	–	–	–	–	–	–	–	–	25	28	31	24
	Endurance	58	66	73	55	66	75	84	63	75	84	94	71
	Race/pace	–	–	–	–	–	–	–	–	–	–	–	–
	Intervals	–	–	–	–	22	25	28	21	50	56	63	48
	Overdistance	232	262	292	222	243	275	306	232	248	281	313	238
	Up/vertical	19	22	24	18	22	25	28	21	50	56	63	48
	Strength	77	87	97	74	88	100	111	84	50	56	63	48

1	Four-week cycle		**4**			**5**				**6**			
2	Training stage	INTENSITY			PEAK/RACE				RACE				
	Week numbers	13 – 16			17 – 20				21 – 24				
3	Actual dates	5/24 – 6/20			6/21 – 7/18				7/19 – 8/15				
4	% of year hours	9.5			8.5				8				
5	Hours/cycle	38			34				32				
	Week number	13	14	15	16	17	18	19	20	21	22	23	24
6	Periodization	23	26	29	22	22	27	33	18	20	30	20	30
7	Hours/week	7.60	11.40	7.60	11.40	6.80	10.20	6.80	10.20	6.40	9.60	6.40	9.60
8	Below: Total minutes per week of each SERIOUS component												
	Speed	23	34	23	34	20	31	20	31	19	29	19	29
	Endurance	68	103	68	103	61	92	61	92	38	58	38	58
	Race/pace	23	34	23	34	41	61	41	61	58	86	58	86
	Intervals	46	68	46	68	41	61	41	61	38	58	38	58
	Overdistance	205	308	205	308	204	306	204	306	192	288	192	288
	Up/vertical	46	68	46	68	–	–	–	–	–	–	–	–
	Strength	46	68	46	68	41	61	41	61	38	58	38	58

allowed you to think carefully about your training. Now you have documentation that outlines what you are planning to do, how often, how much, and at what intensity. Every workout relates closely to the others. If you need to make changes in the plan, such as with total year hours, you can make the changes quickly while maintaining the integrity of the entire plan and clearly seeing how the changes affect the overall plan. Now you have detailed plans that you yourself designed and can change at any time. Also, you have recorded these plans so that next year you can reflect on them and make changes to strengthen the areas needing improvement and further improve your strongest characteristics. Refer to chapter 9 for more guidance on adjusting your plan.

ADJUSTING WEEKLY PATTERNS

A reminder: It's all right to change the weekly pattern within a cycle. For example, one week you may want to plan Wednesday as your day off because of a dentist appointment, and the next week keep Friday as the planned day off. Or, you may wish to make a daylong overdistance hike one week that will use up the entire week's overdistance time allotment. In this case, it would be best to steal some overdistance time from the other week or take off one of the planned overdistance workouts from the same week.

You'll find, as the year progresses, that weekly patterns will begin to make more sense to you and that a steady routine will work best, both with your body's adaptation and lifestyle logistics. Make the pattern fit these considerations at the outset, and your training will truly enhance your lifestyle. If it feels as if you are "pushing the river," then step back from your plan, make some changes in scheduling, and get back into the training. Remember to go with the flow.

CHOOSING A WINNING TRAINING PLAN

From appendix B, find the training plan that matches your activity, level, and year hour range. If no plan is listed under your

Spreadsheet Calculations with Percentages for Each Sport

Training plan for   March 1st – August 15th

Name   Rob Sleamaker

Projected year hours to train   400

Objective   Olympic distance triathlon and multisport preparation

	1 Four-week cycle	1				2				3			
	2 Training stage	BASE				BASE				INTENSITY			
	Week numbers	1 – 4				5 – 8				9 – 12			
	3 Actual dates	3/1 – 3/28				3/29 – 4/25				4/26 – 5/23			
	4 % of year hours	7				8				9			
	5 Hours/cycle	28				32				36			
	Week number	1	2	3	4	5	6	7	8	9	10	11	12

9 Below: Multiply total minutes per week of each SERIOUS component by the designated percentage for each sport activity

	1	2	3	4	5	6	7	8	9	10	11	12
Speed[1]												
Swim @ 0%	–	–	–	–	–	–	–	–	–	–	–	–
Bike @ 50%	–	–	–	–	–	–	–	–	12	14	16	12
Run @ 50%	–	–	–	–	–	–	–	–	12	14	16	12
Endurance[2]												
Swim @ 20%	12	13	15	11	13	15	17	13	15	17	19	14
Bike @ 50%	29	33	37	28	33	37	42	32	37	42	47	36
Run @ 30%	17	20	22	17	20	22	25	19	22	25	28	21
Race/pace[3]												
Swim @ 20%	–	–	–	–	–	–	–	–	–	–	–	–
Bike @ 50%	–	–	–	–	–	–	–	–	–	–	–	–
Run @ 30%	–	–	–	–	–	–	–	–	–	–	–	–
Intervals[4]												
Swim @ 35%	–	–	–	–	8	9	10	7	17	20	22	17
Bike @ 35%	–	–	–	–	8	9	10	7	17	20	22	17
Run @ 30%	–	–	–	–	7	7	8	6	15	17	19	14
Overdistance[5]												
Swim @ 20%	46	52	58	44	49	55	61	46	50	56	63	48
Bike @ 50%	116	131	146	111	121	137	153	116	124	140	157	119
Run @ 30%	70	79	88	67	73	82	92	70	75	84	94	71
Up/vertical[6]												
Swim @ 0%	–	–	–	–	–	–	–	–	–	–	–	–
Bike @ 60%	12	13	15	11	13	15	17	13	30	34	38	29
Run @ 40%	8	9	10	7	9	10	11	8	20	22	25	19
Strength[7]	77	87	97	74	88	100	111	84	50	56	63	48

Sample Worksheet 3.5
(continued)

	Four-week cycle		4				5				6		
2	Training stage		INTENSITY				PEAK/RACE				RACE		
	Week numbers		13 – 16				17 – 20				21 – 24		
3	Actual dates		5/24 – 6/20				6/21 – 7/18				7/19 – 8/15		
4	% of year hours		9.5				8.5				8		
5	Hours/cycle		38				34				32		
	Week number	13	14	15	16	17	18	19	20	21	22	23	24

9 Below: Multiply total minutes per week of each SERIOUS component by the designated percentage for each sport activity

	13	14	15	16	17	18	19	20	21	22	23	24
Speed[1]												
Swim @ 0%	–	–	–	–	–	–	–	–	–	–	–	–
Bike @ 50%	11	17	11	17	10	15	10	15	10	14	10	14
Run @ 50%	11	17	11	17	10	15	10	15	10	14	10	14
Endurance[2]												
Swim @ 20%	14	21	14	21	12	18	12	18	8	12	8	12
Bike @ 50%	34	51	34	51	31	46	31	46	19	29	19	29
Run @ 30%	21	31	21	31	18	28	18	28	12	17	12	17
Race/pace[3]												
Swim @ 20%	5	7	5	7	8	12	8	12	12	17	12	17
Bike @ 50%	11	17	11	17	20	31	20	31	29	43	29	43
Run @ 30%	7	10	7	10	12	18	12	18	17	26	17	26
Intervals[4]												
Swim @ 35%	16	24	16	24	14	21	14	21	13	20	13	20
Bike @ 35%	16	24	16	24	14	21	14	21	13	20	13	20
Run @ 30%	14	21	14	21	12	18	12	18	12	17	12	17
Overdistance[5]												
Swim @ 20%	41	62	41	62	41	61	41	61	38	58	38	58
Bike @ 50%	103	154	103	154	102	153	102	153	96	144	96	144
Run @ 30%	62	92	62	92	61	92	61	92	58	86	58	86
Up/vertical[6]												
Swim @ 0%	–	–	–	–	–	–	–	–	–	–	–	–
Bike @ 60%	27	41	27	41	–	–	–	–	–	–	–	–
Run @ 40%	18	27	18	27	–	–	–	–	–	–	–	–
Strength[7]	46	68	46	68	41	61	41	61	38	58	38	58

[1] **Note.** Swimming intervals incorporate speed training.

[2] **Note.** It's OK to use EN time allotments as warm-up for intervals, up/verticals, speed, or race/pace sessions.

[3] **Note.** Combine race/pace times for 2 weeks and do this workout twice per month.

[4] **Note.** It's OK to combine bike and run interval times with up/vertical interval time to create one workout when time allotments are small.

[5] **Note.** Plan to do all three sports or a bike/run "brick" in at least one session per month.

[6] **Note.** Do these sessions in terrain that is similar to the terrain in which you will race.

[7] **Note.** Sports-specific exercises recommended whenever possible.

Determining the Weekly Pattern for Each 4-Week Cycle

Training plan for <u>March 1st – August 15th</u>

Name <u>Rob Sleamaker</u>

Projected year hours to train <u>400</u>

Daily workouts	Base stage: Sample Week #1			Intensity stage: Sample Week #12		
	Objective	% of total	Mins	Objective	% of total	Mins
1A	OD–Bike	60%	70	OD–Bike	60%	71
1B	OD–Run	60%	42	OD–Run	60%	43
1C				SP–Run	100%	12
2A	Day off			Day off		
2B						
2C						
3A	OD–Swim	100%	46	OD–Swim	100%	48
3B	EN–Run	100%	17	EN–Run	100%	21
3C	ST–Circuit	50%	38	ST–Circuit	50%	24
4A	EN–Bike	100%	29	EN–Bike	100%	36
4B	UP–Bike	100%	12	IN+UP–Bike	100%	38
4C						
5A	EN–Swim	100%	12	EN–Swim	100%	14
5B						
5C	ST–Circuit	50%	38	ST–Circuit	50%	24
6A	OD–Run	40%	28	OD–Run	40%	28
6B	UP–Run	100%	8	IN+UP–Run	100%	33
6C						
7A	OD–Bike	40%	46	OD–Bike	40%	62
7B				SP–Bike	100%	12
7C						

SP = Speed
EN = Endurance
RP = Race/pace
IN = Intervals
OD = Overdistance
UP = Up/vertical
ST = Strength

Sample Worksheet 3.6
(continued)

Daily Workouts	Peak stage: Sample Week #17			Racing stage: Sample Week #21		
	Objective	% of total	Mins	Objective	% of total	Mins
1A	OD–Bike	60%	61	OD–Bike	60%	58
1B	OD–Run	60%	37	OD–Run	60%	35
1C	SP–Run	100%	10	SP–Run	100%	10
2A	Day off			Day off		
2B						
2C						
3A	OD–Swim	100%	41	OD–Swim	100%	38
3B	IN–Run	100%	14	IN–Run	100%	13
3C	ST–Circuit	50%	20	ST–Circuit	50%	19
4A	EN–Bike	100%	31	EN–Bike	100%	19
4B	IN–Bike	100%	14	IN–Bike	100%	13
4C	EN–Run	100%	18	EN–Run	100%	12
5A	OD–Run	40%	24	OD–Run	40%	23
5B	IN–Run	100%	12	IN–Run	100%	12
5C	ST–Circuit	50%	20	ST–Circuit	50%	19
6A	OD–Bike	40%	41	OD–Bike	40%	38
6B	SP–Bike	100%	10	SP–Bike	100%	10
6C	EN–Swim	100%	12	EN–Swim	100%	10
7A	RP–Swim	200%	20	RP–Swim	200%	29
7B	RP–Bike	200%	51	RP–Bike	200%	72
7C	RP–Run	200%	30	RP–Run	200%	43
	Note. Combine weeks 17 + 18 times for RP.			**Note.** Combine weeks 21 + 22 times for RP.		

SP = Speed
EN = Endurance
RP = Race/pace
IN = Intervals
OD = Overdistance
UP = Up/vertical
ST = Strength

year hours and type of event, it indicates that the year hour totals are too low to realistically compete in the event. For example, it is unrealistic to train for the Ironman distance triathlon if your training volume is less than 450 hours.

FROM EXPERIENCE

RAY BROWNING, MS

The foundation for creating a training plan that will work best for you is dependent on matching your objectives, your fitness level, and the amount of time that you really have to train. One of the most common problems I have seen with athletes is a mismatch of goals, fitness level, and available time. Be very conservative when estimating your training year hours. If you think that you have 10 hours per week, plan your training by estimating 8 to 9 hours per week. Table 3.5 provides some guidelines for setting performance goals based on the time you have available. If you do not have the minimum number of hours available, it would be wise to reconsider the event and choose a shorter event or realize you may not be able to achieve a top performance.

Use caution when setting performance goals that specify a specific result in an event, like winning a local road race. A better method is to specify a target effort and focus that you want to maintain. A key to effective goal setting is to have self-acceptance goals for performances. These goals specify that you will accept your performance regardless of the outcome and will not belittle yourself or take out postrace frustrations on those around you. It is ironic that the people who have been the most supportive throughout the preparation stages will often feel the brunt of our performance frustrations. Have a strategy to deal with a subpar performance. I have learned that I need some time by myself (10 to 15 minutes) immediately after a race to cool down psychologically. I use this time to remind myself that I did the best I could, and that it is not appropriate to unleash whatever frustrations I may have on those around me.

Remember to schedule a variety of activities, locations, and training partners into your program. Make a list of the alternative activities available to you, and plan one of these activities at least once per month. Several years ago I made a list of potential training types and came up with 47 activities I could do. This eliminated all of my excuses for boredom, procrastination, or avoidance of training. As I plan the upcoming season, I will use my list at the outset to add several fun sessions into my plan. That way, I will not need to give myself a jump start during the season. It's a strategy that prevents burnout and promotes maximum fun and the best results.

Doing SERIOUS Workouts

Now that you've created your training plan in chapter 3, you'll need more specific guidelines on how to do each SERIOUS training component. Remember, the SERIOUS acronym stands for the seven types of training you will do during your training and racing season: speed, endurance, race/pace, intervals, overdistance, up/vertical, and strength.

Training for endurance sports has a language of its own, with many different words, phrases, and definitions. When it comes to endurance sports training, we speak a variety of dialects. For example, *speed training* may imply high-intensity track intervals to one athlete yet may mean relaxed, high-speed, short-distance 200-meter sprints to another. In this chapter we will discuss the specifics of each type of SERIOUS training, so that you may fully understand the format of your training sessions.

COMPONENTS OF A WORKOUT

We created the SERIOUS systematic approach to training to provide a universal translator, even though people may continue to speak slightly different dialects of the training language (fig. 4.1) Every SERIOUS workout has four primary components that are predetermined in the overall plan. These include

- the SERIOUS objective,
- the sport activity,
- the intensity, and
- the duration for each training session.

These components are intended to elicit specific physiological responses from the workout. Standardizing workouts by these four components allows you to objectively measure the relative value of other variables, such as the method of training, the technique, or the equipment used for the workout. Maintaining this level of objectivity allows you to make informed adjustments in the training plan expeditiously either at the beginning of a new planning phase or during a particular training stage.

We created the SERIOUS acronym to serve as a teaching tool that gets everybody talking the same language and promotes faster learning about the variables that improve training and racing. Table 4.1 illustrates each component and its primary objectives.

These seven training components, each defined by physiological objective, sport activity, intensity, duration, and technical purpose, can be used to compose any conceivable training plan for an endurance athlete. Incorporating them into a systematic plan

© John Kelly

Fig. 4.1. Communicate with other athletes who have a systematic training plan. You can share ideas and fine-tune your plan.

Table 4.1

SERIOUS Training Components and Objectives

Intensity		Primary objective during each stage of training			
Level	Range	Base	Intensity	Taper	Competition
SPEED	2-5	Body speed Tempo speed bursts	Body speed	Peaking	Maintain
ENDURANCE	2-3	Easy cruise	Easy recovery	Easy recovery	Easy recovery
RACE/PACE	3-4	None	Training	Race prep	Best races
INTERVALS	4	Build AT	Build AT	Tune AT	Maintain AT
OVERDISTANCE	1	Base building	Base building	Maintain	Maintain
UPHILL INTERVALS	4	Build AT	Build AT	Tune AT	Maintain AT
STRENGTH	1-2	General	More specific	Specific	Maintain

carefully directs the purpose, eliminates language barriers, and expedites learning. For example, if two athletes are training systematically, they can effectively communicate with each other regarding various ways to accomplish a given objective. Knowing the duration and intensity of a workout allows you to clearly understand its purpose and enhances its outcome. As you accumulate experiences, you'll quickly learn more about the impact each component has on your fitness.

SERIOUS WORKOUTS DEFINED

Each of the seven SERIOUS components has been referred to in many ways by various coaches, physiologists, and athletes over the years. This part of the chapter defines each SERIOUS component by its physiological purpose, time, and intensity. We attempt to describe the various synonyms that others have used. Included with these definitions are descriptions of how to accomplish each type of workout and to apply these concepts to your chosen sport.

Speed

An endurance athlete in training is preparing the body to move fast over a given distance. Sustained speed is what racing is all about. To maintain speed in racing, we need to teach the muscles to move fast during speed training (fig. 4.2). Sharkey (1984) defines speed as the combination of reaction time (time from stimulus to the start of movement) and movement time (time to complete the movement). We like to think of speed as the body's ability to move at a high tempo (strokes or strides per minute) with maximum efficiency for a prolonged time. Every sport has its requirements for speed. Speed varies among individuals. Your goal is to become faster relative to yourself.

A key variable for generating speed rests with your muscle fiber types. Each of us is born with a certain number of muscle fibers that are either *fast-twitch* or *slow-twitch* in nature. Fast-twitch (FT) muscle fibers can contract, or fire, rapidly upon stimulation. These fibers allow the body to generate speed. Typically, fast-twitch muscle fibers exhaust rather quickly when used at maximum effort, usually tiring within the first two minutes of speed-burst activity, depleting their energy stores within this time. It takes only a few minutes of recovery, however, to replenish those

Fig. 4.2.   Speed work is a necessary ingredient for your training plan.

energy stores. In races, you'll rely primarily on your fast-twitch fibers in swim starts, on the first running leg in duathlons, during sprint surges when passing another racer, and at the finish.

Actually there are two types of fast-twitch fibers. Fibers of the first type, described above, are pure speed-generating fibers with limited endurance. Fast-oxidative glycolitic (FOG) fibers are the second type, which you can train to have both speed and endurance characteristics.

I was always one of the fastest kids on my sports teams in school. In high school and college I was a sprinter in track and the fastest sprinter on the soccer team. Once I got to graduate school, my interests turned to endurance sports like running, triathlon, and cross-country skiing. After a few years of long-distance training for these sports, my performance in competitions improved steadily until I was consistently finishing in the top 25 percent of the pack. However, when I jumped into a pickup soccer game one day, my legs just didn't have the raw sprinting speed that they once had. My mind said "go," but my body said "no!" Physiologically, all the endurance training I'd done had "converted" my FOG fibers from sprinters to sloggers.—Rob

Slow-twitch (ST) muscle fibers can contract at a moderate speed over a prolonged time. At moderate intensity, these fibers might contract repeatedly for hours before fatiguing. These rely on the aerobic energy system for supplying fuel for contraction. Oxygen enters the blood, is carried to the muscle cells, and mixes with glycogen (and free fatty acids) within the cell in a process called *oxidation*. Energy is released so the muscle fiber can contract. The cycle can continue over a long time, given enough fuel and oxygen. This is the system primarily used for all endurance activities.

Most people have a fairly even mix of fiber types. Elite endurance athletes tend to have about 90 percent slow-twitch fibers, while top sprinters have 90 percent fast-twitch fibers. For example, Costill (1979) conducted muscle biopsy tests revealing that among elite U.S. distance runners, 90 percent of gastrocnemius (calf) muscle is composed of ST fibers, whereas elite sprinters may have 90 percent FT fibers. If as a kid you were the fastest sprinter and highest jumper in your neighborhood, then you're probably more of a fast-twitcher. But if you were the weird kid who could lap the rest of your PE class in the mile run, you're most likely predominantly slow-twitch. It is important to understand that your body is composed of a certain percentage of fast-twitch and slow-twitch muscle fibers. Genes determine the proportions; you cannot change them. However, as in Rob's example, you can improve the endurance capacity of your FOG fast-twitch fibers.

If you want to get an idea of your muscle fiber composition, the following may give you some clues:

- Vertical jump: If you can jump more than 16 inches upward from a standing start, you probably have more FT fibers than ST fibers in your thigh and calf muscles.
- If you were always the fastest runner on the block for short distances but couldn't keep up over longer distances, you may be a fast-twitcher.

- If you can run, bike, swim, or hike all day at a moderate intensity without tiring, you're probably more of a slow-twitcher.

Regardless of your fiber type composition, if you've been training only endurance and little speed, you can resurrect what fast-twitch muscle fibers you do have and train them to go faster, to have more available energy, and to recover more quickly after exhausting training. Most importantly, you can teach your entire musculoskeletal system to move faster. The neuromuscular pathways used for coordinating fast movement will be improved, facilitating smooth, relaxed, and coordinated swimming, cycling, running, skiing, and so forth. Whether it be for passing a competitor, avoiding a determined dog, or regaining some or all the speed of your youth, you should incorporate speed in your plan.

The need for neuromuscular speed training is an integral part of endurance training. We all have brain-to-muscle (neuromuscular) pathways. These pathways can be likened to a path across a meadow. If the path is walked on frequently, the grass cannot grow over the path, and the way remains clear. If we discontinue using the path, the grass will grow over, and it will become difficult to find the way. Thus, it is important to use speed training throughout the year to develop and maintain clear neuromuscular pathways employed in fast swimming, cycling, running, etc. You can also refer to this type of training as *skill speed*, implying efficient technique at race speed.

Neuromuscular speed training, or skill speed, must always be accompanied by a certain state of mind. When we think of speed, an image of gritted teeth, clenched fists, and tense muscles often comes to mind. These images imply forced, hard effort. Speed work for improving neuromuscular coordination in sports, however, must be accomplished with as little muscle tension as possible while moving the arms and legs as fast as possible. This sounds contradictory, but you can do it by focusing on being efficient and economical, using only the primary mover muscles and relaxing the nonmovers.

Speed training is essential for (1) improving the neuromuscular coordination and maximum speed, (2) improving your anaerobic energy systems, and (3) gaining a better sense of pace per kilometer at race intensity.

Many coaches and athletes use the word *speed* as a universal term for several different types of training. People have used speed to describe short, intense, 15- to 30-second repeats; longer intervals (one to six minutes long) at high intensity; racing and pace workouts; easy and relaxed 200-meter speed intervals; and easy five-second pickups (acceleration periods) used during distance training.

In the SERIOUS system, we like to use three types of speed training, each with its own distinct purpose. They are (1) tempo speed bursts, (2) body speeds, and (3) peaking sprints. Only a small portion of the total training volume will be devoted to speed. The amount of speed work in a given cycle will depend on the stage of the year and the number of hours you are training that year. Typically, you will use tempo speed bursts all year during overdistance sessions, body speeds during the intensity, taper and competition stages, and peaking sprints only during the taper and competition stages.

Endurance

Endurance is defined as the ability to withstand stress over prolonged periods—in the case of endurance sports, prolonged physical stress. Endurance training, often called easy distance, accomplishes many things. It increases your body's ability to consume oxygen ($\dot{V}O_2$max), increases the size and number of mitochondria in muscle cells (mitochondria are little powerhouses within each cell), increases the size and number of capillaries, and improves aerobic enzymes for carbohydrate and fat metabolism. These changes are described in greater detail in the discussion of overdistance training and in the section in chapter 2 on intensity. In short, endurance exercise improves your body's ability to deliver the goods to your muscles so that they adapt, grow stronger, and become better at prolonged effort.

All training plans must include a certain amount of endurance exercise. In the SERIOUS system, endurance and overdistance training are important components for developing and maintaining aerobic endurance. The endurance workouts outlined for your sport are primarily dedicated to improving aerobic capacity. *Aerobic* describes exercise that takes place in the presence of oxygen supplied to the muscle tissues through the cardiorespiratory system. This type of exercise is at minimum 10 continuous minutes in duration.

The other type of exercise is called *anaerobic*, meaning without oxygen. Anaerobic exercise occurs whenever the oxygen demands exceed the oxygen supplies of the cardiorespiratory system. Usually anaerobic exercise consists of short-burst, high-intensity effort, which produces lactic acid, a metabolic by-product. If accumulated in significant quantity in the system, lactic acid may cause fatigue, labored breathing, discomfort, and a sense of distress. It is important to note that exercise is never completely aerobic or completely anaerobic (except for the first 10 to 30 seconds of movement). It is a continuum where at low intensities the energy is primarily derived aerobically, while at the highest intensity the energy is primarily supplied anaerobically.

We recommend that endurance workouts be accomplished at low intensity (see chapter 2). Endurance and overdistance workouts differ in their duration and intensity, with endurance workouts being shorter and at slightly higher intensity than overdistance training (fig. 4.3). You should do most of SERIOUS training either with low-intensity and long-duration (overdistance) training, or at high-intensity, anaerobic threshold pace; therefore, you'll devote only a small percentage of the total training volume to endurance training.

Race/Pace

Races are opportunities to test the results of your diligent SERIOUS systematic training. Competitions, regardless of size, form, place, or time, are also opportunities to meet "problems" as challenges, to notice the small, nonoutcome goals you've accomplished, and to have a lot of fun! They are a culmination of the training process and are the goals to strive for as you play at this game of endurance sports and fitness. In the striving, you will learn many things about yourself and your capabilities. Competitions can be as serious as you make them. Remember to keep them in perspective with all the other aspects of your life (fig. 4.4).

During the intensity and taper stages before the racing season, some races or time-trial pace workouts will be scheduled at least once per month. Use these workouts as benchmarks for determining your fitness, your ability to maintain a faster pace, and the effectiveness of your training plan. They will also maintain motivation for training before the racing season and help you work out the bugs in technique, equipment, and strategy.

During the early part of your program, remember to keep your sights on your long-term goals for competition. The primary goal of early race/pace workouts is to help you measure the sustainable

© John Kelly

Fig. 4.3. Endurance training offers a great opportunity to try cross-training with alternative exercises.

pace at a predetermined heart rate and perceived exertion at that pace. It is important that you recognize the difference between maximum effort and the effort possible at your current fitness level. *Current fitness level* assumes that you are still building your conditioning and that your body is not quite ready to be pushed to an all-out effort. *Maximum effort* means an all-out effort, which you will use during the racing season.

© John Kelly

Fig. 4.4. Races test the effectiveness of your plan. Here's Ray looking very SERIOUS!

The keys to becoming a better racer are efficiency, control and self-discipline with pace and intensity, and the knowledge you gain by listening to your body. The most accomplished endurance athletes have been competing for many years. The lessons they have learned have come by many hours of practice, trial and error, and a systematic approach to analyzing their performance through objective testing and self-reflection.

Intervals

The popular training jargon describing intervals can be variable and inconsistent. In the SERIOUS system, intervals and uphill intervals are essentially the same, except for differences in terrain. Both help your body perform physiological magic, since they will get you very fit, very fast. Intervals are recurrent periods of

© John Kelly

Fig. 4.5.   Intervals can be done on a measured course, fartlek style, or for set times.

high-intensity exercise ranging from 1 to 10 minutes, followed by recovery intervals of varying time (see chapter 2 for intensity guidelines). Intervals are done on terrain that is flat, rolling, or slightly downhill; on running tracks; on treadmills; or in a pool. Treadmills are great for doing tightly controlled running intervals or to beat bad weather. The intensity is the same for intervals and uphill intervals.

Interval training challenges your body's ability to carry and deliver oxygen to the muscle cells for short periods of fairly intense work before too much lactic acid builds up. Remember those fast-twitch fibers—fast glycolytic (FG) and fast oxidative glycolytic (FOG)? FG fibers are not able to use oxygen in the fueling process. They use only the fuel stored in their cells. Once that fuel is spent, the fibers fatigue until a period of recovery allows the fuel to be replenished.

On the other hand, FOG fibers do have the potential to use oxygen if trained appropriately. FOG fibers contract somewhat more rapidly and fatigue faster than slow-twitch fibers do. Interval training recruits the FOG fibers to perform the faster, more intense efforts experienced in a 2- to 10-minute bout of exercise. Training at the appropriate intensity stimulates the FOG muscles to adapt and improve their aerobic capacity. The outcome of interval training is that your FOG fibers will improve their oxidative capabilities, and you improve your ability to work at a higher percentage of maximum oxygen uptake capacity.

Let's look at an example. Suppose you train at the same intensity, pace, and duration all the time, such as 30 minutes of endurance, five times per week. If you try picking up the pace significantly, you will likely find that your breathing will change and you'll fatigue rapidly. This is because those FOG fibers you are recruiting to make you go faster are not trained to handle the newly imposed demands. Their oxidative energy supplies are limited, and an accumulation of lactic acid occurs, resulting in a variety of subjective feelings that tell you that you won't be able to keep up the pace for long. This the anaerobic threshold (AT) or onset of blood lactate accumulation (OBLA), described in chapter 2. But you can improve your AT and thus improve your performance. How?

Doing intervals and hills is the way to improve your AT. Training with intervals will raise your AT significantly, especially if you have not been pushing the intensity over 75 percent of maximum effort. Top endurance athletes maintain an AT of 80 percent to 90 percent of $\dot{V}O_2$max, as contrasted with unfit individuals, who maintain an AT around 50 percent of $\dot{V}O_2$max. We've worked with elite cross-country skiers who have recorded ATs as high as 95 percent of $\dot{V}O_2$max. This means they can race at near maximum intensity before fatigue from lactic acid accumulation limits their performance.

It makes good sense to include a healthy dose of interval training in your weekly plan. How much you include depends on the stage of the training year and your yearly training volume. Typically, intervals and uphill intervals make up about 10 percent of training time in the base stage and 20 to 25 percent of total training volume during the intensity, peak, and racing stages.

Intervals take several forms (figure 4.5), described in detail later in this chapter. Each type of interval has much the same

© John Kelly

Fig. 4.6. Overdistance workouts make up the base of your training pyramid. Though they are low intensity, don't underestimate their importance.

function—to place a demand on your muscles so that the FOG fibers are recruited and their oxidative capabilities improved. The result is that you'll be able to go farther and faster with less fatigue.

Overdistance

Herein lies the foundation of the SERIOUS system for endurance sports. In every stage of the year, overdistance (OD) training comprises the greatest percentage of the total training volume.

Overdistance does not mean overdoing it. Think of OD training as the foundation of your aerobic mansion; you want to build it so that it will last forever and support the expensive structure you'll construct above it. OD sessions are long-duration, low-intensity sessions—usually lasting at least an hour and up to six to eight hours, depending on your fitness and your plan. See figure 4.6.

The secret of OD is in the physiological changes it causes. Basically, there are two adaptations the body makes in response to OD training. First, you'll be training your body to increase its efficiency for releasing and burning free fatty acids over long distances, as enzymatic and hormonal changes in the muscle cells make it easier for fat to be used as fuel during long-duration exercise. This will prove valuable for long events. Also, you'll improve the body's circulatory characteristics in the peripheral muscles—those that do the work in races to help move waste products away from muscle tissue and bring new blood, oxygen, and fuel to the muscle for more work. The mitochondria, the power-houses of the muscle cells, will increase in number and efficiency.

These physiological changes build the cardiovascular "plumb-ing network" on which all other SERIOUS workouts rely. A solid aerobic base will facilitate the delivery of oxygen and fuel to the muscles and the removal of harmful, fatiguing metabolic waste products from the muscle cells. The body will be able to function at high intensities for longer periods before the debilitating effects of high-intensity effort cause fatigue and slow you down. OD workouts during the competition stage enable proper active recovery from racing and intervals as well as maintain a solid aerobic base.

The key to overdistance training is that you make it fun and particularly easy. It's difficult sometimes to learn the true mean-ing of *easy*. Many athletes have the tendency to train at medium to high intensity all the time, never allowing their bodies to rest and catch up from the rigorous training they do on other days. If you're not used to OD pace, your patience and self-discipline may be taxed at first, since the natural tendency for most of us hardheaded, overachieving Americans is to think that if some is good, then farther and faster must be better. OD training requires us to take the hills in stride and slow down to maintain low intensity, even if this means a very slow pace up the hills during the early stages of your program.

The intensity must be very low, about 55 percent to 65 percent of $\dot{V}O_2$max, as described in chapter 2. Any harder than this, and you are not doing an OD workout. It is very common for endurance athletes to mistakenly train at intensities that average about 70 percent to 75 percent of maximum ($\dot{V}O_2$) for the bulk of their training. The problems with this approach are several. First, you do not usually race at this low an intensity (unless you're doing an Ironman or ultra event). Second, training at this intensity depletes muscle glycogen faster than at lower intensity, such as OD training intensity (55 percent to 65 percent $\dot{V}O_2$max). Third, a higher production of lactic acid occurs at this intensity than at OD intensity.

Up/Vertical

A detailed description of the physiology of interval and up/vertical training is provided in the interval section above. Uphill intervals are specifically used on moderate to steep hills to recruit the muscle fibers used in climbing (fig. 4.7).

If you know your races will be held in hilly territory, then plan to do some hills in training. The benefits of hill training are many.

© John Kelly

Fig. 4.7. Uphill intervals are hard efforts designed to train the body to adapt to the uphills and downhills.

First, the specificity principle becomes especially self-evident as the body makes the necessary physiological adaptations to climbing concerning technique, efficiency, and muscle fiber recruitment.

The psychological factor of doing hills is probably even more crucial. Every time we do uphill intervals with our buddies, we seem to find the toughest hills around. Sometimes, we'll play a game with ourselves during the workout. At an unspoken cue, one will push the others by slightly picking up the tempo as we crest the hill. This way, we increase our speed over the top of the hill. As we cruise down the other side, someone always says how much he loves those hills, and someone else will concur at what delightful little training gems they are and how lucky we are to be living in hilly country. This training is perhaps the most rewarding of all. Sure, we become tired, but the psychological lift is surpassed only by race days. The feelings of accomplishment, confidence, and greater self-esteem are tremendous. Every hill presents a new challenge, a new dimension in our ability to handle the odds against us. One gains mental toughness from hill-training sessions.

Strength

Strength is the ability of the muscle to exert force. Maximal strength is the maximal amount of force the muscle can exert in a single contraction. All endurance sports require strength to some degree. How much is necessary for optimal performance? We think the answer rests with each athlete as well as with the technical requirements of the sport. We emphasize strength training in all SERIOUS programs for three reasons: (1) to increase the amount of force your muscles can generate per stroke, per stride, et cetera, over and over again; (2) to maintain or increase the amount of mass to consume more oxygen and generate more energy; and (3) to prevent injury and overuse problems. If your musculoskeletal chain has weak links, you may eventually face debilitating problems.

Proper strength training elicits significant changes in the muscle fibers. It seems that each fiber has a portion that generates tension. This part of the fiber is composed of the contractile proteins of the muscle fiber called actin and myosin. Strength training increases the amount of actin and myosin in the fiber so that it can generate a greater force with every contraction. Our fast-twitch fibers have a greater potential for increasing the contractile proteins than slow-twitch fibers. Conversely, slow-twitch fibers have more mitochondria than do fast-twitch fibers. Ironically, endurance training leads to a decrease in contractile proteins in the fiber, whereas strength straining causes a decline in the endurance characteristics. Therefore, if you train exclusively for either endurance or strength, you may experience a loss of one or the other.

Specificity training leads to sport-specific changes in the body, changes related to the particular exercise or training used. Endurance training leads to increases in the size and number of mitochondria in the cell and the enzymes necessary for the aerobic energy process. Speed training improves the neuromuscular pathways and the energy supplies of the muscle fibers. Strength training improves the amount of contractile proteins, actin and myosin, in the fibers. Thus, each type of training stimulates particular adaptations in the muscle fibers.

Strength training can be either nonspecific or sport-specific. Nonspecific strength training involves conditioning the muscles, tendons, and ligaments by using motions that do not exactly duplicate those used in competition. This includes weight training with machines or free weights and an assortment of calisthenics. Specific strength training involves conditioning the muscles, tendons, and ligaments by using motions that closely or exactly duplicate those used in the sport (fig. 4.8). This includes a variety of methods, depending on the sport. Swimmers and triathletes commonly use the Vasa Trainer. Cross-country skiers use rollerboard devices to duplicate double-poling technique or skating slideboards for leg strength. Cyclists ride up hills using hard gears. Rock climbers do fingertip chin-ups on doorjambs.

In general, it is a good idea to incorporate both nonspecific and specific strength training into the training plan. As the competition season nears, you should use more specific (versus nonspecific) strength training. Depending on your initial strength and areas that need improvement or rehabilitation, plan to devote the following percentages of your total hours to strength training: base stage—20 percent; intensity stage—10 percent to 15 percent; peak and racing stages—5 percent to 10 percent.

Since most endurance athletes do not need to add bulk to improve performance, we recommend a high-repetition, low-to-moderate resistance method for all strength training. This rule applies regardless of the types of machines, calisthenics, or other strength exercises you use.

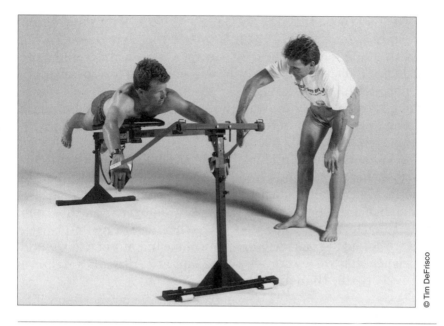

Fig. 4.8. Strength can be increased by lifting weights or by using sport-specific strength-training machines, such as the Vasa Trainer for swimming.

It is important to emphasize sport-specific strength training if you have the facilities or creativity to do so. One interesting story describes how important sport-specific strength is to some elite endurance athletes. U.S. biathlete Josh Thompson, former World Championship silver medalist, gained a reputation for his superb strength workouts. On one trip to the Dachstein Glacier in Austria, he impressed people with several workouts that involved double-poling on roller skis up a paved road, called the Dachsteinstrasse, that steadily climbs 1,000 vertical meters in only five kilometers—that's a 20 percent grade! He didn't even use his legs to propel him up the hill, only his upper body for poling. He said shamelessly, "I want to be ridiculously strong."

HOW TO DO *SERIOUS* WORKOUTS

Please remember that the SERIOUS system of training is one of many methods for training in endurance sports. Since we've given you the guidelines of intensity, duration, and objectives for each SERIOUS training component, you'll now be able to translate the way you have been training previously to see how it relates to our guidelines. We're the last people to tell you that the following workout guidelines are the only way to become a faster and more fit athlete. This method, however, will allow you to add structure and purpose to your program.

Time and intensity are the two critical factors for making a training session purposeful. As long as you consider these with your overall plan, you'll do well.

The following descriptions of each SERIOUS component outline the benefits, methods, and types of training sessions used to generate specific physiological responses. They are based on current advice and knowledge of sports physiologists, coaches, and elite athletes the world over. If you've been training and racing for a while, you've also acquired a wellspring of knowledge and experience that we encourage you to dip into. After all, you know your body better than anyone else.

Speed

Goal: Speed sessions are designed to improve neuromuscular coordination, economy, and raw speed.

Method of activity: Always do speed sessions using the sport(s) in which you will be racing. It's best to have a decent base of exercise before starting speed training.

Warm-up guidelines: Do a minimum of 15 to 20 minutes of low-intensity aerobic exercise in the same sport activity and some light stretching midway through the warm-up.

Cool-down guidelines: Do a minimum of 10 minutes of low-intensity aerobic exercise in the same sport activity and thorough stretching afterward.

Types of speed workouts: As mentioned, there are three types of speed workouts: (1) tempo speed bursts, (2) body speeds, and (3) peaking sprints. Table 4.2 outlines when during the training

The key to speed training is the ease with which you accomplish the workouts. It is essential that you learn to release your speed, rather than forcing it with powerful movements. Maintain economy of movement, performing each speed session with light, easy, yet fast motion.

Table 4.2

When to Do Speed Sessions

Types of speed	48-week plan	24-week plan
Tempo speed bursts	weeks 1-48 during OD	weeks 1-24 during OD
Body speeds	weeks 9-48	weeks 5-24
Peaking sprints	weeks 33-48	weeks 17-24

program you perform each type of speed. Tempo speed bursts are done during OD sessions and thus the warm-up and cool-down guidelines above do not apply to this type of training.

Tempo Speed Bursts

These are very brief, 15- to 20-second speed releases during overdistance workouts. Every 20 or 30 minutes during OD sessions, gradually increase your pace until it is equal to or 10 percent faster than your fastest race pace. The buildup to this pace should take about 10 seconds. Once attained, hold that speed for 5 to 10 seconds maximum; then resume OD workout pace.

Your heart rate will definitely increase over level one during and after the tempo speed burst. Your heart rate will usually decrease gradually back into your level one zone a few minutes after you resume the OD pace. If you are doing OD sessions in hilly terrain, consider doing the tempo speed bursts on all terrain—uphills, downhills, and flats.

Tempo speed bursts will help you maintain good neuromuscular coordination at fast tempos throughout the training program. As you approach the competition season and more high-speed training, your "muscle memory" won't be on vacation.

Concentrate on ease of movement. Your intensity must remain aerobic. Let the muscles be relaxed—this is when the learning takes place. These are not hard sprints.

Body Speeds

Body speeds are done as a specific speed workout generated by your SERIOUS training plan. Following a proper warm-up, begin this type of training by moving smoothly and easily. Gradually increase your pace, concentrating on releasing the speed and removing tension. You should feel a floating sensation. There are two ways to do body speed workouts—by set distance and by set time. Feel free to alternate between them for each body speed session. Typically, it is easier to do set distance body speeds for sports like swimming, running, rowing, and cross-country skiing. Set time body speeds work best for cycling, mountain biking, and in-line skating.

Set Distance Body Speeds. In this type, you do the body speeds over a set distance. You cover the set distance in a prescribed time, which is determined by your goal racing pace. Upon completing the distance, do active recovery for a period that is two to three times what it took you to cover the body speed distance. While some athletes like to recover until heart rate decreases below 120 beats per minute before starting the next body speed, we recommend an active recovery period that is two to three times the body speed interval length.

Repeat this sequence until your allotted time for the speed session is complete or until you've done between 8 and 15 repeats, whichever comes first. Remember that the active recovery time is included as part of the total time for the session. Use table 4.3 to determine the appropriate body speed pace depending on the goal pace and training week.

Tables 4.4, 4.5, and 4.6 provide a guide for set distance body speeds:

Table 4.3
Set Distance Format for Body Speeds

Activity	Distance	Recovery time	Recovery type
Swimming	50 m	30 sec	Rest, easy swim
Cycling or rowing	400 m or 1/4 mile	<120 bpm HR or 60 sec	Easy cycling, easy rowing
Running, cross-country skiing	200 m or 1/8 mile	<120 bpm HR or 60 sec	Walk or easy run, slow skiing

Table 4.4

Swimming Body Speed Table

Goal pace		Week (48 week, *24 week*) time for 50 m (sec)							
100 m	1.5K	1-4 *1-2*	5-8 *3-4*	9-12 *5-6*	13-16 *7-8*	17-20 *9-10*	21-24 *11-12*	25-28 *13-14*	29-32 *15-16*
1:00	15:00	37	36	35	34	33	32	31	30
1:05	16:15	39	38	37	36	35	34	33	32
1:10	17:30	42	41	40	39	38	37	36	35
1:15	18:45	44	43	42	41	40	39	38	37
1:20	20:00	47	46	45	44	43	42	41	40
1:25	21:15	49	48	47	46	45	44	43	42
1:30	22:30	52	51	50	49	48	47	46	45
1:35	23:45	54	53	52	51	50	49	48	47
1:40	25:00	57	56	55	54	53	52	51	50
1:45	26:15	59	58	57	56	55	54	53	52
1:50	27:30	62	61	60	59	58	57	56	55
1:55	28:45	64	63	62	61	60	59	58	57
2:00	30:00	67	66	65	64	63	62	61	60
2:05	31:15	69	68	67	66	65	64	63	62
2:10	32:30	72	71	70	69	68	67	66	65
2:15	33:45	74	73	72	71	70	69	68	67
2:20	35:00	77	76	75	74	73	72	71	70

Step 1: Find the goal race pace that you wish to achieve by the competition period.

Step 2: Determine the current week of your training plan.

Step 3: Cross-reference your goal pace with your training week. This is the pace you need to use for doing body speeds.

Set Time Body Speeds. These body speeds are done by gradually increasing speed, as above, for 30 seconds followed by 60 to 90 seconds of recovery (table 4.7). Repeat this sequence until the allotted time is up. The pace should be similar to set distance body speed pace, and HR should not go above level three for these workouts. This type of body speed allows you to use any type of terrain, but flat or downhill terrain is best. Table 4.7 provides a guide for set time body speeds.

Peaking Sprints

These are all-out efforts at your fastest speed while maintaining good form. Peaking sprints are used only during the taper and

Table 4.5
Cycling Body Speed Table

Goal pace		Week (48 week, *24 week*) time for 400 m (sec)							
Mph	40K min	1-4 *1-2*	5-8 *3-4*	9-12 *5-6*	13-16 *7-8*	17-20 *9-10*	21-24 *11-12*	25-28 *13-14*	29-32 *15-16*
15	99	67	66	65	64	63	62	61	60
16	93	63	62	61	60	59	58	57	56
17	87	60	59	58	57	56	55	54	53
18	82	57	56	55	54	53	52	51	50
19	78	54	53	52	51	50	49	48	47
20	74	52	51	50	49	48	47	46	45
21	71	50	49	48	47	46	45	44	43
22	67	48	47	46	45	44	43	42	41
23	64	46	45	44	43	42	41	40	39
24	62	44	43	42	41	40	39	38	37
25	59	43	42	41	40	39	38	37	36
26	57	41	40	39	38	37	36	35	34
27	55	40	39	38	37	36	35	34	33
28	53	39	38	37	36	35	34	33	32
29	51	38	37	36	35	34	33	32	31
30	49	37	36	35	34	33	32	31	30

competition stages. Peaking sprints are designed to be quite difficult, yet they refine your muscular coordination at maximum speed, improve anaerobic fuel systems, and improve muscular tone. They are the finishing touches on your training and will help you ride a peak for 8 to 12 weeks as you use them during the competition stage. You should perform peaking sprints at level four or five intensity.

Step 1: Choose average race course terrain.
Step 2: Warm up very well for 15 to 30 minutes.
Step 3: Alternate 15-second, all-out sprints with 30-second easy recovery exercise. Do sets of five peaking sprints. Then do five minutes of easy recovery. Repeat the peaking sprint set twice more maximum.
Step 4: Cool down for 15 to 30 minutes.

Endurance

Goal: Endurance workouts are designed to improve the aerobic system, while allowing you variety in activities and playful, less

Table 4.6
Running and Cross-Country Skiing Body Speed Table

Goal pace Min/mi	10K	Week (48 week, *24 week*) time for 200 m (sec)							
		1-4 *1-2*	5-8 *3-4*	9-12 *5-6*	13-16 *7-8*	17-20 *9-10*	21-24 *11-12*	25-28 *13-14*	29-32 *15-16*
8:04	50:00	67	66	65	64	63	62	61	60
7:55	49:10	66	65	64	63	62	61	60	59
7:47	48:20	65	64	63	62	61	60	59	58
7:39	47:30	64	63	62	61	60	59	58	57
7:31	46:40	63	62	61	60	59	58	57	56
7:23	45:50	62	61	60	59	58	57	56	55
7:15	45:00	61	60	59	58	57	56	55	54
7:07	44:10	60	59	58	57	56	55	54	53
6:59	43:20	59	58	57	56	55	54	53	52
6:51	42:30	58	57	56	55	54	53	52	51
6:43	41:40	57	56	55	54	53	52	51	50
6:35	40:50	56	55	54	53	52	51	50	49
6:27	40:00	55	54	53	52	51	50	49	48
6:19	39:10	54	53	52	51	50	49	48	47
6:11	38:20	53	52	51	50	49	48	47	46
6:03	37:30	52	51	50	49	48	47	46	45
5:55	36:40	51	50	49	48	47	46	45	44
5:46	35:50	50	49	48	47	46	45	44	43
5:38	35:00	49	48	47	46	45	44	43	42
5:30	34:10	48	47	46	45	44	43	42	41
5:22	33:20	47	46	45	44	43	42	41	40
5:14	32:30	46	45	44	43	42	41	40	39
5:06	31:40	45	44	43	42	41	40	39	38
4:58	30:50	44	43	42	41	40	39	38	37
4:50	30:00	43	42	41	40	39	38	37	36
4:42	29:10	42	41	40	39	38	37	36	35
4:34	28:20	41	40	39	38	37	36	35	34
4:26	27:30	40	39	38	37	36	35	34	33
4:18	26:40	39	38	37	36	35	34	33	32
4:10	25:50	38	37	36	35	34	33	32	31
4:02	25:00	37	36	35	34	33	32	31	30

structured days in the training schedule. These workouts can provide a sense of pace for longer races such as marathons and triathlons. You can use endurance type workouts as warm-up and cool-down time in conjunction with more intense peaking sprints, intervals or race/pace sessions, or for strength training.

Table 4.7
Set Time Body Speed Format

Activity	Time	Recovery time	Recovery type
Swimming	30 sec	30 sec	Rest, easy swim
Cycling, mountain biking	30 sec	60-90 sec	Easy cycling
Running, cross-country skiing	30 sec	60-90 sec	Rest, easy run, ski

Method of activity: Do swimming, cycling, running, cross-country skiing, or other activities. Also, this is a great opportunity to use a variety of activities or exercise machines at home or the club to warm up for strength training or to provide variety in your program.

Warm-up guidelines: During the first 5 to 10 minutes of the session gradually work up to level two intensity, and include this time as part of your allotted workout time.

Cool-down guidelines: As you near the last 5 minutes of your allotted time, gradually slow your pace. Stretch after these sessions.

Types of Endurance Workouts:

1. **Continuous:** The endurance workout is done as a continuous session for the allotted time without stopping.
2. **Endurance interval or aerobic interval:** The endurance workout is done as an interval workout with long work periods followed by short recovery periods (table 4.8). However, unlike intervals and hills, endurance intervals are completed at level two intensity.

Table 4.8
Endurance Interval Format

Activity	Time	Recovery time	Recovery type
Swimming	5-15 min	15 sec	Rest
Cycling, mountain biking	5-30 min	15 sec	Easy cycling
Running, cross-country skiing	5-20 min	15 sec	Walk or jog

Race/Pace

Goal: Time trials, pace workouts, race simulations, and organized races are designed to provide both training benefits and learning experiences from actual competition.

Race/pace workouts performed at maximal effort during early stages of training will offer only a quick fix of gratification and will detract from a planned peak, if one is reached at all. Always do race/pace workouts at the prescribed level of intensity at your current fitness level.

Method of activity: As you near your competition stage, plan to do race/pace (RP) sessions using the sport in which you will be racing. It's best to have a decent base of exercise in that sport before starting RP training. If you cross-train and are reasonably proficient in several sports, it's OK to do races in any of those sports in the months before the competition stage.

Warm-up guidelines: Warm up for a minimum of 15 to 20 minutes with low-intensity aerobic exercise in the same sport activity and do some light stretching midway through the warm-up.

Cool-down guidelines: Do a minimum of 10 minutes of low-intensity aerobic exercise in the same sport activity and thorough stretching afterward.

Types of race/pace: There are two basic types of RP workouts—time trials (TTs) and organized races. Usually, you'll do TTs on your own or as part of a club's regular activities. Plan to use either a set time or set distance format, approximating the allotted time for the session from your training plan.

Time Trials

A TT is a workout in which you perform at the specified intensity over a measured distance or time. You can alternate among the

Time trials provide opportunities to expand your concentration on technique, practice race tactics, formulate the best fluid and feed schedules, and improve your discipline in maintaining the prescribed intensity and duration. Perform TTs and races with control and relaxed efficiency. Concentrate on moving smoothly and gracefully, while listening to your body's inner wisdom about pace and intensity.

several types of time trials throughout the training program. You can perform TTs outside in typical racing terrain or on indoor training equipment such as bike trainers, rowing machines, and treadmills.

Set Distance Time Trials. Use a predetermined distance and preferably a location that you will be able to use often throughout your program (table 4.9). This way you'll be able to monitor your improvements monthly. Choose a distance that you can perform in a time that is reasonable for your current level of training and fitness and which approximates the allotted RP workout time from your plan. Don't be unnecessarily concerned about the time allotment for the session. Instead, focus on doing the chosen distance and notice your race heart rate intensity, feeling of exertion, and pace. Record your time in your training log, noting weather and other conditions. There are some key factors to make set distance TTs work for you:

- Use the same distance, location, equipment, and environmental conditions once per month to control variables and monitor progress.
- Use your AT heart rate level each month. Set your HR monitor alarm at this level to help you stay in the proper zone.

This way you'll eliminate variables and be able to compare your performances from one session to the next. Also, setting limits on the distance and heart rate forces you to concentrate on using excellent form, technique, or riding position for the duration of the TT. This is the way you'll perfect your technique, get faster, and improve your ability to hold efficient form for the duration of the TT.

If you will be racing triathlons or duathlons, plan a few TTs that combine appropriate distances in each sport.

Set Time TTs. This type of TT is performed for a predetermined time while the distance is measured. These are useful if you don't have a convenient location to do set distance TTs. If your RP sessions are designated as using a combination of activities, you can use this method easily. To do an RP TT using more than one activity, you will need to divide the time according to your planned race distance (table 4.10). For example, if you are planning to do an Olympic distance triathlon in three hours, and the swim will take 30 minutes, the bike 90 minutes, and the run 60 minutes, the

Table 4.9
Set Distance Time Trial Distances

Type of Racing	Swimming	Cycling	Running, cross-country skiing
Sprint triathlon	500 m	20 km	5 km
Olympic triathlon	1,500 m	40 km	10 km
Longer triathlons	Start with 50% of race distance and build up to 80%		
Duathlons		30 km	5 km
Run 10K			8 km
Run half-marathon			16 km
Run marathon			30 km
Cross-country ski			80% race distance

swim is 17 percent of the total time, the bike is 50 percent of the total, and the run is 33 percent of the total. You can use these percentages to split your available TT time to match a typical race time. Single-sport athletes will need to find a location that simulates typical race terrain and use that location often. You'll be able to monitor your progress by noting the distance you cover in your set time for the TT at a set intensity. With all conditions equal, you should see improvement from month to month as your fitness improves.

Racing. Once you reach the taper and competition stages, you'll be well prepared to race in earnest. You will perform your races with personal bests in mind. The training program you have followed to date will have prepared you to unleash your best. Now will be the time to go for it, listening to your body's signals along

Table 4.10
Dividing RP Time Depending on Race Type

Type of Racing	Swimming	Cycling	Running
Sprint triathlon	14%	53%	33%
Olympic triathlon	18%	50%	32%
Longer triathlons	11%	56%	33%
Duathlons		56%	44%

the way. You will reach level three, four, and five intensities during racing, depending on the length of the race.

During racing season you may want to adjust your schedule so that you are racing only once or twice per four-week cycle. This will depend on the length of your races. Add your total RP time allotment for each four-week cycle and use this total racing time as a guide to schedule your races. It's OK if you don't meet the time allotment for the cycle. Instead, focus on having good racing efforts.

The goal of every SERIOUS training program is to allow you to train effectively and achieve your performance goals. For many of you, this will include a goal time in which you plan to complete your events. For others, simply completing the events comfortably will be the goal.

Each RP session has a prescribed level of intensity, and you will need to determine the appropriate pace for your activities to match the intended RP level of intensity, usually between levels three and four. You can do this simply by monitoring your heart rate (HR) and pace during each TT and RP workout. You will quickly learn the pace that elicits the desired HR.

As your level of fitness improves, the training paces you will use will increase. It is important to monitor HR regularly during training to make sure that you are training at the proper intensity.

As the racing season approaches you will be able to predict racing paces based on the pace you've used successfully in training. The pace you will be able to sustain during a race will depend on your fitness and the distance of the event. Use table 4.11 as a guide.

Your knowledge of appropriate racing pace will alert you to the possibility of unrealistic early season goals. Don't attempt to race at a pace that you know you will not be able to sustain. You'll have a better performance and more satisfaction if you follow these guidelines:

1. Do a proper warm-up, ending the warm-up as close to the race start as possible, preferably within 5 minutes of the start.

Table 4.11
Racing Intensities

Race length	Intensity level
Up to 1 hour	4-5
1-2 hours	4
2-4 hours	3-4
Over 4 hours	3

2. Start the race at a pace (and heart rate) that you know you can sustain (many athletes invariably start out much too fast, only to have a "bear jump on their backs" after the first 10 minutes).

3. Plan and do an evenly paced race. Ideally, the first half of your race will be at the same or slightly slower pace than the last half of your race.

Intervals and Uphill Intervals

Goal: These training sessions will enable you to race at or above a level four intensity and will improve your anaerobic threshold as your training progresses.

With all intervals pay strict attention to maintaining a level four intensity or slightly below the elusive anaerobic threshold (AT). For this reason, heart monitors are very useful for intervals. Your arms and legs should not feel spent or rubbery during or after intervals. If they do, you have trained too hard and you must either slow your pace for the next intervals or stop the workout altogether and cool down.

Intervals versus uphill intervals: Essentially, uphill intervals (UP) are done exactly the same way as intervals (IN). The only difference is the type of terrain you choose for your workouts. If you will never race in hilly terrain, then do all the scheduled UP sessions in terrain similar to that in which you will compete. This also includes simulating the weather. If you know your race course will be windy, then do your IN into a headwind part of the time to prepare yourself physically and mentally. IN training is intended for flat or rolling terrain. However, if you know that you'll be racing in very hilly territory, then we highly recommend that you do some of your IN sessions on hills that simulate race conditions. Remember, it's a lot more fun if you are prepared for race conditions before you get to race day.

Method of activity: As a rule, do IN and UP sessions using the sport(s) in which you will be racing. It's best to have a substantial base (four to eight weeks) of aerobic exercise before starting this type of training.

Warm-up guidelines: Warm up with a minimum of 15 to 20 minutes of low-intensity aerobic exercise in the same sport activity and do some light stretching midway through the warm-up. Cool-down guidelines: Do a minimum of 10 minutes of low-intensity aerobic exercise in the same sport activity and thorough stretching afterward.

Maximum time for IN or UP sessions: Even though your SERIOUS training plan will include varying time allotments for these sessions, it's best to limit the total maximum amount of time for each IN or UP session, since these are difficult and stressful. Use the following as a guide for each sport. Each time includes work intervals and recovery times.

Swimming	60 minutes
Cycling	90 minutes
Running	75 minutes
Cross-country skiing	75 minutes

Of course, you will gradually build up to these times. Use any additional allotted workout time as warm-up and cool-down.

Types of interval and uphill interval training: We recommend three types of intervals: fartlek, set distance, and set time. Each has its purpose and methods.

Fartlek

This is the Swedish term for speed play. This type of IN session is continuous for the allotted time on your schedule. Intervals of increased pace occur virtually whenever and wherever you like—on the flats, up hills, and down hills—since it's very useful to learn how to go fast on each type of terrain.

As the name suggests, plan to play, so leave your watch and HR monitor at home. Instead, use your senses and your subjective feeling of exertion and pace for these sessions. Go fast when you feel like it and for as long as you want. Then recover until you feel ready to go fast again. Use variations in the terrain to make the workout more playful and imaginative. Accelerate on the downhill using long strides. Then increase the tempo, bursting up short hills. Pick a landmark and concentrate on using smooth, rhythmic movement to get you there. Consider doing some calisthenics along the way, too. Push-ups, pull-ups, sit-ups, and lunges are great exercises to insert into a fartlek workout. Fartlek is a great workout to do with a training partner, too. Have fun!

Set Distance

These are intervals in which you use a predetermined distance and recovery, shown in table 4.12. Recovery time *is* included in the allotted time for the session. There are some key factors to make set distance intervals work for you:

1. Use the same distance, location, equipment, and environmental conditions once per month to control variables and monitor progress.
2. Use your AT heart rate level each month. Set your HR monitor alarm at this level to help you stay in the zone. This way you'll eliminate variables and be able to compare your performances from one session to the next. Also, setting limits on the distance and heart rate forces you to concentrate on using excellent form, technique, or riding position for the duration of the interval. This is the way you'll perfect technique, get faster, and expand your ability to hold efficient form for the duration of the interval.

Set Time

These are intervals in which you use a predetermined interval and recovery time. Tables 4.13 and 4.14 describe this type of interval training and the recovery times for each length of interval. Gradually increase the set interval times every two to four weeks.

Triathletes and duathletes may wish to use table 4.15 to schedule the different types of IN or UP workouts for each sport. If you train with only one sport activity, or if you are training in a sport other that those listed below, then alternate each type of IN workout throughout your program.

Table 4.12
Set Distance Interval Format

Activity	Distance	Recovery time	Recovery type
Swimming	400 m	<130 bpm HR or half of interval time	Rest, easy swim
Cycling, mountain biking	3 km or 2 mi	<130 bpm HR or half of interval time	Easy cycling
Running, cross-country skiing	1 km or 1/2 mi	<130 bpm HR or half of interval time	Rest, easy run, easy ski

Table 4.13
Set Time Interval Format

Interval time	Recovery time	Recovery type
1-3 min	<130 bpm HR or equal to work interval time	Easy active recovery
3-5 min	<130 bpm HR or 75% of work interval time	Easy active recovery
5-10 min	<130 bpm HR or 50% of work interval time	Easy active recovery

Table 4.14
Set Time Interval Table

48 week	24 week	Interval time	Recovery time
1-4	1-2	2:00	2:00
5-8	3-4	2:30	2:30
9-12	5-6	3:00	3:00
13-16	7-8	3:30	3:00
17-20	9-10	4:00	3:00
21-24	11-12	4:30	3:20
25-28	13-14	5:00	3:45
29-32	15-16	6:00	3:00
33-36	17-18	6:30	3:15
37-40	19-20	7:00	3:30
41-44	21-22	7:30	3:45
45-48	23-24	8:00	4:00

Overdistance

Goal: Overdistance training will develop a strong aerobic foundation through low-intensity, long-duration training sessions.

Overdistance serves as the foundation for all other training. It prepares the body for much higher intensity work in other components of SERIOUS training. Allow yourself some time to become used to doing OD training. You'll need some self-discipline, since the natural tendency for newcomers to OD will be to think it is too easy. Pay close attention to intensity; do not exceed level one for these workouts. We highly recommend use of a heart rate monitor.

Method of activity: Use your primary sport activities for overdistance training most of the time. However, occasionally consider using a variety of activities in combination for these workouts. Water running, preferably with a Wet Vest or Aqua Jogger, is an ideal way to maintain running-specific volume without the stress on the legs. Use a combination of several sports such as hiking, cross-country skiing, stair-climbing, and rowing to condition supportive muscles while reducing the stress on the

Table 4.15

Scheduling Monthly IN and UP Workouts

Week of cycle	Swimming	Cycling	Running
1	Fartlek	Set distance	Set time
2	Set distance	Fartlek	Set distance
3	Set distance	Set time	Fartlek
4	Set time	Fartlek	Set distance

muscles primarily used in your sport (or to beat bad-weather blues).

Warm-up guidelines: No warm-up is required, since this intensity is warm-up level intensity.

Cool-down guidelines: No cool-down is required, but do some stretching afterward.

Maximum time for OD sessions: Use the scheduled time allotment. Avoid doing any extra long distance that is more than 10 percent longer than your longest OD to date.

Types of overdistance: The session should contain a variety of movements or technique changes. By doing this, energy systems are used in a greater percentage of muscle fibers, thereby producing the desired effects in more fibers.

If you'll be doing competitions that will take over two hours, it's a good idea to gradually build up to doing one of your OD workouts each month that takes between two and five hours. This will build up conditioning, confidence, fluid and nutritional awareness, and mental toughness.

Remember that tempo speed bursts are employed in the OD sessions, with one occurring every 10 to 15 minutes. The personality of every OD workout, however, must be one of relaxed, refined effort, with no concern for power, speed, or intensity. Use the OD workouts as easy, comfortable, and enjoyable exercise— you'll be very tired by the end of the session.

Uphill Intervals

Goal: Vertical training is exactly like interval training, except that the terrain is different, thereby requiring different muscle fibers.

If you will never race in hilly terrain, then you should do all or most of your interval and uphill intervals in the terrain and conditions in which you'll race. If you'll be facing headwinds often in races, then use your uphill time to do your intervals into the wind.

Types of interval and uphill interval training: See IN training section.

Strength

Goal: Strength training will help you generate more force, maintain muscle balance and flexibility, and prevent injuries. Pay particular attention to the core abdominal, hip, and back muscles to maintain the integrity of the lower back while improving balance and posture.

A list of the major muscles used in particular activities follows.

Swimming muscles: latissimus dorsi, deltoids, triceps, pectorals (chest), abdominals, hip flexors, quadriceps, tibialis anterior.

Cycling muscles: gluteals (butt), quadriceps, hamstrings, calf, abdominals.

Running muscles: gluteals (butt), quadriceps, hamstrings, hip flexors, calf, pelvic stabilizers, abdominals.

Cross-country skiing and rowing muscles: entire body.

Method of activity: Many devices and exercises may be used to develop strength. Base stage classic strength training is done with free weights, weight machines, and calisthenics. Plyometrics, rubber tubing, and sport-specific machines like the Vasa Trainer all work well to improve sport-specific strength.

Warm-up guidelines: Warm up for a minimum of 10 minutes with easy aerobic activity, light stretching, and calisthenics.

Cool-down guidelines: Cool down for a minimum of 10 minutes with easy aerobic activity and thorough stretching.

Maximum time for strength sessions: Disregard your calculated ST time allotments and concentrate on completing the routine of 8 to 12 exercises with one to three sets of each. Sixty minutes should give you enough time to complete most routines. It's better to choose a series of 8 to 12 exercises that will improve the muscle strength where you need it. Do these exercises in sets of 12 to 20 repetitions to make up the total strength session. It's reasonable to progress to doing three sets of 12 to 20 repetitions of each exercise in a given ST workout. As it becomes easy to do 20 reps, increase the resistance.

Types of Strength Training: Use the recommended ST circuit outlined for your sport in table 4.16. The table suggests strength routines to use during the different phases of the year. When doing the routine, start with one set of 15 to 20 repetitions of each exercise (except for plyometrics). Rest 30 to 60 seconds between exercises. After you become accustomed to the routine, increase the sets.

FROM EXPERIENCE
RAY BROWNING, MS

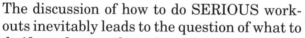

The discussion of how to do SERIOUS workouts inevitably leads to the question of what to do if you frequently train with a group. Ideally you will be so enthusiastic about your training plan that you will soon have all your training partners converted to the SERIOUS system and scheduling their weekly patterns similar to yours. Even in this best-case scenario, problems will arise with group training. Differences in fitness level, ability, and genetic talent make training different for each individual in the group. Although your training partners may be maintaining their prescribed HR, yours may be higher or lower than your plan suggests. Therein lies the most challenging aspect of group training— finding training partners who are not only willing to do the type of training on your schedule, but will benefit equally. Davis Phinney and Scott Tinley are the only two individuals with whom I can do long OD training sessions without the session losing its value by becoming a hammer session.

I am not advocating that you refrain from all group training. In fact, group training can be an excellent time to do high-intensity efforts. A regular group run or bike ride as a fartlek or interval session is appropriate, as long as you maintain the proper intensity, pace, and effort. Swimmers may want to consider an organized swim program, such as masters workouts. These are regular, structured practices that provide an opportunity for stroke technique feedback and variety. You can be true to your training plan by controlling the intensity with

Table 4.16
Strength Routines for Endurance Sports

Exercise	Triathlon (duathlon)		Cycling (mountain biking)		Running		Cross-country skiing (rowing)		Swimming	
Stage of year	B	I,T,C	B	I,T,C	B	I,T,C	B	I,T,C	B	I,T,C
Bent-knee sit-up	✓	✓	✓	✓	✓	✓	✓	✓	✓	✓
Abdominal crunches	✓		✓		✓		✓		✓	
Lower-leg raises	✓	✓	✓	✓	✓	✓	✓	✓	✓	✓
Back hyperextensions	✓	✓	✓	✓	✓	✓	✓	✓	✓	✓
Wide-stance squats	✓		✓		✓	✓	✓		✓	
Narrow-stance 90% squat		✓		✓		✓				
Lunges			✓	✓	✓	✓				
Leg extensions	✓		✓	✓	✓	✓	✓			
Leg curls	✓		✓	✓	✓	✓	✓			
Hip abduction/adduction	✓	✓	✓	✓	✓	✓	✓			
Calf raises	✓		✓	✓	✓	✓		✓		
Bench press	✓		✓		✓		✓		✓	✓
Sitting military press	✓						✓		✓	✓
Lat pulldown	✓	✓					✓		✓	✓
Sitting rows	✓		✓		✓		✓		✓	✓
Biceps curls	✓		✓		✓				✓	✓
Triceps press									✓	✓
Vasa Trainer	✓	✓								
Rollerboard								✓		
Slideboard								✓		
Plyometric leg press w/Vasa	✓	✓		✓						
Plyometric hops	✓	✓		✓		✓		✓		✓
Plyometric skate hops						✓		✓		

Note. (B=base, I=intensity, T=taper, C=competition)

which you swim. For example, if you have an OD session planned, you can swim in a slower lane or adjust the workout pace to suit your intensity levels.

The SERIOUS system allows you to have structured variety in your training program. You can accomplish overdistance sessions in several ways. One particularly memorable OD experience included Rob Sleamaker, Don Kelly, and me. We had one mountain bike between us and we would rotate with two of us running and one riding through the hills of Vermont. When we finished the session we all reflected on how great it was to break up the normal long run with this type of variety. The underlying message is be creative with your training sessions. This chapter has provided you with an outline of how to do SERIOUS workouts and the unlimited combinations for training the SERIOUS way.

5

Warming Up, Cooling Down, and Stretching

What you do before each training session or competition as a warm-up has a significant impact on the results you achieve. To return to the chili analogy, not many of you would prefer to eat cold chili; it tastes much better when it's warmed up. Many of us learned that warm-up was synonymous with stretching. We considered that 15 minutes of jumping jacks, bouncing, toe touches, and various other contortions were enough preparation before a vigorous workout. We now know that these are not safe and proper forms of warm-up. As important as what you do before your training is what you do after each session. A proper cool-down and stretching will ensure you begin the recovery process quickly, allowing your body to better adapt to the training and minimizing the risk of injury.

In this chapter, you will learn

- physiological and psychological basis for proper warm-up,
- how to warm up properly before training and competition,
- how cool-down exercise and mental review helps speed recovery,
- benefits of stretching for improved flexibility,
- basic guidelines for stretching properly, and
- common stretches for the athlete.

All of these are worth serious consideration by every endurance athlete.

WARMING UP

Most of us have been guilty of insufficient warm-up for one reason or another. Perhaps we were late to a race start or didn't have enough time in a day. The results are predictable—a terrible start to the training session or race, often without much improvement through the course of the training or racing session. Athletes warm up both to enhance athletic performance and prevent injury.

Physiology of Warm-Up

Warming up is designed to increase muscle and tendon suppleness, stimulate blood flow to the periphery, increase body temperature, and enhance free, coordinated movements. Warm-up can be achieved through active or passive means. Active warm-up consists of low-intensity aerobic muscular exercise, such as an easy jog, during which metabolism increases. The metabolic processes of the muscle cells are temperature dependent, with increases in metabolism noted at higher temperatures. Åstrand and Rodahl (1977) indicate that the metabolic rate of the cell increases by 13 percent for every degree Celsius of temperature increase in the muscle. The exchange of oxygen from the blood to the tissues is increased at higher intramuscular temperatures. Asmussen and Boje (1960) discovered that physical work capacity is increased following proper warm-up.

Karvonen (1978) studied the physiological effects of warm-up in cross-country runners and skiers, showing that proper warm-up improved performance for these athletes. He tested athletes with and without warm-up routines in various competitions and measured objective data, such as performance times, rectal temperature, heart rate, and venous blood lactic acid concentration, and registered the athletes' subjective performance evaluations. The results showed that the athletes subjectively felt their competition was easier following warm-ups. Most important, actual race results were significantly better for athletes who warmed up versus those who did not.

Passive warm-up involves the use of external means to elevate body temperature, such as saunas, hot showers, whirlpool baths, heating pads, and massage. DeVries (1959) showed that although passive warm-up has been shown to improve performance times, active warm-up has resulted in better performances (fig. 5.1). Thus, this discussion will focus on active warm-up methods.

Injury prevention is another important reason for including proper warm-up before vigorous training. Increases in muscle temperature increase the elasticity of muscle tissue, reducing the risks of strains or tears. Also, it appears that gradual warm-up preceding vigorous activity is important in prevention of cardiac injuries. Barnard (1973) reported that warming up properly can prevent certain electrocardiographic abnormalities that some-

© John Kelly

Fig. 5.1. Include a proper warm-up prior to training and racing to prevent injury and perform at your best.

times occur even in seemingly healthy persons at the beginning of intense running performances. Athletes over 35, especially those with a family history of heart disease, should consider this evidence.

Professional cyclist Ron Kiefel has learned through 18 years of racing that a warm-up is critical to good performance, especially in the all-important time trials of major stage races like the Tour de France. He will typically warm up for one to two hours before a time trial, with some race intensity efforts. Only after this type of warm-up does he feel ready to perform at his best.

Psychology of Warm-Up

The warm-up period is an ideal time to review the objectives of the training session or competition at hand. In training, assess the format of the workout, such as interval lengths and rest periods. Take time to reflect on your training plan goals and how this workout fits into these goals. Before a race, use the warm-up to review nonoutcome goals of technique, pace, and mental focus. Warming up for a training session without mental preparation may result in training that has little focus or enthusiasm. If you take a moment during warm-up to reflect on your overall goals, you'll generate much motivation, focus, and positive energy for the day's workout.

> Through my training and racing, I have learned the importance of positive self-talk to achieve good results. My warm-up routines always include a reminder to think positively during the workout or race—to say "yes I can!"—Ray

Use the warm-up as a time to clear your mind of distracting thoughts, such as work or family issues. With practice you can develop association techniques that help you focus on what you are doing. The checklist later in this section will guide you in achieving the right mental state. Chapter 11 discusses mental strategies for training and racing in more detail.

Proper Warm-Up Before Training Sessions

Preceding all speed, interval, and up/vertical training sessions, plan to incorporate 10 to 30 minutes of moderate-intensity (level one or two heart rate) aerobic activity using the planned training activity. If the intensity or speed during the training session is to be high, then the warm-up can include several short bursts (10 to 30 seconds) of faster movements. These are sometimes referred to as speed pickups. Technique drills, such as one-arm swimming drills, running form drills, or cross-country balance drills, are also appropriate forms of warm-up and will help you to maintain good technique during your training session. It is best that the warm-up end as close to the start of your training session as is practical, preferably within five minutes before beginning. This is particularly important before the start of a time trial or interval training session. A longer lag time will result in a cooling of tissue, a reversion of metabolic processes toward resting states, and ultimately a less effective training session.

You can achieve a proper warm-up for strength-training sessions with one activity or you can include a variety of aerobic activities such as rowing or cycling. Be sure to warm up for 10 to 30 minutes, especially if the intensity of the strength training is to be moderately high, such as during circuit weight training. If you do strength training at low intensity, you can use abdominal and lower-back exercises, technique drills, yoga, or calisthenics as warm-up for your strength routine. You may elect to do one set of your exercises as a warm-up by using light weights for 25 to 50 repetitions. A warm-up is not required for overdistance and endurance training because they are performed at low intensity. Instead, just begin all OD or EN sessions conservatively for the first 5 minutes.

If at any time during a warm-up period you feel pain or unusual discomfort that doesn't go away in 5 to 10 minutes, stop the workout. Many athletes develop injuries by ignoring these signs in the warm-up period. As the body warms up, these signs of overuse may be masked and continuing the workout will only increase the severity of the injury.

Proper Warm-Up Prior to Competitions

Before a race—or a race/pace or time-trial workout—you should warm up for 10 to 40 minutes. The warm-up intensity is medium, with some higher intensity, faster tempo bursts (pickups), or body speeds incorporated in the middle of the warm-up period. Houmard, et al. (1991) tested different warm-up routines before a high-intensity 400-meter swim. This study found that a mild-intensity (65 percent $\dot{V}O_2$max), long-duration (1,300-meter) swim was beneficial compared with no warm-up or warm-up consisting of high-intensity short-duration swims.

Be sure to arrive at the race site with plenty of time to get organized and warm up. Experiment with different warm-up routines and record your warm-up and resulting performance in your training log. A warm-up routine that works well for your high-intensity training will most likely serve you well as a prerace warm-up.

It is imperative that the warm-up before competitions include the activity with which you will compete. This may seem obvious, but on many occasions we have witnessed triathletes standing around at the water's edge before the start of the swim. The ideal warm-up for the triathlete includes optional cycling or running and at least 10 minutes of swimming. It is important to end the warm-up as close to the start of the race as possible (maximum of 5 minutes before the start), especially for short races. A proper prerace warm-up routine also serves as an excellent time to review your equipment, transitions, and nutritional needs.

It seems that the intensity and duration of the warm-up must also be adjusted for environmental conditions. Robinson (1963) observed that road runners who warmed up in 90-degree heat before a 10K race had rectal temperatures 1.5 degrees higher than those who did not warm up. The increase in temperature before racing in the heat may be a detriment to performance due to problems associated with overheating. The reverse condition is often a problem for the swimmer, triathlete, or cross-country skier. A warm-up in cold air or water may actually decrease body temperature and is thus not recommended. For swimmers or triathletes, if the air temperature is below 60 degrees or the water temperature is below 65 degrees, then the proper warm-up would consist of running for 5 to 10 minutes followed by some upper-body calisthenics, such as push-ups and arm swings. Proper dress will adequately prepare the athlete for cold prerace conditions. Prepare to keep your warm-up clothing on until just minutes before the start.

Warm-Up Checklist

 Review training plan goals; identify some nonoutcome and outcome goals.

 Commit to using proper technique.

Commit to proper pace and perceived exertion. Identify how you will monitor intensity and race your race.

Commit to being relaxed and powerful. Focus on efficient movements.

Commit to saying positive things—think positive! Focus on what you want to happen, not all the things you don't want to happen.

Commit to focusing on what you are doing—one stride or one stroke at a time, doing each one perfectly.

Acknowledge yourself and your efforts as valid in themselves.

Do 10 to 40 minutes of low- to moderate-intensity activity before training.

Do tempo speed bursts or body speeds before high-intensity training or racing.

Adjust the warm-up for environmental conditions.

End the warm-up within 5 minutes of the start of the training or race.

COOLING DOWN

The cool-down is as important as the warm-up. While the warm-up period prepares your body for high-intensity training, the cool-down prepares the body for the rest and regeneration that is to come. Many of us neglect this important aspect of training. By failing to cool down we slow the recovery and adaptation necessary for continued improvements in performance. Regard the cool-down as a part of the training session, not an optional addendum.

Physiology of Cool-Down

Intense exercise is usually accompanied by a buildup of metabolic waste, such as lactic acid, and often may cause slight tears or ruptures in the connective tissue. Both conditions can lead to soreness. In particular, it is necessary to remove metabolic waste to enhance recovery from training. A warm-down period following exercise has been shown to markedly speed removal of lactic acid.

Shevciw (1986) reported a study of the German National Junior Hockey Team, the members of which performed a 3,000-meter run that brought them to a condition of high lactic acid buildup. Immediately after the run, a 20-milliliter sample of blood was taken from each athlete. Three additional blood samples were drawn at 3 minutes, 6 minutes, and 30 minutes after the run. Between the 6-minute and the 30-minute blood samples, half the athletes ran a 15-minute cool-down at subthreshold intensity, while the other half of the group rested. The blood samples taken at 30 minutes postrun showed that the athletes who used the cool-down run had significantly lower levels of lactic acid than the athletes who rested.

The multisport athlete may not benefit from the cool-down process as much as the single-sport athlete. Costill and Saltin (1975) have shown that cool-down periods may further deplete the glycogen stores of the athlete and thus may hinder the recovery for the next training session. This is particularly important for the multisport athlete who may have scheduled training several times during the day or hard sessions on successive days. Our experience has led us to recommend a cool-down for 5 to 10 minutes after a hard training session if the next hard training session is scheduled during the next 24 hours. If you have an easy day following, cool down for 15 to 30 minutes at a very easy pace.

Psychology of Cool-Down

Just as the warm-up is an excellent time for a review of goals and mental state, the cool-down serves as a time to evaluate the workout. Review the mental checklist provided earlier in this chapter and examine the mind-set you achieved. Did you stay positive and focus on what you could control? If not, why not? What can you do differently next time? Remember that this evaluation is a tool for technical correction, not a time to belittle yourself. Use the cool-down as the time to put the workout away—that way you don't carry it around with you the rest of the day. A great workout can serve as a motivator, but a bad one can set the stage for a terrible day if you dwell on it. If you commit to using the cool-down as the time to deal with any frustrations, the rest of your day and your interactions with those around you will be much more pleasant. Record your feelings in your training journal and re-member to acknowledge your accomplishments.

Cool-Down Routines

We have observed several top athletes consistently using a cool-down after all hard training and racing. At the 1987 World Biathlon Championships, American Josh Thompson won the silver medal in the 20K race—the first medal ever won by an American male in World Cup biathlon competition. After a brief celebration with coaches and teammates, he had the presence of mind to change into a dry warm-up suit and ski a 30-minute cool-down before facing the deluge of fans and reporters.

Ideally, you perform the cool-down in the same manner as the warm-up (fig. 5.2). Plan to do 15 to 30 minutes of level one exercise, using the same activity you used for training that day. Fifteen to 30 minutes of easy aerobic activity should follow strength workouts, too. There's no need to cool down after OD or endurance training because they are accomplished at low intensity.

© John Kelly

Fig. 5.2. A cool-down is a necessary part of most workouts and races and can include some play.

It's a good idea to change into dry clothing (and a dry hat if it's cold) before you start the cool-down. This will prevent you from becoming chilled. If it is very cold outside, you can elect to cool-down inside with some easy activity followed by stretching. On hot days, your primary concern will be to replace fluids lost during training. Begin drinking fluids during your cool-down or delay the cool-down if you feel very thirsty or dizzy. If you have just completed a long workout or event such as the Ironman, the cool-down is not recommended. After you've cooled down enough, find a warm, dry place to start your stretching routine and replacement of fluids and fuel.

Cool-Down Checklist

☑ Review the mind-set achieved—did you accomplish good focus?

☑ Put the workout away. Accept the result and yourself.

☑ Do 15 to 30 minutes of level one exercise.

☑ Stay comfortable while you cool down—avoid getting too hot or cold.

☑ Stretch.

STRETCHING

Intense physical training generally strengthens the specific muscle groups associated with the training activity. However, these muscle groups and the connective tissue surrounding them usually become less flexible as they strengthen. The decrease in flexibility is accompanied by an increase in muscle fiber and connective tissue tension, which can increase the probability of injury. Another result is a decreased range of motion, which inhibits proper technique. All athletes need to be concerned with injury prevention, and achieving greater range of motion may help improve performance (fig. 5.3). Examples of improved performance include longer strides in running, greater pull strokes in swimming, improved ability to ride a flat ski in cross-country skiing, and more aerodynamic form in cycling.

© John Kelly

Fig. 5.3.   Regularly stretching your muscles, tendons, and ligaments can help prevent injuries and enhance your performance.

General Guidelines for Flexibility Exercises

• Stretch regularly, every day if possible. Gymnasts and aerobics instructors become flexible only by spending hours each day stretching. We know one instructor who claims that she often watches TV or reads the newspaper while in a split with her elbows on the floor in front of her.

• Use slow, static stretches. Avoid ballistic or bouncing stretches, which increase the likelihood of overstretching and straining the muscles and connective tissue. Instead, relax the muscles and ease into the stretch, *never* to the point of pain. Breathe in and out regularly, releasing any tension you may be feeling. Hold each stretch for 15 to 60 seconds, increasing the stretch gradually.

• Once in a stretching position, make an inventory of your body's condition, relaxing those muscles not involved in the primary stretch, and then refocusing on the muscles you are trying to stretch.

• Set realistic goals for stretching. There is no need for you to outstretch anyone or to improve much over the previous day. Just release the muscular tension in a comfortable way, and your flexibility will gradually improve.

• Increases in flexibility will be greater if you stretch after activity when the muscle temperature is high.

You'll soon determine a formula that works well for you. You may find that stretching works best if done after workouts or at the end of the day, after you have been active. Sitting in a sauna, Jacuzzi, or hot bathtub will warm up muscles and enhance stretching. It is important to consider flexibility training something that will give you long-term benefits besides being a specific warm-up or injury prevention exercise before intense training.

Stretching Before Vigorous Training

Stretching is not synonymous with warming up. Generally, we do not recommend stretching as part of the warm-up routine. The likelihood of injury may increase if stretching is initiated before the muscles are properly warmed up. If you plan to stretch before vigorous training, especially before speed or strength sessions that require substantial range of motion, always warm up first according to the guidelines presented previously. Stretch the muscle groups that you will use during the training session, following the general guidelines above.

Postexercise Stretching

This is the optimal time for stretching because the muscles are warmed up. Follow these steps:

1. Cool down with low-level activity for 10 to 30 minutes following any hard exercise. Change into dry clothing and

put on a warm-up suit or wind suit (and a dry hat in cold weather).

2. Find a warm, dry place to stretch. Some relaxing music may be helpful.

3. Following the general guidelines for stretching, concentrate on those muscle groups used hardest in training. This is a good time to stretch all other areas, too.

4. You may want to jostle and massage the major muscle groups a bit before you stretch them. This can help relax them.

5. If you plan to ice an area, stretch the area first, while it is still warm, and then apply ice.

6. Stretching in a whirlpool or shower is fine, preferably done shortly after the training session, but make sure you stretch all the muscles used during training.

Stretching Routines

Alter (1990) has provided a good reference for learning flexibility exercises and techniques. Also, qualified aerobics, gymnastics, and dance instructors, as well as athletic trainers and physical therapists, can show you proper stretching techniques. Figures 5.4 through 5.13 illustrate the most common stretches. Choose the ones that stretch the muscles you use most often in your training.

Ten General Stretches for the Athlete

Fig. 5.4.   **Groin stretch.** Sitting upright on the floor, bring the heels and soles of your feet together as you pull them toward your buttocks. Place your elbows on the inside of the upper thighs and slowly push your legs toward the floor.

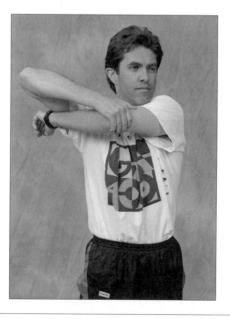

Fig. 5.5.   **Lateral shoulder stretch.** Grasp your raised elbow with the opposite hand. Exhale and pull your elbow backward.

Fig. 5.6.   Hip flexor stretch. Standing upright, flex your left knee and roll the right foot under so the top of the instep rests on the floor. Place your hands on your hips while slowly leaning or pushing your left hip toward the floor.

Fig. 5.7.   Standing quadriceps stretch. Standing upright, flex one leg and raise the foot to your buttocks. Grasp your raised foot with one hand and pull your heel toward your buttocks without overcompressing the knee.

Fig. 5.8. **Sitting hamstring stretch.** Place your heel against the inside of the thigh of the extended leg. Exhaling, keep your left leg straight while you bend at the waist. Extend your arms and upper body toward the ankle of your extended leg.

Fig. 5.9. **Crossing legs twist.** Crossing your left foot over your right leg, slide your heel toward your buttocks. Reach over your left leg with your right arm and place your right elbow on the outside of your left knee. Exhale and look over your left shoulder while turning your trunk and pushing back on your knee with your right elbow.

Fig. 5.10. **Adductors squat stretch.** Squat with your feet about 12 inches apart and your toes turned slightly out. Exhale and slowly push your legs outward with elbows. Keep your feet flat on the floor to reduce strain on the knees.

Fig. 5.11. **Calf stretch.** While standing four or five steps from a wall, bend one leg forward and keep the other leg straight. Lean against the wall keeping your rear foot down flat and push against the wall with your arms.

Fig. 5.12.   Pectoral stretch. Rest your interlocked forearms on top of a barre or chair at knee height. Drop your head beneath the supporting surface and exhale, letting your head and chest sink to the floor.

Fig. 5.13.   Lower back stretch. Grasp behind your thighs to prevent hyperextention of the knees. Exhaling, pull your knees toward your chest and shoulders and elevate your hips off the floor.

FROM EXPERIENCE
DAVIS PHINNEY

Davis Phinney, two-time Tour de France stage winner and U.S. Pro cycling champion, may have more warm-up and cool-down experience than any other athlete. His 18-year cycling career has included as many as 100 races annually, not to mention countless hours of training for these races. We figured there was no better person to give advice on warming up, cooling down, and stretching.

While a competitive cyclist in Europe, Davis developed what he calls his ritual: "I would get to my hotel room, lay out my racing clothes, and sit on the floor doing stretches. At the same time I would be clearing my head, taking away all the stress and getting in a focused state of mind for the upcoming race. By moving my body and focusing my mind, I was able to integrate the mind-body connection and visualize what I needed to do out on the race course." Davis found the best time to do his ritual was when he was calm, one to two hours before the start of the race. Because the races were long and on consecutive days, he learned that riding a long warm-up didn't help his performance "Right before the start of a bike race there is too much going on. It worked better for me to do my ritual early and then come to the start line knowing I was focused on what I wanted to do."

The stretching that Davis does before an event or hard workout ranges from slow, gentle movements to active, rapid movements designed to increase the range of motion while increasing the blood flow to the muscles. The active stretches are held for 5 to 10 seconds; they include muscle groups on the medial and lateral sides of the body. "I will stretch my iliotibial bands and groin muscles prior to a hard effort because they are the ones most likely to get tight. These side-to-side stretches go against the normal straight-ahead movements I do in cycling, but I find them very important to open my joints and improve my range of motion. The key to the stretching part of my warm-up routine is getting all my muscles to work independently and to increase the mobility of the muscles, that way I know I will have the most efficient movements."

6

Fueling the Body for Training and Performance

Two key ingredients to every overall training plan recipe are nutrition and fluids. How well you nourish your body before, during, and after exercise is nearly as critical as how well you plan and do your training. Sport nutrition is a relatively new science. There are many approaches to eating to improve performance, and we agree that finding the best approach is important. Yet food is a very personal issue, subject to many factors that influence choices. We suggest that you consider food and fluids by how they meet the body's requirements for endurance sports performance. Therefore, we will cover the basics of food as fuel for endurance exercise. We recommend that you look to other references, such as *Ergogenics* by Lamb and Williams, if you desire information about nutritional aspects not covered in this book. See the bibliography for other sources regarding nutrition.

We've found that in endurance sports the major limiting factor from a nutritional perspective is chronically inadequate carbohydrate intake. Gollnick (1985) determined that carbohydrates (CHO) provide the primary fuel during intense muscular endurance activity. Therefore, we recommend high CHO consumption by endurance athletes on a daily basis. We have found no scientific evidence to support recent recommendations proposing a higher fat-lower carbohydrate diet.

SERIOUS systematic training provides us with an overall perspective regarding energy expenditure and the respective energy requirements for different types, duration, and intensities of daily exercise. This chapter will review the following topics:

- Overview of the energy nutrients: carbohydrates, proteins, and fats
- Benefits of the high-carbohydrate diet
- The carbo factor: how to get the right stuff(ing)
- Pre-, during, and postexercise diets
- The fluid factor: water, the essential nutrient

OVERVIEW OF THE ENERGY SYSTEM NUTRIENTS: THE RIGHT MIX

High-performance nutrition involves a definite combination of carbohydrates, fat, protein, vitamins, minerals, and water (fig. 6.1). The mixture will be approximately the same for most endurance athletes, with some variation, of course, depending on food choices, gender, and other characteristics. It is helpful to understand how each of these nutrients contributes to optimal performance and good health (fig. 6.2).

Carbohydrates: The Predominant Energy Nutrient

Carbohydrates and fats are the predominant fuel nutrients. Carbohydrates are found in a number of foods including table sugar, whole grains, starches, vegetables, and fruits. Once digested, these foods are used for energy in basically the same way. Processed carbohydrates are found in the bloodstream as glucose or stored in the muscles and liver as glycogen. Excess supply is converted to free fatty acids and stored as adipose tissue (body fat).

According to Holloszy and Booth (1976), the body will burn carbohydrates as the major source of energy during intense (over 65 percent $\dot{V}O_2$max) endurance exercise. In the SERIOUS system,

Fig. 6.1.   Include a healthy balance of carbohydrates, protein, fat, vitamins, minerals, and water in your high-performance diet.

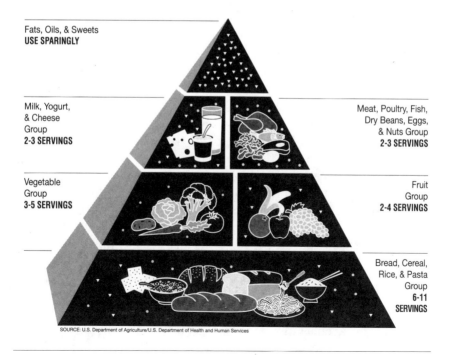

Fats, Oils, & Sweets
USE SPARINGLY

Milk, Yogurt,
& Cheese
Group
2-3 SERVINGS

Meat, Poultry, Fish,
Dry Beans, Eggs,
& Nuts Group
2-3 SERVINGS

Vegetable
Group
3-5 SERVINGS

Fruit
Group
2-4 SERVINGS

Bread, Cereal,
Rice, & Pasta
Group
**6-11
SERVINGS**

SOURCE: U.S. Department of Agriculture/U.S. Department of Health and Human Services

Fig. 6.2.   The food pyramid can guide you in planning nutritional meals.

this means that you'll be using predominantly carbohydrates with some fat whenever you are exercising above level one intensity.

Carbohydrates are the fuel most readily available to the muscle cells. The only problem is that we can store only a limited amount of carbohydrates in the body. Scientists estimate that the average 150-pound, well-trained male endurance athlete can store some 1,800 kilocalories as glycogen and glucose. A well-trained female endurance athlete weighing 120 pounds can store about 1,550 kilocalories.

This energy reserve translates into about 90 to 180 minutes of continuous exercise, depending on the athlete's efficiency, intensity, and environmental conditions. Heavy training and competition will deplete these glycogen stores in about two hours. You may be familiar with the marathoner's dilemma of "hitting the wall," which occurs when the body depletes its glycogen stores during training or races. The condition is characterized by feelings of severe fatigue, dizziness, local muscle pains, and abnormal heart rate. The body is able to continue exercise, but at a much reduced intensity or rate because now the body's fat stores must almost single-handedly meet the energy requirements. Burning fat alone is a very inefficient way to fuel exercise. The best ways to prevent this situation are to raise the preexercise muscle glycogen content to the highest possible level and to ingest a fluid containing carbohydrate (CHO) during exercise.

You will increase your glycogen storage capacity through proper training and diet. Daily endurance training will partially deplete the glycogen in the muscle tissues. As you consume a proper carbohydrate-fat-protein mix, the muscle cells will gain the capability to store slightly more glycogen than they did before you began training.

There is a limit, however, to how much glycogen each person can store. Highly trained endurance athletes will usually be able to store about 1,800 to 2,000 kilocalories. By stimulating your body to adapt to increasing demands, systematic training will improve glycogen storage capacity (if you make CHO available in the diet). Of course, you accomplish this with a gradual, long-term process; don't expect that you will just load up on carbohydrates and do well in a triathlon.

How much of your diet needs to be carbohydrates? Most sport nutrition research concludes that between 50 percent and 65 percent of the calories in the endurance athlete's diet should consist of carbohydrates. During a long endurance event, athletes may need to get more than 70 percent of their energy from carbohydrates, depending on the length and intensity of the event. There are two types of carbohydrates—complex and simple. Complex carbohydrates are found in plants and are considered a better form of carbohydrate due to their vitamin, mineral, and fiber content. Simple carbohydrates, such as table sugar, have little nutritional value and are often referred to as providing "empty calories."

The typical American diet contains less than 50 percent carbohydrates. Economic and social influences have helped condition Americans to eat large amounts of meat and dairy products, both of which are high in fat and protein and relatively low in carbohydrates. Athletes subject to such eating habits often fail to adequately replenish glycogen stores with carbos on a day-to-day basis. Chronic glycogen depletion, or even a few days of deficiency, can result in overtraining, injuries, and subpar performances.

A recent experience illustrates this point well. An elite runner came to us for advice regarding his downward-spiraling performances. He described constant fatigue and lethargy during training and recovery. His last four races had been terrible, and in one 15K race he began to black out as he ran the last few kilometers. Otherwise, he was sharp mentally, working productivity, and enjoying a good family life. Yet he couldn't figure out the reason for his pitiful performances.

We started asking questions. Hypohydration was not a factor, because he was doing well with fluid replacement. We turned the pages of his training log. Two weeks before racing season he had been sick with the flu. When he recovered, he jumped right back into his high-intensity training stage to peak for the big races. Speed work, intervals, and race/pace workouts made up the bulk of his training—all of which burn carbohydrates at higher rates than low-intensity exercise.

We analyzed his diet by having him keep accurate records of everything he consumed for a week. The analysis revealed what we had suspected all along—constant glycogen depletion due to inadequate replenishment. He was consuming a diet that was 40 percent carbohydrate, 17 percent protein, and a whopping 43 percent fat. When he had resumed training after his illness, he dove headlong into his chronic state. No wonder he was bonking in races!

We quickly gave him a crash course in sport nutrition and provided him with a diet plan that included 65 percent carbohydrates. We worked hard to improve his nutritional awareness and his skills in identifying foods that would give him the right amount of carbohydrates and reduce the high-fat foods from his diet. Within a few weeks, he was back to racing and training at his potential.

Ellsworth, Hewitt, and Haskell (1985) identified similar circumstances in elite cross-country skiers. The point is that many athletes believe they are consuming adequate amounts of carbohydrates, but analysis of their intake would reveal otherwise. Later in this chapter we will give you guidelines on how to analyze your dietary intake.

The Protein Factor

Are you one of the millions who were brought up on a training table heaped with steak and eggs? You may remember Sylvester Stallone as Rocky Balboa downing three raw eggs before his morning run. If muscles are made of protein, isn't it logical that a high-protein diet will help build muscles?

Sounds good, but it isn't true. Of course, muscle *is* in constant need of repair and rebuilding, especially in athletes training hard, and protein for these functions, in the form of essential amino acids found in certain foods, must be present in the diet. However, most Americans consume 50 percent to 100 percent more protein than their bodies need for the rebuilding functions. The excess protein they eat will only be excreted as urea. This causes our organs, particularly the kidneys, to work overtime metabolizing the extra protein. In addition, any excess kilocalories from the protein may simply be stored as fat. Thus, eating too much protein wears out our precious organs and adds to unwanted fat.

Animal products do have the virtue of being complete proteins—they contain all the essential amino acids in one package. However, they also contain cholesterol and increased amounts of saturated fats. Used in moderation and with discretion, animal sources of essential amino acids (building blocks for muscle cells) can be a useful part of the endurance athlete's diet.

If you don't want to worry about having to get the essential amino acids from a combination of several vegetable protein sources, make an effort to choose the leanest of meats. Trim away any visible fat, remove the skin from poultry, discard the egg yolks, and buy only skim or low-fat milk, yogurt, and cheeses. "Free-range" animal products tend to be leaner and are less likely to be filled with unknown chemicals and hormones that are often fed to other animal stock. Wild or farm-raised fish and game are excellent sources of protein that are usually low in fat content and high in trace minerals, such as iron.

These foods will then have a much reduced fat and cholesterol content, and the protein will be of high quality. The key is that you don't need to eat a very large serving of any of these in a day. The amount depends on your body weight and training requirements. Generally, our bodies need one to one and one-half grams of complete protein per kilogram (0.45 to 0.675 grams per pound) of body weight on a daily basis. However, when in heavy training, you may need as much as two grams of complete protein per kilogram (0.9 grams per pound) of body weight daily. Another key component of animal proteins, especially lean red meats, is the iron content available and easily assimilated by the body. Endurance athletes, especially runners and female athletes, may have a higher predisposition to anemia or low iron and serum ferritin levels. Vegetarian endurance athletes are even more susceptible to this condition. Therefore, take special care to get enough iron through your food, through supplements, or both.

There are many alternatives to eating animal products as the sole source of dietary protein. Vegetables, legumes, and whole grains in appropriate combinations will provide adequate quantities of essential amino acids. Whole grains such as oats, barley, wheat, and millet contain all the 44 known essential nutrients (except vitamins B_{12}, C, and D). Grains usually have protein contents ranging between 8 percent and 15 percent protein by weight, compared to 30 percent for beef. However, grains typically contain low levels of essential amino acids tryptophan and lysine. The careful consumer can remedy this by combining dried beans with the grain dish or by adding a small amount of low-fat animal protein to the meal. Several excellent sport nutrition references listed at the end of this book can help you determine appropriate sources and combinations of proteins.

The extent to which it is possible to use fewer animal and more vegetable sources of protein is exemplified by Vermont's elite runner Jim Miller, who has developed his own "dinner of champions." We affectionately refer to Jim's evening cuisine as the "Miller Compound," and, believe me, his compound sticks to your ribs! Jim starts with a base of brown rice and lentils cooking in water. As the rice grains become tender, he

*adds some herb seasoning, vegetables, a can of tuna packed
in water, and occasionally some vegetable soup stock. I've
witnessed the creation of the Miller Compound on numerous
occasions and have seen many variations on the basic recipe;
he's even been known to throw in a dab of peanut butter, some
low-fat cottage cheese, and raisins. He gets a diet that is very
high in complex carbohydrates (about 65 percent), meets
enough of his daily protein requirements through the tuna
and the complementary rice and lentils, yet has very little
fat.—Rob*

Fat in the Diet: How Much Is Necessary?

At most, 30 percent of your calories should be from fat sources.
Most Americans consume 40 percent to 45 percent of their diet
from fatty foods. Endurance athletes following such a diet will fail
to replace precious glycogen in sufficient quantity to meet heavy
training demands. Also, by eating a high-fat diet, they are subject
to increased risk of excessive blood cholesterol, heart disease, high
blood pressure, diverticulosis, cancer, obesity, and other diseases.

Fats are generally either overt or "hidden." Overt fats are foods
such as oils, butter, margarine, lard, and visible fat on meats.
Hidden fats are found in combination with other foods—fried
foods, baked goods with lots of oil or butter, snack foods (like
tortilla chips, candy bars and donuts), fatty meats, whole-milk
dairy products, eggs, nuts, and nut butters. It's often difficult to
recognize fats in the diet, but they sure add up. If you eat any of
the foods just listed on a regular basis, especially meats and dairy
products, without attention to their fat content, you're probably
eating too much fat.

Some fat in the diet is necessary. It is used for insulating nerves,
in the manufacture of certain hormones, and for cell membranes.
It is an important energy source too, especially at low exercise
intensities.

"Fat is burned in the flame of carbohydrates" is an expression
used to describe the energy utilization mechanism of the muscle
cells. At low- to moderate-intensity exercise, there can be a
glycogen-sparing effect if fat can contribute to the energy supplied
to the muscle. However, note that abundant fat is stored in
adipose tissue even in the trimmest of athletes. A 150-pound
athlete with 5 percent body fat has 31,500 kilocalories of stored

fat. This fat can be used for energy. Therefore, most sport nutritionists feel that there is no need to plan diets especially to fulfill a fat intake requirement. Rather, they are concerned with too much fat in the diet. Josh Thompson, formerly one of the top biathletes and cross-country skiers in the world, once referred to himself as a "fat-o-phobe"—one who very carefully screens every scrap of food he puts into his mouth to make sure he's not consuming a high-fat item. It is a good idea for all endurance athletes, as well as the general population, to adopt a bit of "fat-o-phobia." Individuals who have the tendency toward anorexic or bulimic behavior are the exception.

Our recommendation is that few (less than 15 percent), if any, of the fats you consume be from animal products. These include red meats, poultry, dairy products (skim-milk products are acceptable), eggs, and animal-fat-based shortenings or margarine. The reason for this is that cholesterol and most saturated fats are present only in animal fats. High-cholesterol, high-fat diets contribute to heart disease and other ailments, and the body does not require dietary cholesterol because it manufactures its own. Change your diet to include the lowest cholesterol and fat levels possible. We are not telling you to avoid animal products. In fact, lean meats are an excellent source of complete proteins as well as iron. Simply learn to moderate the fats that you do eat.

BENEFITS OF THE HIGH-CARBOHYDRATE DIET

We recommend a high-carbohydrate diet for several reasons. First, a high-carbohydrate diet provides the body with the most available energy for training and competition. Next, it may speed up the recovery process. Finally, it seems that a high-carbohydrate diet can promote good health.

Fuel for Training and Racing

As mentioned before, the glycogen stores in the body can fuel intense exercise for up to two hours. You can maintain glycogen stores by consuming a diet high in CHO (50 to 70 percent). Bergstrom, Hermansen, Hultman, and Saltin (1967) found that endurance (time to exhaustion) is significantly improved when a high-CHO diet is consumed, as illustrated in figure 6.3.

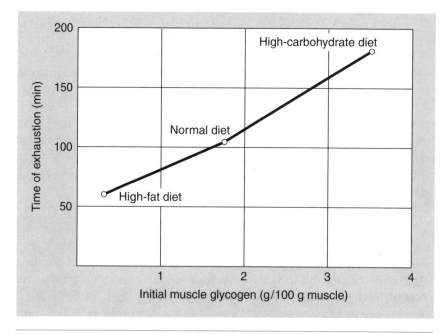

Fig. 6.3.   Effects of various diets on time to exhaustion in endurance athletes.

Restoration

Restoration does not refer simply to what most regard as recovery, to how you feel after a bit of rest. It refers more specifically to the process of restoring the muscles and physiological processes that you have stressed during a specific training session. Training at all levels and volumes, particularly those exceeding 500 hours, will produce the best results if you implement proper restorative measures. Diet is an integral part of the restoration plan. Costill and Miller (1980) determined that failure to replenish glycogen daily will likely result in constant depletion and fatigue, as illustrated in figure 6.4.

General Health Maintenance

In most cases an optimal-performance diet high in CHO will also be a healthful, nutritious one. The athlete following a performance-enhancing, high-CHO diet will likely consume copious quantities of complex carbohydrates in the form of whole grains, whole grain breads, and fresh fruits and vegetables. These foods, especially whole grains, are excellent sources of such other essen-

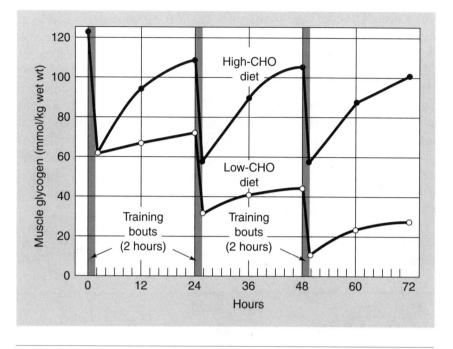

Fig. 6.4. A diet high in carbohydrates speeds recovery from training.

tial nutrients as protein, vitamins, minerals, fiber, and essential fats. They provide a wealth of CHO for replenishing muscle and liver glycogen.

Used sparingly, dairy products made with skim milk, lean cuts of meat, white meat poultry and fish, and reduced intake of animal products in general, will help you focus on getting enough of the primary fuel source—CHO. These steps will help you eliminate poor nutrition as a cause of poor performance. They will supply your body with "the right stuff(ing)"—enough carbohydrates for fuel, adequate protein for cell structure, a proper balance of vitamins and minerals for optimal cell function, and enough water and other fluids for all bodily functions. Good nutrition is another tool to help you attain personal bests, in athletics as well as health.

PLANNING YOUR DIET: HOW TO GET THE RIGHT STUFF

Besides paying attention to your carbohydrate, protein, and fat intake percentages, there is another way to monitor the CHO in your diet. This method involves determining your daily needs in terms of grams of CHO per pound of body weight for varying activity levels. Blom, Vaage, and Kardel (1980), after looking at glycogen replenishment rates following hard training, suggested that endurance athletes training at high intensity should consume between 3.8 and 5.4 grams of CHO per pound of body weight per day to maximize glycogen replenishment. This was for athletes who were expending between 3,500 and 5,000 kilocalories per day. Athletes training at lower volumes and intensities will require less CHO per day, usually ranging between 2.5 and 3.8 grams of CHO per pound of body weight. Table 6.1 outlines CHO needs for athletes of various weights and activity levels.

Since many athletes are habitually failing to replenish depleted CHO, the most positive approach to getting enough CHO is to focus on grams of CHO per day. Therefore, it is necessary to

Table 6.1
Daily Carbohydrate Requirements of Endurance Athletes

Training volumes and intensity

Athlete's weight (lb)	Low (3-6 hr/wk) 2.5 g/lb	Moderate (6-8 hr/wk) 2.8 g/lb	High (8-10 hr/wk) 3.3 g/lb	Very high (>10 hr/wk) 3.8 g/lb
	Grams of carbohydrate needed per day			
100	250	280	330	380
110	275	308	363	418
120	300	336	396	456
130	325	364	429	494
140	350	392	464	532
150	375	420	495	570
160	400	448	528	608
170	425	476	561	646
180	450	504	594	684
190	475	532	627	722
200	500	560	660	760

Note. These values are based on estimates of actual energy expediture. Variation will depend on the athlete's efficiency of movement and the type of activity employed in training.

become better educated regarding the foods that will give you the most bang for your buck. If you find it difficult to eat the high volumes of CHO that are required to replenish glycogen stores, consider high-CHO fluid products that are now available. These products contain between 60 and 100 grams of CHO per 16-ounce serving and are an excellent way to boost CHO intake, especially immediately following exercise. In addition there are several high-CHO energy bar products that have excellent nutritional value and work well as a dietary supplement.

Interpreting the Labels

Most prepackaged grocery store food items have nutritional information on the package. This can be extremely useful, even though it requires a little bit of translation on your part. Typically, the nutritional information on the package will provide the following information (see table 6.2):

- Servings per container
- Serving size
- Calories per serving
- Total fat in grams, percent daily value
- Sodium in grams, percent daily value
- Total carbohydrate in grams, percent daily value
- Sugars in grams
- Protein in grams
- Various other information, such as sodium or vitamin content, and so forth

The key to deciphering all of this information is knowledge of the energy contribution (in kilocalories) per gram of protein, CHO, and fat. One gram of protein contributes 4 kilocalories, one gram of CHO 4 kilocalories, and one gram of fat a whopping 9 kilocalories (see table 6.3). Thus, fat contributes two and one-quarter times the energy of the same weight of either protein or CHO. For example, a tablespoon of butter, which is 100 percent fat, provides about 100 kilocalories, the same number of kilocalories as a medium-sized apple, which is 100 percent CHO.

Therefore, to determine the relative percentages of protein, CHO, and fat in a food item, simply multiply the number of grams of the nutrient by the kilocalorie contribution per gram and divide this result into the total kilocalories per serving. For example, one

Table 6.2
Nutrition Facts

Serving size 1/2 cup (53 g)
Servings Per Container about 8

Amount Per Serving

Calories 180	Calories from Fat 10

	% Daily Value*
Total Fat 1.5g	2%
Saturated Fat 0 g	0%
Polyunsaturated fat 0.5g	
Monounsaturated fat 0.5 g	
Cholesterol 0 mg	0%
Sodium 0 mg	0%
Total Carbohydrate 40 g	13%
Dietary Fiber 5 g	19%
Sugars 18 g	
Protein 5g	

Vitamin A 2%   •   Vitamin C 10%

Calcium 2%   •   Iron 10%

*Percent Daily Values are based on a 2000 calorie diet. Your daily values may be higher or lower depending on your calorie needs:

	Calories:	2,000	2,500
Total fat	Less than	65 g	80 g
Sat fat	Less than	20 g	25 g
Cholesterol	Less than	300 mg	300 mg
Sodium	Less than	2400 mg	2400 mg
Total Carbohydrate		300 g	375 g
Dietary Fiber		25 g	30 g

Calories per gram:
Fat 9   •   Carbohydrate 4   •   Protein 4

> ## Table 6.3
> ### Caloric Equivalents of Energy Nutrients

Energy nutrient	Energy (kcal/gram)
Carbohydrate (CHO)	4.1
Protein	4.3
Fat	9.3

rice cake, which has 66 kilocalories of total energy, is 1.4 grams protein, 14 grams CHO, and 0.5 grams fat. Total kilocalories of protein are 5.6 (1.4 × 4 kilocalories/gram). This means the rice cake's calories are 8.5 percent protein (5.6 divided by 66 total calories per serving). Total kilocalories of CHO are 56 (14 × 4 kilocalories/gram), or about 85 percent of the rice cake's calorie content. Total kilocalories of fat are 4.5 (0.5 × 9 kilocalories/gram), or 6.8 percent of the caloric content.

Using this approach while shopping will help you determine which foods are high in fat and which are not. It's a good idea to use a nutrition almanac to help with foods without nutritional information on the labels. Table 6.4 identifies various healthy foods, their kilocalories per serving, and the grams and percentages of protein, CHO, and fat for comparison to less healthy choices. Table 6.5 offers some of the top grain and legume energy sources for athletes.

One approach we use when giving a lecture on nutrition or working with a group of athletes is what we call the grocery bag technique. We load two grocery bags with food items that have nutritional information on the packages. We divide the group into two teams, each receiving a grocery bag. One team gets the "low-fat" bag, and the other group gets the "typical American diet" bag. We instruct the teams to calculate the percentages of protein, CHO, and fat of each food item in the bag. Then they average the percentages of these nutrients for all items, giving the relative percentages of protein, CHO, and fat calories they would get if they ate one serving of each item from their grocery bag that day. The results are usually humorous, and everyone learns a lot about the nutrient content of the food they eat and how they might substitute food items that are more nutritionally sound, such as using zero-fat yogurt instead of regular yogurt, which can be as high as 40 percent fat.

Table 6.4

Table 6.4

Healthy Food Choices for High-CHO Diets

Food	Serving size	Kcals/serving	CHO (g)	Protein (g)	Fat (g)	% CHO	% Protein	% Fat
Dairy:								
Skim milk	8 oz	100	13.0	10.0	<1.0	52	43	5
Nonfat yogurt	8 oz	200	42.0	8.0	0.0	86	14	0
Low-fat cottage cheese	4 oz	90	3.0	14.0	2.0	14	67	19
Egg whites	1 large	17	0.3	3.6	0.0	7	93	0
Poultry & Fish:								
Chicken breast	3 oz	74	0.0	14.0	2.5	0	76	24
Haddock	3 oz	67	0.0	15.6	0.5	0	93	7
Swordfish	3 oz	100	0.0	16.3	3.4	0	65	35
Tuna (in water)	3 oz	95	0.0	21.0	0.6	0	88	12
Grains:								
Brown rice (cooked)	8 oz	178	38.2	3.8	1.2	86	8	6
Lentils (cooked)	8 oz	212	38.6	15.6	trace	70	29	1
Kidney beans (cooked)	8 oz	218	39.6	14.4	0.9	70	26	4
Spaghetti (cooked)	8 oz	155	32.2	4.8	0.6	83	12	3
W. wheat bread	1 slice	56	11.0	2.4	0.7	73	16	11
Rolled oats (cooked)	8 oz	132	23.3	4.8	2.4	69	15	16
Shredded Wheat	1 oz	110	23.0	3.0	1.0	81	11	8
Grape Nuts	1 oz	110	24.0	3.0	0.0	84	16	0
Fruits & Vegetables:								
Apple	1 medium	96	24.0	0.3	0.0	98	2	0
Banana	1 average	142	33.3	1.6	0.3	94	4	2
Potato (baked)	1 large	114	25.7	3.2	0.2	90	9	1

Table 6.5
Top Ten Grains and Top Ten Legumes for Endurance Athletes

Best protein sources: >20% protein and <20% fat	Best carbohydrate sources: >70% carbohydrate and <5% fat
Black beans	Brown rice
Kidney beans	Wild rice
Lima beans	Whole barley
Navy beans	Whole buckwheat
Soybeans	Whole wheat
Black-eyed peas	Rolled oats
Split peas	Whole rye
Dried whole peas	Whole corn
Lentils	Foxtail millet
Wheat germ	Pearl millet

Using the Supermarket as a Restaurant

Some supermarkets have delis and salad bars that can provide quick, wholesome carryout meals for the athlete. But most don't provide these services, so it's best to have a strategy for getting nutritious unprepared food at the grocery store. In general, if you stay on the perimeter of the store and refrain from going down most aisles, you'll have good success getting the right stuff. This is because most of the healthier foods—those high in CHO and low in fat—are usually located around the perimeter, in the produce and the dairy sections. If you are traveling, it's a good idea to have some utensils and a small bowl on hand, which will allow you to prepare such items as cereal and milk with fruit, sandwiches, or salads. Following is a list of foods to provide you with more menu ideas:

Vegetables: raw carrots, raw celery, salad bar (easy on the dressing!)

Fruit: all fresh fruits, fruit juices, dried fruit, applesauce, jams and jellies

Cereal: Alpen, Familia, muesli, Grape Nuts, Shredded Wheat, Nutri-Grain, rolled oats, Oatios

Milk products: skim milk, zero-fat plain or fruited yogurt, skim-milk cottage cheese

Whole grain breads: Pepperidge Farm whole wheat, Arnold 100 percent whole wheat, bagels, locally baked whole grain breads

Crackers: Barbara's 100 percent whole wheat pretzels, Wasa Crispbread, Rykrisp, Kaavli Norwegian Flat Bread, rice cakes

Cheese, poultry, fish, and legumes: peanut butter, skim-milk cheeses, chicken or turkey breast, tuna in water

Desserts: raisins, Sunshine Raisin Biscuits, fig bars, frozen yogurt, sorbet, frozen fruit bars, bran muffins

PRETRAINING AND RACING DIETS

Experience will teach you what works best for your preexercise diet. By testing preexercise meals during training, you will be able to select an appropriate prerace diet. Ideally, your prerace meal will leave you feeling satisfied and give you ample energy for the race. Remember to record your preexercise meals in a training log to aid you in selecting the proper prerace meal. You should consider the liquid, high-CHO products mentioned previously as a prerace meal or supplement. Table 6.6 provides guidelines for timing and content of feedings before, during, and after training and racing.

Here are several considerations when planning your preexercise diet:

1. For the 10 days preceding the race concentrate on increasing your CHO intake to 70 percent to 80 percent of your diet's total kilocalories.

2. At 12 to 24 hours before the race eat high-CHO, balanced meals with some fiber to eliminate constipation. Hydrate well with water, juices, and energy drinks.

3. At 2 to 4 hours before the race you may elect to reduce intake of solid foods and use more high-CHO energy drinks. Do not stuff yourself. Use easy-to-digest foods that you have tried in training.

4. At less than 1 hour before the race consume water or fluid replacement energy drinks. Eat something light if you need to fill

Table 6.6
Training and Race Dietary Strategy

Time before race	Race length (hours)			
	<1 hour	1-2 hours	2-4 hours	>4 hours
1-10 days	Normal diet	High-CHO diet (>65% CHO)	High-CHO diet (>65% CHO)	High-CHO diet (>65% CHO)
12-24 hours	High CHO	High CHO	High CHO	High CHO
2-4 hours	Low-CHO fluid or H_2O	Low-CHO fluid or H_2O	Solid or liquid high CHO (1-3 g/kg BW)	Solid or liquid high CHO (3-5 g/kg BW)
1-2 hours	Low-CHO fluid or H_2O	Low-CHO fluid or H_2O	Liquid high CHO (1-3 g/kg BW)	Liquid high CHO (3-5 g/kg BW)
<1 hour	Low-CHO fluid or H_2O	Low-CHO fluid or H_2O	Low-CHO fluid or H_2O	Low-CHO fluid or H_2O
During race	Low-CHO fluid or H_2O	Low-CHO fluid or H_2O	Mix low CHO (fluid rep.) with high CHO (energy rep.) Rate = 1 g CHO/min	Mix low CHO (fluid rep.) with high CHO (energy rep.) Rate = 1g CHO/min
Postrace (1-4 hours)	Mix low CHO (fluid rep.) with high CHO (energy rep.) Rate = .75g CHO/kg BW/hr	Mix low CHO (fluid rep.) with high CHO (energy rep.) Rate = .75g CHO/kg BW/hr	Mix low CHO (fluid rep.) with high CHO (energy rep.) Rate = .75g CHO/kg BW/hr	Mix low CHO (fluid rep.) with high CHO (energy rep.) Rate = .75g CHO/kg BW/hr
>4 hours	High-CHO diet (>65% CHO)	High-CHO diet (>65% CHO)	High-CHO diet (>65% CHO)	High-CHO diet (>65% CHO)

Notes. Fluid replacement fluids contain 5-15% CHO; energy replacement fluids contain >10% CHO (>100 kcal per water bottle). BW = body weight, 1 kg = 2.2 lb.

your stomach, such as an energy bar, bread, bagels, bananas, and so forth. Be certain to experiment with the foods of choice during hard training sessions or practice races well before race day.

En Route Consumption

The length of a training session or race will determine whether it warrants en route feeds. Exercise, particularly intense exercise, lasting over 90 minutes generally warrants en route consumption of CHO. Theoretically, the body will have enough glycogen stored to complete any exercise session shorter than an hour, and if fully loaded with CHO, to complete a session as long as two and one-half hours.

In practice, as Macaraeg (1983) has demonstrated, en route feedings of scientifically formulated fluid replacement energy drink products during intense exercise delay the onset of exhaustion. Thus, for exercise sessions or races lasting over 90 minutes, we recommend consumption of CHO to prevent fatigue and restore depleted glycogen. Replenish glycogen by consuming approximately one gram of CHO per minute, which is about 240 kilocalories of CHO per hour, or one bottle of high-CHO energy drink or high-CHO energy bar.

Carbohydrates After Exercise

The foods you eat after exercise should generally be the same as those you eat before exercise. But there are guidelines regarding when after training you should sit down to the table. Depletion of muscle glycogen from training and competition produces an increase in enzyme activity called glycogen synthetase, which raises the muscle cells' receptivity to storing glycogen. Glycogen synthetase activity is at its highest level for 2 to 4 hours directly following exercise, and then falls to normal preexercise levels within 12 to 24 hours. In other words, the body can most efficiently convert carbohydrates to stored glycogen immediately following intense exercise.

When you are training hard, it is important to take advantage of this opportunity for glycogen intake. Otherwise, even if you eat a high-CHO diet containing 400 grams of CHO per day, you may not fully replenish preexercise glycogen levels during peak training periods. For example, if during a training session a third of your muscle glycogen is depleted, a CHO-rich diet will restore muscle glycogen in 24 hours; whereas a moderate- or low-CHO diet will not replenish muscle glycogen. This means your body will not be adequately prepared for another training session. A marathon racer depletes about 150 millimoles of glycogen per kilogram of muscle tissue in a race; only 50 to 60 millimoles of glycogen per kilogram of tissue will be replenished in 24 hours. Subsequent recovery from this type of effort will take several days.

FLUID FACTOR

Of all the nutrients to consider, water is the most important. Yet fluid intake often receives inadequate attention.

No matter what your level of sport participation, you have one important similarity to the elite athlete: You will get thirsty. In most adolescents and adults, 60 to 70 percent of the lean body weight is water. Many of the body's functions depend upon water. During vigorous exercise this dependence is pronounced, and the need for fluid replacement becomes crucial. Of the available chemical energy of foods, only 20 to 25 percent is used to perform work; the remainder is dissipated as heat. As a result, exercise increases the body's internal core temperature (the temperature around your spine and organs). Vigorous exercise, especially during hot weather, double-session training, or competitions, markedly elevates your core temperature. For example, running at a two-and-a-half-hour marathon pace produces enough heat to raise the body temperature 1 degree Celsius (1.8 degrees Fahrenheit) every five minutes, which would cause severe problems if not for the body's air-conditioning system—sweating and its evaporative cooling effects.

Your brain's hypothalamus—the body's thermostat—senses the rise in core temperature and sends messages to the muscles and skin to begin the cooling process. When your hypothalamus senses an increase in core temperature above 37 degrees Celsius (98.6 degrees Fahrenheit), the hot blood at your core moves toward your skin. The sweat mechanism is activated, and the air moving across your damp skin produces the cooling effect of evaporation. Your skin temperature decreases to several degrees below the core temperature, so that hot blood from the core passing through the skin becomes cooler. The blood then moves back to the core to reduce the core temperature, and the cycle continues.

This process costs the body a great deal of precious water. In fact, perspiration is the major cause of water loss. During vigorous activity, such as running, cross-country skiing, cycling, and so on, a person can lose between 1 and 6 liters (1.1 and 6.3 quarts) of water per hour. If the process continues for an hour or more, the body cannot execute its cooling and other basic functions adequately. Fatigue sets in, and performance is affected. Even relatively mild dehydration reduces performance. Fink (1982) demonstrated that losing only 2 to 3 percent of the body's fluid through dehydration (about three or four pounds of body weight) will decrease performance by 3 to 7 percent in runners competing in 1,500-, 5,000-, and 10,000-meter races. Figure 6.5 illustrates the effects of dehydration on physical performance.

Increased respiration also contributes to dehydration. As the steam from your breath on a cold morning shows, the air you expire contains a good deal of water. You lose more if the air is dry or hot, or if you are breathing large volumes of air (as in endurance exercise). During exercise it is possible to lose between 150 milliliters to 300 milliliters (5 to 10 ounces) of water per hour through respiration alone.

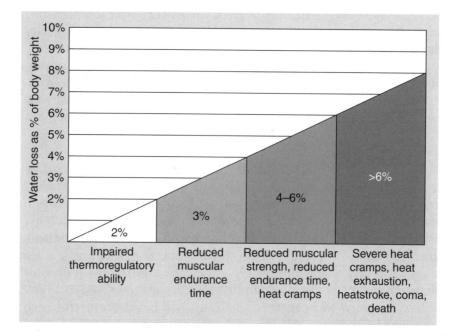

Fig. 6.5. Effects of various levels of dehydration on endurance performance.

Longer training sessions or competition mean more water loss. Theoretically, a marathon runner, a triathlete, or a marathon cross-country skier will lose an average of 160 ounces of water over the course of a two-and-one-half-to-three-hour race. That's 10 pounds of water! Even if the athlete consumed 40 ounces of fluids along the way, a 120-ounce deficit would remain.

How can you replace so much fluid over the course of the race or practice session? You can't. You must properly hydrate your body before the event so that you can depend on stored water as well as on water consumed during the race or training session. Stored water is released as follows: For every gram of carbohydrate (glycogen) stored in the muscles, liver, and blood, the body stores three to four grams of water. During oxidation (combustion) of this glycogen to provide energy, the water is liberated as well and can be used in the cooling process. This is why athletes who properly hydrate themselves before practice or competition can go the distance without replenishing all fluids lost. Of course, elite athletes can accomplish this more efficiently than average athletes can.

Water will always be a good replenisher. Commercial sugar-and-electrolyte solutions can be effective if they include appropriate sources of glucose. Macaraeg (1983) has shown that use of polymerized glucose replacement fluids (as compared to no fluids or just plain water) will delay the onset of exhaustion in well-trained athletes (see figure 6.6). These *fluid replacement* products contain between 5 and 10 percent glucose (approximately 50 to 100 kilocalories per 16-ounce water bottle), as compared with *energy replacement* products, which contain more than 10 percent glucose. Most fluid replacement products have small amounts of sodium chloride, which is necessary to allow adequate fluid absorption during exercise. If the solution has a high concentration of glucose, such as an energy replacement solution, the body treats it as a source of energy and not fluid, and dehydration will not be prevented. Some fluid replacement products use glucose polymers (many linked glucose chains) while others use one-chain glucose. There is no scientific evidence that one type is absorbed more completely during exercise. Use products that are palatable to you in a variety of environmental conditions, such as heat. You will take in more of a product that tastes good. Also, make sure you are familiar with the fluids served at feed stations in any race you enter. If you have not used them before or feel uncomfortable with their concentrations, prepare your own fluids and arrange to have them available. Some basic principles that apply to fluid replacement include the following:

• Every day, especially the day before competitive or long events, drink 8 to 10 eight-ounce glasses of water or fluid replacement product. If you know you need more than that, drink more.

• Drink up to 32 ounces of water or fluid replacement drink one to two hours before practice or competition. Immediately before your event or workout, drink up to 16 additional ounces of water or fluid replacement product.

• If a competition or workout will last over an hour, it is best to replace fluids by consuming 100 to 200 milliliters of water (3 to 6 ounces) every 15 to 20 minutes. Typically, you will be able to tolerate larger fluid intakes while cycling compared to running. For triathletes, this means consuming more fluid during the cycling segment to prevent dehydration. Keep in mind that environmental conditions influence fluid requirements; if it is hot, humid, or windy, you will need to consume larger quantities of fluids.

• Don't wait until you are thirsty to drink; if you do, you will fall far behind your body's water needs. This is why it is so essential to replace water regularly throughout the day as well as during exercise. Your urine color should always be clear. If your urine is chronically cloudy or yellowish in color, you are probably underhydrated (unless you take B-complex vitamins, which give urine a bright greenish yellow color). Check your urine color frequently and replace fluids appropriately.

• After a hard training session or competition, it may take 10 to 20 hours to fully rehydrate with water, fluid replacement products, fruit juices, skim milk, or herb teas. Caffeine drinks such as coffee, tea, or cola, as well as alcohol (such as the postworkout beer), are diuretics—they cause the body to eliminate water. Consume them in moderation. Check your weight loss every morning and night to estimate fluid losses; a five-pound weight loss over 24 hours means you've lost about two and one-half quarts of water. If you have morning weight loss of more than 2 percent, reduce your training for the day or take a day off and concentrate on fluid replacement.

• Determine a plan for fluid replacement and try it several times in training before you try it in an important race.

• The dryness that comes with altitudes above 5,000 feet, coupled with the increased workload the lower partial pressure of oxygen puts on the body, raises fluid requirements. Make sure extra water is available if you live or train at a high altitude.

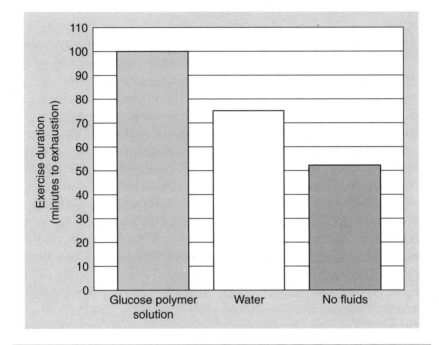

Fig. 6.6. Water and fluid replacement energy drinks improve performance.

Recovering Effectively From Training

If creating the SERIOUS training plan, implementing it, and supporting it with proper diet and nutrition are considered the training recipe for your winning chili, then the recovery process could be considered how well your body digests and assimilates the chili. Recovery deserves considerable attention; we see it as a very important ingredient in the total training and performance process. *Restoration* and *recovery* can be considered synonyms in this context, and describe this essential component of the training process.

Athletes and coaches commonly oversimplify and disregard the recovery process. They may feel adequate recovery happens as long as the athlete gets enough sleep at night and has enough time between workouts to feel fully rested. Little thought goes into what the athlete actually does during this downtime. Restoration refers to the active process of restoring the muscles and physiological processes that the athlete has stressed during a specific training session. Additionally, thorough restoration considers the various psycho-emotional stressors associated with daily living, such as work, school, personal relationships, or financial situation, and creates a heightened awareness of the effects of these stressors. Likewise, restoration is not to be confused with rehabilitation from a specific injury, which is a totally different matter. For additional information regarding the restoration process see the discussions on the importance of the cool-down and stretching in chapter 5, nutrition to aid recovery in chapter 6, and postrace recovery in chapter 10.

Consider the training process to be like a balance scale (fig. 7.1). A small percentage of the time we achieve a stable balance. It is through this process that we learn. We learn about the effects of various stressors, about their relationship to other factors in life, and ultimately about strategies to use in refining our daily balancing act. Without awareness of and attention to life's stressors, athletes would continue to train full-speed ahead, with little regard to the intuitive and learned checks and balances our bodies and minds are capable of administering.

As discussed in chapter 2, the body will respond positively to an imposed overload, given opportunities to recover. Most athletes' lives, however, involve a lot more than training. Most have other stressors that affect their restoration process. The factors that affect the progress of restoration may occur individually or simultaneously. Although it is beyond the scope of this book to venture into the

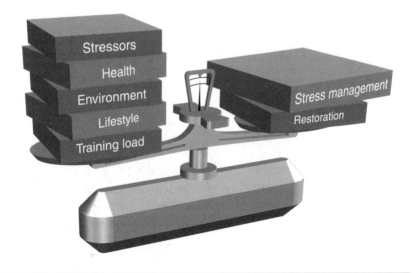

Fig. 7.1.   Maintaining a balance between stressors and restoration requires constant awareness of the effects of stress and the necessary recovery techniques.

psycho-emotional ramifications of various stressors, let alone to list the multitude of stressor variables, it is a good idea for you to outline the stress factors that are most common in your life. This will enhance your awareness of how they might affect the training and restoration process.

Much of the available information regarding training for endurance sports concentrates on appropriate training volumes and methods. Contemporary coaches and athletes usually equate larger training loads with increases in performance, provided that the athlete gradually increases training loads over several years, as well as within a given training and competitive season. Our experience, however, is that most athletes and coaches do not employ a systematic approach to training plans, so that the total training volume is often inappropriate for the individual athlete. Of course, some may follow a "hard-easy" approach to training patterns, alternating high-intensity days with low-intensity days, but few pay close attention to such stress signals as those outlined in chapter 8 (morning pulse, morning weight, sleep hours, feel of the workout, and completion of the workout).

RESTORATION AND TRAINING LOADS

Adequate training loads (as measured in year hours) are indeed necessary for increasing the functional capabilities of the body. Systematically increasing the training volume from year to year as well as within the training year is best accomplished by observing the following:

1. A gradual increase in hours trained per year—usually 5 to 15 percent per year, depending on your level of development.
2. Use of qualified coaching, scientific, and medical assistance, with proper adherence to the training plan and scheduled rest.
3. Use of a combination of current training methods and devices, psychological preparation, and effective methods for restoration from training bouts.

It is true that the body will improve its ability to recover as part of its adaptation to increased training loads. However, as training programs become more demanding, experienced coaches and sport scientists are finding that recovery time may not keep pace with increases in training. Therefore, many progressive sport scientists and coaches have been urging that all training be planned and regulated according to a simple yet thorough restoration program aimed at accelerating the recovery process.

Many world-class endurance athletes train between 700 and 1,000 hours per year. Some athletes in sports such as the triathlon train as much as 8 hours on certain days! Such training clearly improves race performances. However, as the Russian coach Zalessky says (quoted in Yessis, 1986), "further increases in physical loads lead to such changes in the athlete that they go beyond physiological norms, worsen the functional state and lower the athlete's capacity for work" (p. 2). He goes on to say that the most effective way for correcting this is through various restoration methods. Russian coaches, athletes, and scientists employ a systematic approach to recovery methods, making it possible to increase training load and intensity without injury or overtraining. In fact, a well-thought-out training plan coupled with proper restoration methods reduces the incidence of injury.

Planning training so that you recover well from that training is beneficial in several ways. First, the body (and perhaps the mind) recovers more rapidly between training sessions. In other words, the body adapts to the imposed demand more readily. Second, you can sustain a higher training volume, which ultimately will result in higher work capacity. Third, you enhance awareness of the effects of stressors, making appropriate adjustments to those stressors possible.

Typically, a hard day of training, such as intervals, should be followed by an easy day (endurance or rest) to allow recovery. You can experiment with different weekly patterns depending on the stage of the season, the training volume, and your experience. In general, the more intense the training stage becomes in terms of volume and character of workouts, the greater the need for patterning the week after the hard day-easy day format. You may even wish to employ a hard day-easy day-easy day pattern, allowing two easy days between intense days. The benefit of the training session and the active rest may increase if you plan different equipment, activities, or training environments into the weekly pattern. Cross-training (the use of a variety of sport activities to accomplish a training plan) may decrease stress on the musculoskeletal system, decrease the likelihood of psychological burnout, and increase the restorative capabilities of the body.

Multisport athletes, such as triathletes, will need to pattern more than one type of activity. It is best to adopt the hard-easy approach mentioned above for cycling and running. Plan your hard cycling and running training on the same day or close together during the week (table 7.1). This will allow maximum recovery, as the training week will not include hard training day after day.

Mark Allen and Kenny Souza have experimented with alternating hard weeks of cycling and running as a way to recover fully from training. They emphasize cycling one week, through increased intensity and volume, and emphasize running the following week. They have indicated this method works well, especially during periods of a high volume of training, such as before the Ironman.

RECOVERY PROCESS

Yessis (1986) described the recovery process as consisting of three phases: *ongoing recovery*, which happens in the course of a training session; *quick recovery*, which commences at the end of the session and involves metabolic waste removal; and *deep recovery*, which is where adaptation occurs and the athlete's physiological and psychological resources become greater than before. The desired physical improvements seem to depend heavily on this deep recovery phase.

Table 7.1
Sample Weekly Pattern for the Multisport Athlete

	Sun	Mon	Tues	Wed	Thur	Fri	Sat
Swim			OD		IN	EN	
Bike	OD			IN	OD		OD/SP
Run	OD		OD	IN		SP	EN
Other			ST		ST		ST

It takes longer for some bodily systems to recover than it does for others. Connective tissue (tendons and fascia) and supportive tissue (ligaments and bone), because of decreased vascularization, usually take longer to recover than do the metabolic and cardiovascular systems. Likewise, mending of muscle proteins and replenishment of muscle glycogen typically take longer than replenishment of other biochemical substances. It is essential that restoration practices be directed at those systems that require more time to recover.

Muscular acidosis is a primary performance-limiting factor for endurance athletes. As explained before, accumulations of lactic acid in the muscle tissue cause the feeling of muscle fatigue. These accumulations can be detected by corresponding increases in blood lactic acid concentrations. Scientists have been analyzing blood lactate in athletes for some time, and these measurements are now routinely used to identify an athlete's state of training and recovery. Several methods for accelerating the clearance of lactate from the musculature have been developed and tested and are used today by athletes and coaches. For example, a simple warm-up and cool-down at easy intensity has been shown to speed removal of metabolic wastes.

Shevciw (1986) reports that passive methods of recovery can also speed removal of blood lactate. Relaxation baths (water temperature at 36 degrees Celsius [97 degrees Fahrenheit]) and relaxation massage (30 minutes in length) administered to a group of elite handball players after 30 minutes of vigorous play significantly decreased blood lactate levels in comparison with those found in players who went without regenerative measures after playing. These studies indicate that lactic acid reduction is accelerated when the restorative methods of bath and massage are employed postexercise.

The overall goal of the training plan and restoration program is to induce the best possible training effect, both physiologically and psychologically, while avoiding overtraining. Overtraining is caused by a host of factors, such as neglect of recovery needs within the training cycle, too much training at or near the threshold intensity, an excessive number of competitions, poor planning, poor diet, or stressful living, job, school, or personal situations. You can avoid overtraining with the correct restorative methodology.

RESTORATION METHODS

Athletes currently practice many restoration methods. Clinical and practical research is investigating the timing and frequency of implementation of the various methods. Although it is beyond the scope of this book to offer a conclusive methodology for application of restoration, we will describe several recovery methods currently used by athletes, coaches, and scientists. These are characterized as either *active* or *passive restoration* practices.

Active Restoration

Active restoration involves the physical exertion of the athlete. This is also referred to as *natural restoration*. This category includes the following:

Cool-Down Activity

As described in chapter 5, measures such as taking a 15-minute cool-down run seem to improve blood perfusion of muscle tissue, which accelerates removal of lactic acid. The cool-down is usually necessary only after intense effort, such as speed, race/pace, interval, and up/vertical training sessions. It is important that the intensity of the cool-down activity be low (at or below level one, described in chapter 2). Logistically, it is easiest to extend the workout activity by cooling down using the same activity, but it may also be beneficial to switch activities for the cool-down. For example, a runner might wish to finish the workout with a 15-minute, easy cycle on a cycle ergometer. Multisport athletes need to avoid extended cool-down periods after training sessions to reduce continued depletion of muscle glycogen. If you are doing multiple training sessions per day, shorten cool-down periods to 5 to 10 minutes.

Fluid Replacement

You must consume fluids, preferably water or a fluid replacement product, before, during, and after all training. The urine should be relatively clear and pale. Remember not to confuse liquid energy replacement products (greater than 15 percent CHO) with fluid replacement products. You must replenish lost fluids as well as energy. If you're training indoors, on a treadmill or bike trainer, fluid losses are substantial, and you must replace the fluid during and immediately after exercise.

Nutrition

The diet must be high in complex carbohydrates, which you should consume both directly after training and between sessions. It is a good idea to use an energy replacement bar or an energy replacement drink during and after long workouts to replenish lost carbohydrates (see chapter 6). Also, recommended daily allowances of trace minerals, such as iron, zinc, chromium, selenium, calcium, potassium, sodium, and magnesium, which are necessary for normal biochemical reactions, should be consumed as part of the foods selected.

Walking

Simple walks, taken with an attitude of leisure and relaxation, are useful in restoration (fig. 7.2). Usually evening walks after the day's training are most effective.

Fig. 7.2. Take a walk to recover and as a "getaway."

Passive Restoration

Passive restorative techniques do not require your active physical involvement. There are many passive methods of restoration therapy. The relaxation baths and relaxation massage are particularly popular in sport applications.

Sleep

Maintain normal sleep amounts and patterns, particularly during high-intensity training periods. Bedtime and hours of sleep should be consistent if possible, and the bed should be comfortable and firm. If you plan two training sessions in one day, naps between workouts, if time allows, are beneficial in promoting recovery. Avoid napping late in the afternoon, as it may affect your evening sleep patterns. Also, caffeine late in the day can disrupt your normal sleeping routine. Avoid it or use it in moderation.

Massage

Perhaps one of the most widely used methods for recovery is massage. Massage can take many forms, and several techniques are popular with and useful for athletes (fig. 7.3). Proper massage accelerates recovery from workouts and can increase your total work capacity. The increased blood flow to the muscles during massage promotes lactate removal and nourishment of the muscle tissue. Regular massage is also effective for discovering areas of particular tightness or soreness, which can be an early signal of a developing overuse injury. Make a mental note of potential trouble areas and continue with your training carefully.

Sport massage by a qualified professional is the most effective. However, you can derive considerable benefit from self-massage techniques. The main techniques for self-massage involve jostling, kneading, and stroking the muscles with slow, soft movements directly after a workout or competition. You can use self-massage several hours after the workout as well, when it typically is longer in duration. For more information about massage, refer to the bibliography that appears near the end of this book.

Relaxation Baths

These are one of the oldest known forms of restoration. It is on record that Aristotle enjoyed relaxation baths. However, it is not clearly known how baths work to regenerate the body. They seem to promote blood circulation and muscle relaxation. Whirlpool or

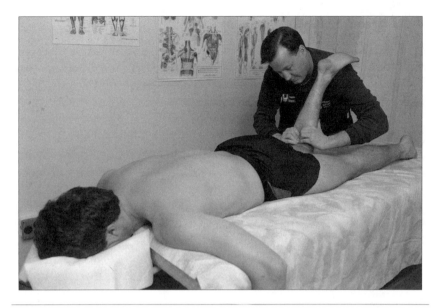

Fig. 7.3.   Sports massages can reduce recovery time between workouts.

Jacuzzi hot tubs, with water at 36 degrees Celsius (97 degrees Fahrenheit), effectively accelerate blood lactate removal and heart rate recovery (fig. 7.4). Use care when using hot tubs with higher temperatures (above 100 degrees Fahrenheit), as prolonged exposure can lead to dehydration and possible heat illness such as heat exhaustion. Limit your exposure to 10 to 15 minutes per session.

One of our favorite winter routines is to relax in a hot tub for 5 to 10 minutes followed by an exhilarating roll in the snow, and then back into the hot tub for a skin-tingling few more minutes. This spices up the relaxation bath considerably!

Progressive Muscle Relaxation

You can enhance relaxation of the muscles by employing techniques to progressively reduce muscle tension. You may use a variety of techniques, including self-hypnosis, visualization, and muscle tensing and releasing. We recommend that you learn techniques from qualified professionals, either in person or by audio tape. The benefits are improved blood circulation, speedier removal of metabolic wastes, and improved nourishment of tissue by nutrients in the blood.

Fig. 7.4. Whirlpools (in moderation) can offer a fun way to relax and speed up the recovery process.

Other Methods

Russian coaches report very sophisticated methods for restoration, including massage during workouts; various water procedures, such as showers, saunas, and baths; ultrasound and electrostimulation; autogenic psychoregulation relaxation therapy; and special pharmacologically derived diet and fluid replacement therapies. Many of these procedures require careful administration and may be logistically difficult for the average athlete to employ.

You may discover that even with the proper restorative techniques, you are still not recovering from your training properly. Several incomplete workouts or a poor feeling for several consecutive days can mean you are overtrained. Overtraining does not always indicate too much training; it could easily result from other stressors. Table 7.2 outlines some of the various factors that can affect recovery and induce a state of overtraining. Be aware of these factors and be prepared to make adjustments in your training plan if you find that some of these apply to you. See chapter 9 for further information on adjustments to your training plan.

Table 7.2

Causes of Overtraining

Training method

Inappropriate structure	Recovery neglected in weekly and in 4-week cycle periodization pattern
	Too much volume or intensity too soon
	Too much volume of training at or near AT (threshold intensity)
	Too high an intensity when training for aerobic endurance (OD or EN)
	Excessive competitions, with associated changes in daily routine and inadequate training time
	Insufficient variety of training methods
	Frequent failure due to setting unrealistic goals
Poor plan adjustment to changing circumstances	Failure to alter training pattern or volume to accommodate other stressors such as work, exams, family, etc.
	Too much training too soon after forced interruptions such as injury or illness
Inappropriate planning and teaching methodology	Inadequate knowledge of restoration or stress management or hygiene (i.e., all factors associated with physical and mental health)
	Lack of confidence in training plan or coach
	Too much forced technical instruction that is complicated; not enough opportunity for alternative games and training

Lifestyle

Planning	Hurrying things
	Irregular daily routine
	Not enough fun or leisure time (no relaxation)
	Poor quality or insufficient sleep
Diet	Inadequate balance of CHO, fat, and protein
	Poor fluid replacement
	Excessive alcohol consumption
	Excessive caffeine consumption
	Lack of vitamins and minerals due to poor dietary choices
Housing	Poor housing (noisy, crowded, poor lighting, etc.)
	Disturbed home life

(continued)

Table 7.2
(continued)

Environment

Distractions	Continuous conflict with others (family, coach, etc.)
	Inappropriate stimuli (TV, movies, etc.)
Job/education	Unhappy with job
	Time demands of work
	Conflict with others at work
	Overextended in job or school workload
	Low performance in job or school
Personal	Tension in family
	Unhappy love relationship
	Family responsibilities

Health

Allergies, asthma, colds, flu, gastrointestinal problems, infectious diseases, other chronic problems

FROM EXPERIENCE
MARK ALLEN

Mark Allen, long regarded as the king of triathlon, has won virtually every major event in the sport, including the Hawaiian Ironman and the Nice triathlon. His nickname among his peers, Grip, came from Mark's remarkable ability to get into a zone and push himself very hard. If you were out training with him, you would inevitably end up in his "grip," hanging on for dear life at a pace well beyond your comfort zone. Mark uses a strong mental focus to get into this zone, and he is able to recover from his prior training.

We discussed with Mark the recovery strategies that allow him to train at such a high level. He pays close attention to his attitude toward training. After a couple of hard workouts if he finds himself unmotivated to go out and train later in the week, he will skip the workout or do an easier training session. "I find that I can push through the physical signs that indicate I am not recovered, such as sore legs, but if I watch my attitude toward my training it gives me a better indicator of whether I am ready for another stressful session. I know that I can go out and do a workout, but if I am not in a positive frame of mind, I won't get as much benefit from the training session."

Mark finds massage a valuable tool to aid recovery. He watches his nutrition, also, having learned that an increased protein intake (up to 30 percent of his dietary intake) aids in the repair process during heavy training loads. He contends, in addition, that antioxidants, such as vitamins C and E, help him recover from the demands of training and, especially from poor air quality.

Mark advocates active recovery when it comes to restoring the body after a major competition. Mark swims after a race until his legs feel recovered. "During the Ironman one year I got very sick, and I rested completely for about a month after the event. When I started back into training, I was very tight and stiff. It took a long time to feel relaxed and comfortable training."

Blisters are another benchmark of recovery. "I can't see *inside* my body, but I can see the blisters heal. I use the blisters as an indicator of the healing process going on inside my body." Stretching after an event also helps keep Mark from getting stiff and tight. "As you recover, gradually start with some very easy stretching in areas that aren't sore and increase your stretching to get your flexibility to where it was prior to the event." Alternate activities are another way Mark aids in postrace recovery. To stay active he chooses sports that he doesn't do so often during the season, such as surfing, letting his triathlon-specific muscles get a rest.

After a good race (his 1995 Ironman victory, for example) Mark sometimes gives in to nutritional vices, eating foods he normally wouldn't choose. "It's important to give yourself some rewards for a good performance, as long as you don't go overboard." His attitude is a good reminder to all of us that success itself can be an integral part of the recovery process.

Tracking
Your Training

Next to hard-core baseball fans and accountants, serious athletes and fitness enthusiasts are often the most statistic-conscious people around. We like to know the numbers. What was my time in that race? What was my place in my age group? How much do I weigh today? What's my resting heart rate, especially after yesterday's interval workout? What's my total mileage for the week? For the month?

Yes, many of us love our numbers. Yet all of these facts and figures are of only temporary value unless you take time to record them in a training log that is well organized and designed to allow easy access to your vital numbers. Ideally, the log will become a teacher that is ever expanding in its knowledge and wisdom. One masters cross-country skier, Bob Greg of Escanaba, Michigan, has recorded his training in an impressive detailed log for over 20 years! He's used it wisely to guide his training and racing every year.

Keeping a training log is similar to keeping a personal diary, except this one focuses only on the exercises, workouts, and competitions you perform. Most importantly, it's your own special place for tracking your fitness, your performances, and your experiences. One may even choose to use the log and journal as a method of integrating your physical, mental, and spiritual experiences through your sport activities.

On the practical side, you've invested much of your precious time, energy, and money carefully planning and following your training program. One return on your investment is the objective information that a well-kept training log provides. It is one of the best means for evaluating your progress over the long haul. Unless you have a great memory, it becomes very difficult to objectively view high points and low points in training and to track trends and idiosyncrasies in your training.

Every athlete would do well to keep a log and journal. You may be doing this already. However, if you are like most athletes we've coached, your log could be working more efficiently for you. We've created a log and journal system that will provide invaluable information and a self-monitoring method that will pay for itself repeatedly as you record the weeks, months, and years of your sporting experiences.

BENEFITS OF AN EFFECTIVE TRAINING LOG

We've been fortunate to have worked with many elite athletes over the years. One observation we've made is that the best athletes regularly maintain logs and journals that record vital objective and subjective information. These athletes review their training logs regularly. They search for clues and insights about their successes and setbacks, their progress and pitfalls.

Some years ago, one of the cross-country skiers on the U.S. National team was having terrible results in preseason races and training. She skied the world championship team try-outs but failed to make the World Cup team and became extremely ill afterward. Depressed and confused by her mysterious drop in performance, she came to me for advice. After listening to her story of the events leading up to the racing season, a few pieces of the puzzle came together. Still, we needed hard data on training hours, what those hours consisted of, recovery information, and general comments from her journal entries. Since I had persuaded most of the National team athletes to keep a log, she was able to present a thorough training log on request.

I reviewed her log carefully, searching for insights. Every time I came to a place where I found a clue to solving the mystery, I recorded it. After I finished the investigation, we reviewed my observations. In June she had undergone arthroscopic knee surgery. Although she had been given some guidelines for rehabilitation, it was apparent that she had stressed the knee too much too soon. The journal entries for the four months postsurgery indicated weakness of the knee joint and her fears of reinjury during training. In July she had seen a new coach who placed her on a different training plan. He did not realize the extent of her injury and started her on too much volume for her current fitness level.

In October her relationship with her boyfriend ended. In November she experienced a financial crunch, forcing her to work more to meet some deadlines, and thus creating more emotional stress. She also went to West Yellowstone, Montana, where, like most skiers, she was so elated by the early snowfall that she tossed her training plan aside. She skied far too many kilometers for five days and became exhausted. One could refer to it as the "crash and burn" approach; it was self-destructive. She couldn't resist the temptation of getting out there with her teammates and skiing all day long on consecutive days, instead of gradually building her ski-specific conditioning.

Her log entries during November and December revealed a distinctive pattern in her training. She would feel good and ski hard for three days. During the third day she would "bonk," becoming exhausted in less than 30 minutes. On the fourth and fifth days, she would rest and recover. The sixth day would be a race or timed trial, and because she always felt better by race time, she'd ski at full throttle for as long as possible (in the early part of the season, no less!). The seventh day would mean a nosedive for the bed.

As she started each new seven-day cycle, she would be slightly more exhausted than the week before. When the World Cup tryout series finally arrived in January, she was a wreck. Her immune system was weak. She got the flu almost immediately after arriving at the Olympic Training Center in Lake Placid, a haven for viral infections because so many athletes from around the world are constantly coming and going. She "bonked" midway through each of the four races of the series. No medals, no trip to Europe, no fun.

Our review of her training records suggested that the best prescription for her was to take two to three weeks of total rest. No training. No stress. The rest was followed by a gradual return to her previous levels of training. She followed this prescription and made a strong comeback later that season. Most important, she learned some valuable lessons that would serve her well in future seasons. If she had not kept the log and journal, it would have been extremely difficult to piece together the problems with her training and to develop an effective solution.—Rob

Some endurance athletes and coaches have enjoyed effective record keeping, problem solving, and troubleshooting for years. Sigvart Bjontegaard, head coach of the U.S. Olympic Biathlon team from 1986 to 1988, and a former national champion biathlete in Norway, shared with us the dozen neatly kept training diaries he had used during his 12 years of training with the Norwegian National team (fig. 8.1). Recorded for each week, month, and year were total training hours, the percentages of each training component, recovery data, subjective feelings, and so on. At the end of each booklet was a foldout graph with the 52 weeks on the horizontal axis and the percentage of weekly hours on the vertical axis. The completed chart was detailed with color coding and actual numbers. He had used a bar graph to color code the percentage of each week's hourly volume by training component, such as overdistance, speed, strength, interval, and so forth (fig. 8.2).

Sigvart arranged these yearly graphs next to each other. He went on to explain which years were his most successful and why he thought this. We analyzed his most successful years and concluded that he had discovered training principles and regimens advocated in today's scientific and coaching literature. He had inadvertently become a scientist, a data collector, a keen, objective observer of his training progress. Now he could use that data to help the athletes he was coaching.

There are countless other stories about using training logs to objectify and enhance training. Without this self-monitoring it's easy to lose perspective and become sidetracked by subjective feelings and inappropriate advice from others. A systematic approach to collecting information about training is essential for developing and staying on track with training plans and methods that work best for you.

We developed the SERIOUS training log and journal system to dovetail the record keeping with the SERIOUS training compo-

Fig. 8.1.   U.S. Olympic biathlon coach, Sigvart Bjontegaard (left) and Rob Sleamaker review the log books and performance graphs Bjontegaard meticulously kept during his 12 years of competing at the national level in Norway.

nents. This way, you'll build a personal database and you'll continue to use the same language and intentions as your training plan. This approach will make it easier for you to tailor your log and journal to your specific training plan. It's designed to enable you to track progress, detect trends, balance training, and monitor stress and overtraining with ease and without spending much time recording tedious details. If you regularly use a computer, you'll find that keeping this log and journal on a spreadsheet program will make your job easier and neater.

CUSTOMIZING YOUR TRAINING LOG

As with your training program, you will gradually develop a format for your log that works best for you. For example, you may find that you want to quantify the nontraining stress in your life,

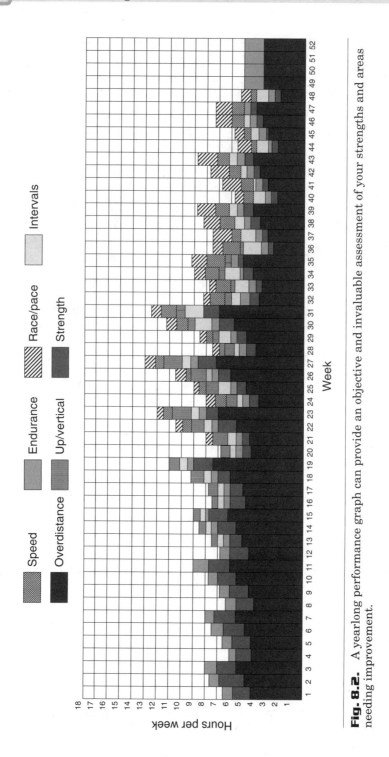

Fig. 8.2.   A yearlong performance graph can provide an objective and invaluable assessment of your strengths and areas needing improvement.

giving it a 1 to 5 rating, so that you can use that as an overstress indicator along with your training. The key to developing an effective log system is to determine the statistics that affect your training, formulate a way to quantify them, and record them daily.

There are now several computer software programs available that will log your training and provide suggestions for future sessions. Some of these programs allow you to input heart rate monitor data, giving you a detailed review of each training session. This can prove to be a valuable tool, especially to determine how well you accomplished the objective of the training session. For example, you can review an interval training session to determine if you stayed in your prescribed heart rate zones and then review the recovery of your heart rate after each interval.

No matter whether you choose to record your training data manually or with the aid of computer software, there are several variables we recommend that you include in your training log. These include date and time of workout, SERIOUS training component, training time, intensity, activity, how you felt, whether you completed the workout, stretching time, and warm-up and cool-down time. In addition, it is important to record recovery indicators such as morning pulse and weight, and sleep hours.

SERIOUS Training Log

The SERIOUS Training Log in figure 8.3 illustrates the design and has been completed to illustrate how to use it correctly. The following is a description of the components of the log and how to complete it:

1. **Week #:** This is the week number of the training plan you are presently following.

2. **Day/date workout:** You may have as many as four different training sessions each day, so you'll need to record each one.

3. **Training time of SERIOUS components:** Record time in minutes for all components trained each day and total at the end of each week.

4. **Intensity:** Mark the intensity either as the actual heart rate value or with a number 1 through 5, 5 being the most intense level, for each workout. Check your training plan to be certain you completed the workout at the prescribed intensity.

Figure 8.3
Training Journal

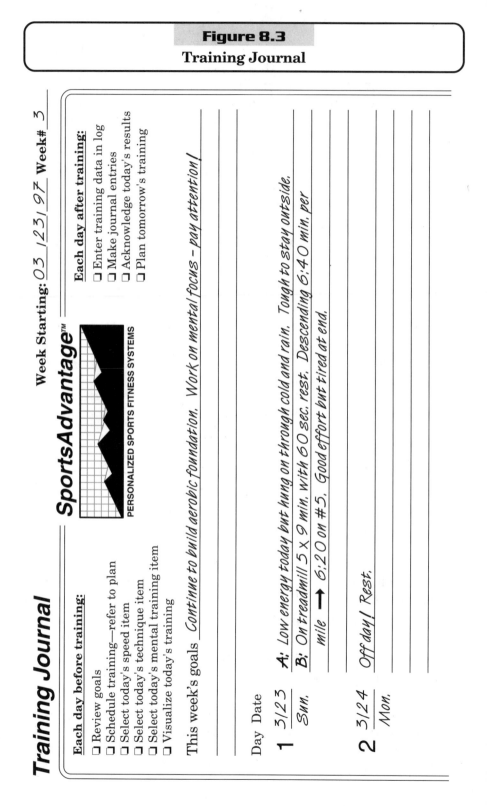

Training Journal

Week Starting: 03 / 23 / 97 **Week#** 3

SportsAdvantage™

PERSONALIZED SPORTS FITNESS SYSTEMS

Each day before training:

☐ Review goals
☐ Schedule training—refer to plan
☐ Select today's speed item
☐ Select today's technique item
☐ Select today's mental training item
☐ Visualize today's training

Each day after training:

☐ Enter training data in log
☐ Make journal entries
☐ Acknowledge today's results
☐ Plan tomorrow's training

This week's goals _Continue to build aerobic foundation. Work on mental focus – pay attention!_

Day Date

1 3/23 Sun.
A: _Low energy today but hung on through cold and rain. Tough to stay outside._
B: _On treadmill 5 x 9 min. with 60 sec. rest. Descending 6:40 min. per mile → 6:20 on #5. Good effort but tired at end._

2 3/24 Mon.
Off day! Rest.

Figure 8.3

(continued)

3	3/25 Tues.	**A:** In deep snow with Colleen; tough going but had fun.
		B: With John – getting stronger.
		C: 300, 200, 100, 100, 200, 300, 300, 200, 100 on 1:20 base – felt strong but not fast.
4	3/26 Wed.	**A:** Turbo trainer 1 min. – 5 min. – 1 min. pyramid by 1 min. interval with 1 – 2 min. rest. Good effort – was hard. HR = 160-164
		B: Treadmill – right after riding. 8 x 800m on 4 min. 5:43 – 5:33 per mile pace. A little tired but getting faster. HR = 165-170
5	3/27 Thur.	**A:** Body speeds 37 sec. with 60 sec. rest – worked on releasing speed.
		B: 3 x 800yd. with some kicking – getting better.
6	3/28 Fri.	**A:** Body speeds 12 x 200m in 42 sec. on 2 min. – getting easier each week, leg speed coming.
		B: Mostly drills, went very easy.
		C: Circuit routine – fast and furious!
7	3/29 Sat.	**A:** Nice long run with Paul and Vicki – enjoyed it.
		B: Rode home after run – long way – good effort.

5. **Training activity:** Record the time spent in each sport activity you use each day. If you use more than one activity to complete the session, such as running and cycling, note the minutes of training for each in the space provided. You'll want to go over your log at the end of the year and figure the amount of time you trained in each activity.

6. **Warm-up and cool-down time:** If you add some extra time to a training session for these, be sure to record the time, since warm-ups and cool-downs are typically at level one or two intensity for 15 to 30 minutes. This time will add up!

7. **Stretching:** Record minutes of stretching. From 15 to 30 minutes per day is best. You may want to note the routine you used in the journal section.

8. **Workout completed:** Mark with a "No" if you do not complete the scheduled workout(s) due to fatigue during the session. Failing to complete a planned workout because of fatigue or injury is usually a sign of overstress. Monitor subsequent training sessions carefully and take a day of rest if you continue to have trouble completing sessions. If you do not complete a planned workout because of a scheduling conflict or another nonphysical reason, there usually is no need for alarm. Just continue with your scheduled training.

9. **Feeling:** This is based on a scale of 1 to 5, with 1 being the absolute worst feeling and 5 being a fantastic race or training session. Basically, it represents your mental set for the training session. Too many entries of 1 may indicate that you are overtraining. Likewise, many entries of 5 could mean that you are about to peak (hopefully not too early!).

10. **Morning weight:** Weigh yourself consistently at the same time in the morning under the same conditions, before breakfast but after voiding. Losses of more than 3 percent body weight usually represent fluid loss. If you have lost 3 percent or more, take an easy day of training and replenish fluids. A loss of body weight in water of more than 5 percent is dangerous and could lead to overheating or even heatstroke.

11. **Morning pulse:** A morning pulse, taken before rising, of more than 10 percent over normal usually means stress or overtraining. Training, family, relationships, work, or financial problems may affect this. Your body is telling you to rest. You'll need to adjust your plan. (Note: you may need to void before taking

morning pulse because a full bladder can sometimes cause an elevated heart rate.)

12. **Sleep:** Record hours of sleep. Ten percent less than normal is a signal to take an easy day and catch up on rest.

Training Journal

It is a good idea to record thoughts, feelings, life situations, or other observations in journal form. A journal is also a good place to record distances covered in training, weather, training partners, and equipment used that day. If you do not like to write, this may not be for you; in this case, keep very accurate log records. However, you can gain a great deal of vitally important information by looking back through a well-kept journal. Journal entries should correspond with log entry dates. Figure 8.4 illustrates the SERIOUS system journal.

READING AND ANALYZING YOUR TRAINING LOG

Keeping a detailed log is not difficult and will provide you with the data you—and perhaps coaches, doctors, or sports scientists—will need to evaluate your training objectively. Perhaps the most important benefit to logging is that it will help you maintain balance between overtraining and undertraining. Disciplined logging will allow you to continuously check your state of training. The SERIOUS training log system is logical and easy to follow. All you need is the commitment to make it work for you.

You will use a well-kept log to identify trends in performance, stress, and other important information. One benefit is the ability to mine your log and journal for gems of information that identify negative trends. Perhaps you really don't like training with Joe Cool Athlete because every time you do, he pushes you to go harder and faster than you have planned on your schedule. Eliminate the stress—either work out a compromise or refrain from training with Joe. Or, you may notice that you are having pains in your knee after about 300 miles on those running shoes. Maybe it's time for a new pair. The list goes on and on.

You will be able to monitor overtraining, stress, and your progress by evaluating your recordings for morning pulse, morn-

Figure 8.4
Training Log

Training Log

SportsAdvantage™
PERSONALIZED SPORTS FITNESS SYSTEMS

Week Starting: 3 / 23 / 97 Week# 3

Day/date	1 A	1 B	1 C	2 A	2 B	2 C	3 A	3 B	3 C	4 A	4 B	4 C	5 A	5 B	5 C	6 A	6 B	6 C	7 A	7 B	7 C	Total
Workout																						
Speed													30			25						55
Endurance		65						60												120		245
Race/pace																						
Intervals										60	30			40								130
Overdistance	225						80										60		150			515
Up/vertical																						
Strength								70										35				105
Intensity																						
Swim									60					65			60					185
Bike	225									90			70							120		505
Run		65					80				55					60			150			410

Figure 8.4
(continued)

Extra warm-up/cool-down time				155	35	40 25	30 25		
Stretching				✓	✓	✓	✓		✓
Workout complete?			yes yes	yes yes yes	yes yes yes	yes yes	yes yes yes	yes yes yes	yes yes

Monitor your stress factors daily:

Feeling during workout	*Best* 5 / 3 / *Worst* 1	
A.M. weight	+5 / 0 / -5	Average= 170
A.M. pulse	+5 / 0 / -5	Average= 40
Sleep hours	+3 / 0 / -3	Average= 8

ing weight, sleep hours, and incompletion of workouts. If any one of these is abnormal according to the descriptions that follow, you should take it as a sign to alter the day's training. Consider it a red flag of warning. If any two of these are abnormal, you should definitely adjust your training for the day, either by reducing the time, changing the intensity, or taking the day off and getting more rest.

These stress monitors are only predictors. Use common sense and listen to your body for the answers. Also, depending on your situation, you may have to make adjustments for outside stressors over which you have little control. As we discussed in chapter 7, travel (especially changing time zones during air travel), altitude, humidity, heat, extreme cold, long work hours, family schedules, and other factors can affect the quality of your recovery from training.

Another valuable discovery you will make will be the recognition of a trend that leads up to breakthrough training days or races. Study the weeks before these days. You may be able to connect key factors to these performances. Think of keeping a log and journal as another way of learning about yourself and how your body, mind, and spirit integrate with your training and racing plans. Have fun discovering these trends for yourself.

BEFORE TRAINING EVERY DAY

Each day, before training, take some time to review your training. I recommend the following checklist:

 Review your goals for this session, for the short term, and for the long term. Imagine yourself actually achieving each of these goals.

Schedule your training into your day. Refer to your daily schedule and decide when and with whom you will train.

 Select a speed item. Choose one thing to work on that will improve your speed.

Select a technique item. Choose one thing to work on that will improve your technique and form.

☑ Select a mental training item. Choose one thing to work on that will improve your ability to concentrate, relax, feel confident, and so forth.

☑ Visualize the day's training. Close your eyes and imagine yourself training, having a great time accomplishing what you love to do!

☑ Remember to include playfulness in your training and racing. Take a moment to reflect on the fun factor of your training and choose to be playful today. Perhaps you'll invent a new way of doing your workout or you'll create a game that you'll play with your training partners. Use your imagination.

AFTER TRAINING EVERY DAY

☑ Enter the day's training data into your log.

☑ Make your journal entries.

☑ Acknowledge the day's results. Give yourself credit when you deserve it.

☑ Plan tomorrow's training.

FROM EXPERIENCE
RAY BROWNING, MS

Ten years of training logs and journals have provided me with an invaluable resource. In 1992, I had perhaps my most consistent triathlon season. I attribute this success largely to looking back over the previous seven years, determining the training sessions that I found to be the most effective, and avoiding the sessions that led to overtraining. Here are a few words of wisdom culled from my experience with training logs and journals:

- A well-kept training log and journal will serve as a window into the vaults of information and experiences you've accumulated through training and racing.
- A good log starts with simply keeping one on a daily basis.
- Failures and mistakes are not bad. They simply represent opportunities to learn and to use your creativity.
- Occasionally, ask a coach, trainer, sports physiologist, or doctor to review your log with you. You'll be surprised at what an objective pair of eyes will reveal.
- If you are not satisfied with your training, it will show up in the log. Do something to change your program, get advice from a professional, read a book, or rely on your wisdom to make the necessary changes.
- Measure and record your daily stress signals, such as morning weight, resting heart rate, sleep hours, and over-all feeling about the day's workouts. Reflect on these and other life commitments and energy drains, and evaluate whether you need to change the day's planned activities.
- Be sure to acknowledge the day's results. Give yourself a pat on the back for good efforts.
- Pay close attention to the enjoyment and fun you are having in training and racing. It's important to plan this into almost every session.

Managing Your Training Program

Unfortunately, it's not a perfect world. The best-made plans, including our SERIOUS system, don't always work out exactly as we would like. Life is a compilation of changes, unexpected events, alterations, and adjustments. Since training and racing are an integral part of your life, you can count on needing to make some adjustments and changes in your SERIOUS training plan. We've designed thousands of training programs for individuals and every one has needed adjustments as part of the total training management picture.

Expecting that you will need to change or reorder your plans is a key ingredient to successful program management. Remaining flexible and easygoing will make these inevitable changes much simpler and smoother. The most successful athletes realize that they will make adjustments to their training plans throughout the season, and the changes do not disconcert them. Worrying that changes will damage your performance may be an unnecessary expenditure of energy. Dwelling in disappointment about an injury or setback will only delay your recovery. Experienced athletes understand this and use their creativity in working around a problem.

In this chapter, we have provided some strategies for identifying areas that need adjustments and for making positive changes in your training plan. We also include a discussion of managing travel and injuries, as well as a troubleshooting guide for common training plan questions.

COMMON REASONS FOR ADJUSTING YOUR TRAINING PLAN

The most common reasons for making adjustments to your training plan are stress, travel, work demands, family commitments, unexpected life circumstances, available time, injury, and illness. For example, a new baby in your family will most likely mean some nights of sleep deprivation and hectic schedules, which may require a reduction in training time or a rearrangement of the schedule.

Most adjustments will be minor and will require simply rearranging your workouts by varying the weekly or daily pattern; for example, you may have to switch Wednesday's intervals with Friday's day off to travel on Wednesday. Occasionally, you may need to make changes in the structure of the plan or in your total training hours.

SERIOUS systematic training provides structure and direction. Your plan will serve you best, however, only when it stretches you enough to produce performance gains and allows you to get up in the morning, look at your plan, and head out the door confident that the workout will help you accomplish your goals. Stress can be created when you are not able to complete your daily training. This undermines the confidence you have in the program and leads to more stress. This cycle continues until you become frustrated and part from the plan. A better solution is to adjust the structure of the plan and your goals if necessary, acknowledge that this is part of the learning process, and be confident that the adjustments will serve you well. Be sure to note the changes in your training log for future reference.

There are two basic ways to make adjustments in your training plan. You make the first type of adjustment on a daily or weekly basis primarily to react to stressful circumstances, such as illness, overtime at work, relationship problems, logistics, weather, or travel.

The second type is by changing the basic structure of the plan in terms of weekly patterns, periodization, volume of training per cycle, and yearly volume. This would entail creating an entirely new training template using the process described in chapter 3.

VARYING THE DAILY AND WEEKLY PATTERNS

The most common way to adjust your plan involves changing it on a daily or weekly basis by monitoring stressors due to various life circumstances. You should be prepared to skip a workout or reduce the time allotment of a scheduled workout. The trouble-shooting guide in this chapter will give you guidance for making changes in your program and provide answers to commonly asked questions.

MANAGING TRAVEL

Travel, whether for business, pleasure, or racing, may affect your training plan. The keys to managing travel well are planning and flexibility (fig. 9.1).

Noncompetition Travel

Before any trips, review your training plan, reflect on what you would like to accomplish, and decide what will be realistic for you considering equipment available and your schedule. Make adjustments in your training plan, if necessary. For example, if the trip will take most of the day, you might plan to take the travel day as your off day from training. It may be better to be conservative by taking a rest day rather than squeezing in training before you leave or after you arrive at your destination.

Prioritize your training by scheduling your most important sessions when you know you will have time available during your trip. Many business trips entail days filled with meetings, appointments, and "power lunches." With this schedule, if all you can manage is one training session per day, consider that a success. Perhaps the best time to get in some training will be early in the morning or just before the evening meal. Just remember that some exercise, even if it means using the hotel's fitness center, will help you release some work stress and maintain some of your fitness.

© Anne Krause

Fig. 9.1. Travel can be fun if you plan ahead.

As a general guideline, 20 to 30 minutes of aerobic exercise (level one to level two HR) at least twice per week will maintain your current level of fitness. Don't be too concerned about the method of activity. You can be creative when you travel and try activities you don't normally do, such as rowing or swimming. Bring a heart rate monitor with you when you travel to help you train at the right intensity and to accommodate differences in environmental conditions.

> *I bring my training log along whenever I travel. Otherwise, if you are like me you will forget what you did after a day or two and won't have an accurate record for future trip planning.—Ray*

Another strategy is to compress the training week into a few days before a trip, especially when you know in advance that you won't have time to exercise during the time away from home. For example, you may wish to combine two days of training into one. However, be careful not to overdo it. Use caution when combining long OD workouts or high-intensity interval or race/pace sessions.

If you cannot train during a trip, avoid compressing a lot of training into the days after you return, since travel is stressful and you may not allow your body enough rest. It is better to start back into training by doing the workouts as scheduled and let the missed sessions go as incomplete. Use your best judgment and listen to your body when deciding how much to do on the return.

An effective strategy is to plan to do your high-intensity and equipment-dependent training before you depart or at least two days after you arrive. For example, it makes more sense to switch workouts around so that you can use your bike to do set distance intervals before your trip, rather than attempting to do them on a health club's exercise bike. If you must do high-intensity training during a trip, be sure to have your heart rate monitor along. The easiest way to perform intervals is by doing fartlek training. This type of interval training lends itself well to travel since the intervals are unstructured. If you happen to be out running in a park, you can choose various landmarks as starting and stopping points for your interval. You can also easily perform intervals on an exercise bike in a health club; go hard when you want and easy when you want. Many exercise bikes now have programs that allow you to do interval training, which also works well for high-intensity training.

Whenever possible, arrange in advance to use the facilities you will need, such as a swimming pool, athletic club, running trail, or safe cycling route. Local colleges or universities are usually a good source, and many hotels now have adequate fitness facilities. The concierge at your hotel often is aware of the city's best clubs, parks, tracks, and so forth. Local bike shops and athletic stores are a great resource, since the employees are often athletes. Be prepared to improvise your training slightly. If necessary, use a treadmill or stairmaster instead of running, or use an exercise bike instead of bringing your bike with you. If you are using equipment or activities you are not familiar with, be careful with high-intensity training, as you may increase your risk of soreness or injury.

Traveling by car? This presents a great opportunity to discover areas you otherwise would not see. If your schedule permits, take the back roads and stop at parks or quiet roads for your running or cycling. Head into a small town to learn if it has a pool available. On a recent road trip through Wyoming and Montana I ended up running alongside a herd of ante-

lope who were as curious about me as I was about them. Take an extra day, load the car with your favorite toys, and see what's out there.—Ray

The reality for noncompetition travel is that you'll need to be creative and organized in planning your travel before, during, and after your trips. If you can manage to do at least half of your planned training sessions, you will avoid losing any fitness. If you will be traveling for an extended period (more than two weeks) and you know you won't be able to train much, repeat those weeks in your training plan when you return and adjust your competition plans accordingly.

Noncompetition Travel Checklist

 Reflect on what you need to accomplish.

 Prioritize your training.

Review your training and travel schedule and make necessary changes.

 Find facilities at your destination—at clubs, universities, or hotels.

Be prepared to improvise your training.

Consider one training session per day as a success.

Competition Travel

For local races, plan to arrive at the race site early. Allow enough time to register, review the course, void, and warm-up properly. Adjusting your training for longer travel to a competition is best done far in advance. For domestic travel by air or by long car trips, plan to arrive at least one day before the event to get adjusted and to review the race course. Use the travel day as a rest day and plan some light training the day before the event. For example, if you are going to race on Sunday, travel on Friday and do some light training on Saturday.

If you are traveling internationally, you will need considerably more time at your destination before the competition. The rule for adjusting to an international destination is one day per hour of time zone change (for example, you'll need six days to adjust to a six-hour time change, such as New York to Paris). Setting your watch to the new time zone when you board your international flight will remind you to begin the adjustment process. Also, to avoid dehydration, remember to consume plenty of water when traveling by air. Pass on the caffeine or alcohol beverages. It may be best to resist the temptation to nap during the day after you arrive so that you can get a full night's rest and quickly readjust sleeping patterns. Chapter 10 will cover prerace training and adjustments for major events.

Plan your travel and training to adapt to stressful environmental conditions, such as high heat, humidity, or altitude. According to Costill (1986) your body will adapt to the heat or altitude gradually with full acclimatization occurring in 7 to 12 days. Plan low-intensity training during the acclimatization period and make it a priority to rest and adjust to the conditions. If you will be competing in the heat of the day, you should do at least 50 percent of your training during the warmest part of the day. If you are not able to arrive at the race destination in time to acclimatize properly, adjust your performance goals and don't expect to have your best race.

Competition Travel Checklist

☑ Plan your travel and training changes far in advance.

☑ For domestic travel, arrive two days early and train lightly the day before the event.

☑ For international travel, arrive one day early for each time zone change.

☑ Consume plenty of water while traveling.

☑ Allow sufficient time for acclimatization to the new environment (8 to 12 days).

☑ Focus on low-intensity training (OD or EN); see chapter 10.

MANAGING INJURIES

Even the best training plan does not preclude the possibility of injury. If you have an injury, either from an acute (such as a crash) or chronic (overuse) source, the primary goal is to get the injury to heal quickly. An injury is another form of stress to the body, and ignoring an injury can be a recipe for long-term problems. Wouldn't it be easier to adjust your training for two weeks to let an injury heal than to spend six months training through the pain of an injury only to be forced to take two months completely off, or worse, to create permanent damage?

Injuries often develop due to a lack of awareness that the body is telling you something is wrong. If you have a persistent pain that lingers through your training, adjust your training and use an alternative activity (see tables 9.1 and 9.2). If the pain persists for more than two weeks or gets worse, see a professional and get a diagnosis and treatment. Many injuries, if detected early enough, can be managed with only a small adjustment in your training. Be conservative and follow the diagnosis and treatment prescribed by your medical professional. Train with alternative activities, such as water running, for the same time and intensity recommended in your plan.

VARYING THE OVERALL STRUCTURE

Use the worksheets in chapter 3 to make any fundamental changes in the structure of the plan and to observe the effects

Table 9.1
Injuries and Training Adjustments

Injury diagnosis	Adjustments to training plan
tendinitis	Do an alternate activity for two weeks, or reduce activity 50% if minor
muscle strain	Do an alternate activity for two weeks, or reduce activity 50% if minor
muscle tear	Cease activity until pain free, repeat missed training, adjust racing schedule
stress fracture	Cease activity until pain free, repeat missed training, adjust racing schedule
joint swelling, pain	Do an alternative activity for two weeks, or reduce activity 50% if minor

Table 9.2
Suggested Alternatives for the Injured Athlete

Activity causing pain	Alternative activities
Running	Water running, running on soft surface (grass), stairmaster, classic style nordic skiing, cycling (road or mountain bike)
Cycling	Classic or skate style nordic skiing, exercise bike, hill walking, running, in-line skating
Swimming	Vasa Trainer, alternative swim strokes, nordic ski double-poling, skate style nordic skiing, rowing
Nordic skiing	Running, water running, cycling, Vasa Trainer

these changes have on the entire program. For example, if you change the periodization pattern in one cycle, you will see the effect in the next cycle by how well you recover between cycles. If you decide that you need a greater percentage of speed training in a cycle, you can see the effect of change in that cycle and, more important, attempt to observe and measure the effect of that change in your speed on race day.

Adjusting one variable in a systematic plan does affect the other variables to some degree. The following are areas you will most likely need to adjust:

Fine-Tuning Yearly Volume (Year Hours)

It has been our experience that many endurance athletes are "extra credit junkies"; they will vastly overestimate the year hours for their training plan and their race objectives. Overambitious goals may conflict with realistic available time per week, since work or school, family commitments, or other factors will require time and energy. As a result, you may need to decrease the training volume. Sometimes, reducing training year hours is a strategy for improving performance. During the 1994-95 World Cup season, Norwegian cross-country ski star Björn Daheile reduced his yearly volume to focus on improving his technique and was nearly unbeatable. Sometimes an increase in year hours is necessary, especially if you have underestimated the amount your body can accommodate. The rule is to increase yearly volume by at most 5 to 10 percent. If adjusting volume is the only change to your plan, the calculations will be straightforward since you'll use the original template.

Adjusting Percentage of Total Volume per Cycle

Sometimes an increase or decrease in volume within a single cycle is necessary because of other commitments, such as a time-consuming project at work or an injury. If you make changes, you must change all the other cycles in their percentages of total year volume as well to maintain a total value of 100 percent. If you need to change the cycle volume by more than 1 percent of your year hours, such as lowering one cycle in the intensity phase from 10 percent to 8 percent, then consider lowering your yearly volume (by 2 percent in this example). It may not be possible for you to increase all the other cycles to make up for the decrease in that one cycle.

Changing Periodization Patterns

It is important to follow the basic guidelines that have been successfully used by others, such as the periodization patterns presented in chapter 3. Try to maintain a similar periodization pattern during the base and intensity stages of the year to allow your body to become accustomed to the changing workloads. You may need to experiment with different patterns to find what works best for you and what may work for a particular time. For example, if races occur every two weeks in a cycle, you might adopt a hard week-easy week format for the cycle, with races falling at the ends of the easy weeks (e.g., a periodization pattern of 30, 20, 30, 20). If your race falls at the end of the third week of a cycle, adjust the periodization by having your highest volume during week 1, with a decrease in volume in the second, third, and fourth weeks (e.g., a periodization of 33, 27, 20, 20). There are many ways to shape the periodization of a cycle, and you should experiment with these by stage of year, volume per cycle, and so on.

Adjusting Percentage of SERIOUS Components

You can adjust the percentages of the various training components used in a given cycle and stage to meet your particular abilities. An experienced athlete who has built a strong base over the years may have better success using a greater percentage of higher intensity training than a less well trained athlete would. By using a systematic approach, you can effectively incorporate these changes into your basic structure by adjusting the percentages of SERIOUS components.

There are several clues to tell you whether you should adjust your percentage of SERIOUS components. Generally, a decrease in performance during a season or consistent fading late in a race indicates a lack of aerobic base, and thus a commitment to a greater percentage of OD and EN training is appropriate. If your technique deteriorates during your training or racing, it may be due to a lack of strength; thus an increase in the percentage of ST training is proper. Remember to test your AT levels regularly; if they fail to increase over time, that may be an indicator of not enough IN, UP, or RP training. Remember that if you increase the percentage of one component you must decrease the percentage of one or more of the other components. After you have made adjustments in your plan, measure the success of these adjustments by racing results (they should improve), performance tests such as the AT test, and your subjective feeling during your training and racing.

Table 9.3 serves as a troubleshooting guide for SERIOUS training.

> ## Table 9.3
> ## Troubleshooting Guide for SERIOUS Training

Question	Solution
Changing the weekly format of the program	First, try to get used to the planned format for three to four weeks. If that is not possible, you can change the days around but remember to follow a hard-easy approach. Determine which are your hardest days and schedule these with easy days between. Switch entire days of training, not just workouts, so that the days stay as planned and only the weekly format changes.
Missing one workout	Missing a single workout is no problem; just go on to the next planned session. Do not try to add a missed workout to the others already planned for the week.
Missing 1-3 training days	Occasionally you may miss more than one training session. If you miss between 1 and 3 days of training, continue on with your program as planned. For example, if you miss days 2-4, start training again on day 5, not day 2.
Missing more than 3 training days	If you miss more than 3 consecutive training days in one week, you should repeat that week. Remember this will affect your planned peak, as it will be one week later. You may want to adjust your racing schedule accordingly.
Unable to complete allotted workout time due to fatigue	An inability to complete one workout due to fatigue is not a problem; just watch yourself to make sure you are getting enough recovery from your training. If you are unable to complete 20% of your planned workouts, change your plan to fewer year hours.
Tapering for race week	During race week you may want to reduce your training volume and intensity a few days prior to the event. Taking 2 consecutive days off 10-14 days prior to key competitions may be appropriate. Taking a day off 2 days before with some light training the day before may be an effective strategy. All IN workouts should be short and sweet (6 × 2 min w/ 2 min recovery). Use a log/journal to record your tapering methods until you find one that works for you. See chapter 10 for race week schedule.
Are you overtrained?	Even the best planned program cannot accurately predict your body's ability to recover from physical and mental stress. An inability to recover can lead to overtraining. Below are some symptoms of an overtrained athlete.

Table 9.3

(continued)

Question	Solution
	• Poor training sessions (a feeling of 1-2 in your training log) • High morning pulse (>5 beats above average) • Disrupted sleep patterns • Irritability • Loss of appetite • Unable to get HR high enough during training • Urine very concentrated The best remedy for overtraining is rest. Start with 1 day of rest and evaluate your condition; it may take 2-3 days of rest to recover. Overtraining is not without warning signals. Learn to pay attention to them and modify your training by reducing volume and intensity. If the problem keeps reoccurring then a reduction in your year hours is necessary (probably 5-10%).
How do you measure intensity?	Use a heart rate monitor.
Your race is 120 minutes long and your race/pace time for the week is only 45 minutes.	Use all of the race/pace time allotted for the four-week cycle. This is a general guide to determine how much racing to do each month. You may use most of this in one race, or you may have some left over at the end of the month—either is OK.

FROM EXPERIENCE

RAY BROWNING, MS

When I look back through my training log and journal, I notice that most of my adjustments in my training plan have been due to travel demands. It seems easy to plan your training while you travel, but actually getting the training done is another matter. I have learned to reduce my training during a trip to 50 to 60 percent of what I would normally do. This training volume is sufficient to keep my mental state intact while accommodating the demands of travel and being away from home. If I will be away from home for more than three days, I usually bring most of my training toys with me, such as my bicycle, running shoes, and swimsuit. On shorter trips, I will do my swimming and cycling at a local health club while exploring the locale by running outside.

Since I've traveled throughout the world over the past 10 years, I have developed a considerable list of training facilities and most often I know a city or area by its training venues. It has been a wonderful way to see places, and I recommend that you explore the places you visit "by train(ing)."

If you do very long endurance events, such as Ironman triathlons, marathon running, cross-country ski races, or cycling stage races, remember to schedule 7 to 10 days of very easy recovery training following these races. The premise behind the SERIOUS system is that you will be in excellent condition once the racing season begins. Avoid the temptation to continue to train hard during the season. Instead focus primarily on doing high-quality, low-quantity training and on recovering from the intense races that take a toll on your body. This may mean that you will need to do all high-intensity training between races as "short and sweet" sessions, especially if you race every weekend during your competitive season.

You will discover, as I have, that your log and journal from training will become indispensable tools. If you take the time to keep them up-to-date, they will come to serve as an accurate reflection of your training program and can guide you to continued success.

Optimizing Your Training for Racing

Racing is the ultimate test many of you will choose to evaluate your training plan. This is the chili cook-off at the county fair. To maximize race performance, you should consider several variables. Proper nutrition and the timing of your travel are two variables, which have been discussed in chapters 6 and 9, respectively. In this chapter you will learn how to adjust your training plan for racing, including setting up a prerace schedule, tapering properly, and achieving the proper state of mind for racing.

TAPERING FUNDAMENTALS: ADJUSTING YOUR TRAINING PLAN

The pre-event taper is a period of reduced training volume and frequency that allows your body to recover from hard training. While there is considerable scientific evidence to support tapering for competitions, the optimal taper will be different for each athlete. A well-executed 7-to-21-day taper has been shown by Houmard (1994) to improve swimming performance 3 to 5 percent compared with no taper. Houmard recommends a 60 to 90 percent reduction in training volume and a 20 percent reduction in frequency of training to accomplish these performance enhancements. Shorter taper periods of 4 to 14 days have been shown to improve cycling and running performance by a similar margin (3 to 5 percent). Interestingly, swim tapers include high-intensity training daily, while cycling and running tapers typically reduce or eliminate completely high-intensity efforts. The most likely explanation for the difference is the relatively low musculoskeletal stress of swimming compared with cycling and running. Also, swimming competitions are typically done at a much higher intensity and shorter duration than cycling or running events, making the high-intensity training more important.

The improvement in performance after a taper period is due in part to increased muscle strength and power. It appears that the reductions in training allow the musculature ample time to recover fully from the endurance training and gain strength. In addition, the taper period improves the body's muscle glycogen stores, giving you extra energy stores. The reduced training demands correspond to reduced demand for glycogen as an energy source, and as a result, more glycogen is stored in the muscles. A high-carbohydrate diet is also important during the taper period to ensure high levels of muscle glycogen. Finally, the oxidative enzymes in the muscle are altered, creating improved aerobic capacity.

Many athletes erroneously assume that any reduction in training volume or intensity will result in a loss of fitness. Fortunately, there is no scientific evidence to support this belief. It is much more difficult to improve endurance capacity than it is to lose it, as long as you maintain at least 50 percent of your normal training volume. One of the side effects of tapering is that the increased muscle glycogen stores also increase the amount of water stored in the body, giving you a slightly heavier feel. In fact, your weight may increase during the taper period. Don't be alarmed and don't convince yourself you need one more long day of training—it will do more harm than good. The key to successful taper is rest. When discussing their training, athletes frequently mention how great they felt considering they had just come off an illness or minor injury. Sometimes the best tapers are not even planned.

The week before the Ironman in Hawaii is always an interesting place to attempt the taper. Most athletes arrive 10 to 14 days before the race to acclimatize to the heat and humidity, so the small town of Kona is full to the brim with endur-

ance maniacs. I have learned from 10 years of experience not to worry about what other people are doing or how fit they look. It is easy to be caught up in the energy that surrounds the race and do too much training, intending to get that extra edge. I have to tell myself continuously that what counts is how fast you are on race day, not any other day. I use a gradual 10-day taper with 2 days off the week before the race. The day before is short and sweet—swim, bike, and run about 20 minutes each with some race pace surges thrown in. I am amazed that a day or two before the race I see people out running or cycling miles from town. Many of these competitors leave their best race on the Kona coast the week before the event.—Ray

There are two general types of event tapers, a gradual taper and a drop-off taper. Typically, you will use a gradual taper for specific events that are the most important on your schedule, such as a national championship. If you have several important races during your season, a drop-off taper can be effective. As with all training, you will have to experiment to find the taper that works the best for you. As a reminder, the taper includes reducing or eliminating strength training.

The gradual taper is a reduction in training volume over a period of 7 to 14 days. Reduce your planned daily workouts by 10 to 20 percent each day for a 7-to-14-day period. Table 10.1 illustrates the changes in your schedule using a 7-day gradual

Table 10.1
Adjustments to Training Volume—7-Day Taper

Training	Day of taper						
	1	2	3	4	5	6	7
Scheduled volume	150 min	180 min	90 min	30 min	120 min	150 min	60 min
Reduction	10%	20%	30%	0%	50%	100%	75%
Taper volume	135 min	144 min	63 min	30 min	60 min	off	15 min

Notes. Race day is day 8. If the scheduled time is for more than one training session, then reduce each training session by the suggested percentage. Do not reduce warm-up and cool-down time for high-intensity training sessions. Day 4 training would be reduced by 40% if more than 45 minutes.

taper. If the scheduled training for the day is less than 45 minutes, do the workout as scheduled. Maintain the same weekly pattern during the taper period. Two days before the event, take a rest day. On the day before the event, do an easy workout with some body speeds or pickups in the middle of the session. You may feel as though you will lose some fitness, but you'll arrive at the race rested and ready to do your best.

The drop-off taper is a rapid reduction in training volume during the three days before a competition. Complete your scheduled training up to three days before your event. Three days before reduce training by 50 percent; two days before take totally off (no training); and the day before your race reduce your scheduled training volume by 75 percent. This taper is a favorite of Dave Scott's and works well if you tend to recover from your training quickly.

The type of taper you use will depend on the length, type, and importance of the event, as well as which taper proves best for you over time. Avoid doing tapers for early season events, unless they are very important qualifiers. For early season events, follow your plan and take a rest day two to three days before the event. For a midseason event, a drop-off taper works well and allows the continuation of your normal training pattern with little disruption. A major event, such as the national championships or a longer event, will most likely require a longer taper period, such as the gradual taper mentioned above.

One common mistake made during a taper period is to succumb to the urge to do just one more hard workout a few days before the race. Avoid the prerace hype and focus on being well rested and mentally ready.

FIVE AREAS OF PERFORMANCE

A good performance will require that you address each of the five areas of performance: physical training, psychological preparation, technical preparation, tactical preparation, and nutritional preparation. When you consider each of these areas, you will optimize race performance. Table 10.2 summarizes performance area guidelines for the three days before race day.

Table 10.2
Race Day Countdown

	Day 3	Day 2	Day 1	Race day
Physical	EN or OD day, no >60 min	Rest day	EN with some SP surges	Good warm-up, start steady
Mental	Practice race focus	Review goals for event	Practice race focus	Stay positive and focused
Technical	All equipment race ready		Test all equipment in training	Take advantage of equipment (position)
Tactical	Review nutritional plan	Develop race strategy	Review course and checklist	Play your plan

Note. See table 6.6 for nutritional preparation guidelines.

RACE PREPARATION

There are many details and distractions on race day, such as inconvenient parking, unexpected equipment glitches, or long lines for the Porta-Johns. Even the most experienced athletes occasionally become confused and forget an important part of the prerace routine. For example, elite triathletes occasionally forget their bike locations in the transition area; they exit the water and initiate frantic searches for their bikes. This slip costs valuable seconds and mental energy that could mean the difference between a great race and a poor race.

You may find it helpful to write out a countdown-to-race-time checklist. Counting backward from the start of the race, list what you will do and an estimated time for each item (be conservative). Have it so that all you do for the 30 minutes before the race is warm up, go to the bathroom, clear your mind to focus on your race, and toe the line on time (fig. 10.1). Include equipment checks, registration, bib numbers, as well as food and water before, during, and after the race. Assume that you will be responsible for doing everything and leave nothing to chance. It's a bit disheartening, for example, to jump on your bike in a triathlon only to realize that you forgot to fill your water bottle. You want to eliminate any surprises. Be familiar with everything, yet be prepared to make changes if necessary.

© Jero Honda

Fig. 10.1.   Prepare for the start of your race by having a prerace checklist to eliminate any last minute surprises.

Sample Countdown-to-Race-Time Checklist

(Estimate time each item will take)

- ☑ Prerace meal
- ☑ Transportation to event
- ☑ Event parking
- ☑ Registration
- ☑ Equipment preparation and placement (including testing)
- ☑ Rest room stop
- ☑ Prerace fluids
- ☑ Fluids, nutrition for event (water bottles full, etc.)
- ☑ Time for mental focus
- ☑ Postrace fluids and nutrition and dry clothing ready
- ☑ Prerace warm-up routine

Course Review

On the day before your race or sometime preceding the competition, review the course. Study the areas that might be troublesome or that will be the best for strategic positioning. Ideally, it is best to do a complete time trial on the course at some point three weeks or longer before the race. With the advent of sophisticated training equipment, such as programmable bike trainers and treadmills, it is now possible for you to program a course at home or in the club and do a course time trial or review. If you cannot do this, get to the race early enough to drive the course. Review course maps with profiles and identify aid station locations and other logistical considerations.

Equipment Considerations

Proper equipment is one way to increase your performance without costing the body more energy. Remember, though, the cardinal rule regarding equipment and race day: Never try something new on race day! The penalty for violating this rule can be severe, and even the best of athletes occasionally make this mistake. In Dave Scott's first "comeback" race of 1994, he was obligated to use a sponsor's new bike that he had ridden only once. The bike was too small and by the halfway point of the cycle leg Dave had debilitating cramps in his gluteals and hamstrings. He was eventually able to finish the race, over an hour behind the leaders! Experiment with new equipment in training, not on the race course.

For cyclists, triathletes, and duathletes, aerodynamic and hydrodynamic gear and riding positions are the latest methods to achieve performance gains. Wind tunnel tests show that an aerodynamic position on the bike can save as much as 30 minutes in an Ironman triathlon. If you are a triathlete or cyclist who does time trials, we highly recommend that you use aerodynamic equipment. Aerodynamic handlebars, helmet, wheels, and tight fitting clothing are the primary products to consider. Also, a bike that allows you to get into a comfortable, aerodynamic position is critical. For the swimmer, a wet suit will improve open-water performance by increasing buoyancy and reducing heat loss. Competitive swimmers will improve efficiency by shaving body hair and wearing a swim cap. Front and rear suspension mountain bike frames allow higher speeds on rough terrain. Cross-country skiers will optimize performance by using the latest advancements in equipment and wax technology. It is beyond the scope of this book to describe the benefits of equipment technology in detail, but be aware of these factors and use them to your advantage, with due consideration of your goals and your pocketbook (fig. 10.2)

Racing Well—A Mind-Set for Performance

Our thoughts before and during an event will have a major impact on how we perform. There are a few simple mental strategies that will improve performance. Practice these strategies in training and they will be available to you during races.

© John Kelley

Fig. 10.2.   For some events having reliable, well-tuned equipment is a must. Test and adjust new equipment in training before racing with it.

1. Focus on what you are doing. Disassociation, or thinking about something other than what you are doing, is a common mind-set during training and racing and does not lead to the best performances. Studies of elite athletes indicate that they focus on what they are doing at all times during an event, while recreational competitors tend to think of other things while racing. Stay in the moment and focus on doing each stride, stroke, pedal cycle, and so forth with your best technique and power, rather than focusing on the person in front or where you will end up on the results sheet.

2. Focus on what you can control. For some, this takes quite a bit of practice. As far as we know, no one has control over nature, so don't use your energy to change the weather. The same is true concerning your competition; you have no control over another person's performance.

3. Think positively. What we say to ourselves dictates how we perform, plain and simple. So find a positive mantra, practice it, and make it a habit.

Mine is simple: "yes". If I repeat "yes" often enough I know that I will eventually start feeling better and going faster.—Rob

POSTRACE RECOVERY

Racing at high intensity, especially if you race often, can be quite taxing on the body psychologically and physiologically. Since there are several things you can do to expedite your recovery, you might as well be proactive about this process. The recovery tactics you use will depend on the length and intensity of your event. As a rule, any event that takes you more than two hours to complete will exhaust your body, and it will take as long as two to three days to recover before you're ready to train hard. If you really push yourself or the event is very long, such as an Ironman, it may take several weeks to recover completely. Studies indicate that elite marathon runners still have muscle damage eight weeks after they complete a marathon. Training at high intensity during this period increases the risk of injury, overtraining, and prolonging complete recovery.

The absence of soreness, a normal resting HR, and normal sleeping patterns are some of the signals that you can use to judge your recovery from racing. A complete recovery will allow your body to adapt to subsequent training and racing demands. Training during the recovery period should be low intensity and short duration, 30 to 60 minutes of level one or two intensity. You may also elect to do alternative activities to enhance the recovery process. Swimming and water running are excellent activities to assist recovery from many types of events, including running, cycling, triathlon, duathlon, and cross-country skiing. A 20-minute easy walk a few hours after a race will promote recovery, too.

Doing body speeds is also a good way to monitor your recovery. They should be easy to complete and not leave you sore or tired by the end of a 20-to-30-minute session. If you cannot complete a body speed session, continue to rest or train easily for 2 or 3 days. Once you feel recovered, continue to train cautiously. Typically you may start to feel better 7 to 10 days after a very hard effort, but if you attempt high-intensity training at this time you will delay your recovery. For races longer than five hours or very hard marathons, allow at least 10 to 14 days of low-intensity training before beginning high-intensity efforts. Also, see chapter 7 for a discussion of recovery methods and chapter 6 for postrace nutritional guidelines.

The recovery period is the time to reflect on the race and evaluate your psychological performance. Did you achieve a good focus and think positively? If not, what could you do differently in the future to achieve a better mental state? Make notes of your strengths and weaknesses, and then formulate new strategies for the future. Take the time to evaluate your performance without harsh judgment, since this process is a tool for better performances. Resist the urge to dissociate while doing the low-intensity training required after racing. This is a great time to focus on how you feel, to monitor your body's response to the training, and to assess the status of your recovery.

FROM EXPERIENCE

DAVE SCOTT
Ironman legend and coach

To give you an idea of how the elite taper for a major competition, we went right to the top: to Dave Scott, who has won the Ironman World Championships six times. When he decided to return to the Ironman in 1994, at the age of 40, many people thought his chances for success were slim. After all, he hadn't raced in the Ironman since 1989. He silenced the skeptics with an excellent race, finishing second, just three minutes behind Greg Welch. How did he do it? Part of his performance success can be attributed to his taper program before the event, which Dave discussed with us.

Dave's last long bike-and-run were 15 to 18 days before race day. His long run was 16 miles and his long ride was 113 miles. Nine days prior to the race he did a 3K time trial in swimming, with the last 800 meters at level four intensity. Eight days before the race he had his last hard combination bike-and-run workout. That session consisted of a three-and-a-half hour bike ride at a steady pace (level three intensity), with about 60 minutes of higher intensity (level four) at the end of the ride. A 7-to-10 minute rest followed the ride, and then Dave did a 90-minute run (14 miles) with a faster average pace than what he wanted to run in Hawaii. The first 7 miles of the run were between 5:40 and 5:50 minutes per mile, and the last 7 miles were at 6:30-6:50 pace. In addition to the bike-and-run session, he did a level-four interval workout in swimming, which lasted one hour. This training day was followed by two days of rest, one of which included travel from Colorado to Hawaii.

The week before the race included his final strength-training session, on Tuesday using moderately heavy weight but not exercising to muscle failure. A two-hour bike ride with 35 minutes of 1.5- to 2-minute intervals at level four intensity, a nine-mile run, with each mile progressively faster (the last three miles at under 6 minutes-per-mile pace), and a swim around the swim course (3.8K) with the last 18 minutes at projected race pace completed Tuesday's training. Wednesday, three days prior to the Ironman, Dave rode for one hour at an easy pace, ran six miles at an easy pace, and swam 40 minutes easy, using a mix of strokes. Thursday's training was 40 minutes of cycling and 20 minutes of running, each with two sets of 6 × 15-second pickups to race speed with 45-seconds recovery. A 45-minute easy swim, mixing strokes and including some pickups was the final workout on Thursday. Friday, the day before the race, Dave ran two and a half miles, rode six miles, and swam 20 minutes, all at an easy pace.

Regarding the general principles of tapering Dave says, "Don't rely just on easy training for two to three weeks; you need to stimulate the neuromuscular system by working at race speed for short periods of time during the taper period. Cut back the amount of freestyle swimming during the taper period, using more backstroke and breaststroke. This gives the muscles used in freestyle a chance to recover."

Staying Motivated to Train

Much of your success using the SERIOUS training approach is dependent on an effective state of mind. To stay motivated to train toward goal events, it is important to create the proper mind-set and practice mental conditioning techniques. Many athletes assume that a mind-set for winning will be developed naturally through the process of training and racing experiences. In reality, our minds follow a path of least resistance, and we are most likely to think and focus based on our habits. You wouldn't expect your body to reach maximum performance levels without effective training. The same is true for mental training.

Mental habits are learned. Changing how we think while training and racing requires a dedication to replacing ineffective thought patterns with a winning mind-set. In this chapter we will discuss methods that will help you stay motivated to train and race, including an introduction to basic sport psychology and the importance of play in your routine.

There are mental states that are most effective for training and racing, just as there is proper technique for each sport. You can develop these states to maximize your training and racing experiences. An understanding of the basis of motivation, knowing how to create a strong motivational foundation, and a dedication to simple mental training techniques will lead to improved performances and more enjoyment from your racing.

FOUNDATION OF MOTIVATION

The first steps in the mental conditioning process are to define what you want (your vision or mission), where you are now (current status), and how you are going to get from where you are now to what you want (goals and process). Let's return to the chili one last time. To make and enjoy your chili, you must first decide that you want some, then do an inventory of what you have at home to make it (recipe, ingredients, etc.), and, finally, begin the process of making it and eating it. If you're not in the mood for chili, you certainly won't be motivated to make some.

Vision (What You Want)

Successful businesses have discovered the importance of having a vision and mission. The vision keeps the corporation on track toward its goals and serves as a check on the activity of the company. You, as an athlete, need to create the same foundation for yourself in the form of a vision. The vision is the foundation of motivation. It provides the answers to the whys of training and racing, which you will inevitably encounter (Why am I doing this?). Inherently, you will not be motivated to do things that you do not want to do. The vision is the picture of what you want to achieve. Take a moment to refer to the goals you established in chapter 1. Think about why these are meaningful to you—what purpose they hold in your life. The meanings you discover will be key to developing your vision.

When creating a vision for yourself, follow the guidelines below:

1. Focus on what you want (rather than on what you don't want).
2. Identify what excites you with possibility and opportunity.
3. Make your vision something you truly want.
4. Make your vision as real as possible.
5. Make your vision specific enough so that you can evaluate whether you are moving toward or away from achieving it.

Creating a vision that has significant meaning may take some time. Consider it a process that will shift and change as your life unfolds. The vision is the dream of what you dare to accomplish; it will provide direction and inspiration. The vision is an expression of who you are and part of your contribution to the world. There is no such thing as a bad or wrong vision; if it has meaning to you it is the right foundation. Revisit your vision regularly and change it if necessary. What excites you now about training and racing may not excite you next year.

My vision is broad and includes why I compete and what contribution I want to make to those I meet. Carpe diem is a central theme in my vision—to live life with a "Seize the Day!" attitude. Competition is an important part of my lifestyle because it fills the need for a sense of adventure and excitement, and allows me to search for my personal boundaries, my "edge." I have a vision of pushing myself, fully concentrating on the present moment, getting the most out of my body and mind, and letting the experience unfold. One of the visions that I have used is putting myself on a new road or trail, not sure what's around the corner, moving forward with a sense of adventure and anticipation, and most of all, really enjoying the process.—Ray

Current Status (Where You Are Now)

To move toward what you want, you must honestly appraise where you are now. In chapter 1, you established your objectives for training and racing. This included an evaluation of your strengths and weaknesses, which indicates where you see yourself now. Be sure to include your mental strengths and weaknesses in this evaluation. Positive motivation comes from the discrepancy between your present reality and where you want to be. Don't be discouraged by your present reality, since it serves only as a starting point. You've got to take the first step before you can walk a mile.

Think of your training and racing experiences. What things do you do well? Are you always excited the morning of a race? Do you look forward to the start? When training or racing, are you focused and thinking about the things you can do to perform at your best, such as proper technique? Most of us have days where we are "on," and we have a great workout or race. What was your mental state during these times? What can you do to achieve this state more often? Taking the time to make these evaluations will give you an excellent view of where you are now and allow you to plot a course to achieve even greater success.

Getting From Current Status to Vision (the Process)

Choose short-term steps (goals) to move you from your present reality to what you want. The process involves focusing on the technical elements of training, such as physical preparation or specific mental techniques (see those suggested below) that you can control. There is no point in focusing your energy on uncontrollable things, such as the weather, equipment problems, or another person's training or racing. How many times have you been milling around before the start of a race and overheard other athletes complaining about the weather? "It's too cold!" "It sure is windy today." The truth is, unless you're very well connected, you won't be able to change the weather on race day. Therefore, focus your precious energy on what you can do to have your best performance. Your competition and environment are just part of the challenge, and because they constantly change you will have a different experience each time you step out the door to train or race.

If you find yourself focusing on the uncontrollable, change your focus to getting information from good sources, such as your support crew or by planting positive messages on your equipment. Sound goal setting and supportive and knowledgeable people in your life will be valuable during the process to provide comments and technical correction.

Supporting the Process

Positive reinforcement is a part of the process of achieving what you want. Motivation comes from the enjoyment of the activity and by feeling rewarded for your accomplishments. To foster a positive approach during the process, focus on and reinforce your successes, convey an optimistic attitude, use humor, and develop a social support network of family and friends.

MENTAL CONDITIONING TECHNIQUES

What you think about affects how you feel, act, and perform. One of the basic psychological principles is that you move toward your most dominant thoughts. Your thoughts may be in the form of words or images. They have a great deal to do with how well you achieve your training and racing objectives. Remember that positive thinking is a skill that can be conditioned (trained).

There are four areas of mental conditioning that you can develop to help create positive performances. These are (1) self-talk, (2) mental imagery, (3) focusing, and (4) relaxation.

Self-Talk

During training and racing you are accompanied by a constant banter from your mind. Too often the mind interprets training or racing stress as negative and sends negative messages to your consciousness, such as "this is uncomfortable; shouldn't we slow down or stop?" By developing and practicing positive affirmation statements, you can develop new habits that will lead you to think positively during training and racing. As you develop positive statements to repeat to yourself, keep in mind some guidelines.

1. Use brief, direct statements (for example: Yes, Strong, Relaxed, and Powerful).
2. Use positive terminology (avoid terms of obligation: I must, I should).
3. Focus on your strengths.
4. Focus on possibilities.

Develop several positive affirmation statements that have personal meaning to you and practice them regularly during training. As a reminder, you may choose to make up index cards with your statements on them. Each day, select a card and use that affirmation statement during your training. Remind yourself during the warm-up period to practice these statements.

One important, yet often overlooked, element of human nature is the natural up-and-down pattern to our moods. Low moods and high moods are as normal as night and day, rain and sunshine, winter and summer, life and death. Typically, if we are experiencing a naturally occurring low mood, then the lens we see life through becomes a bit distorted. If we give this too much energy, we can be very hard on ourselves and our self-talk can become very self-destructive.

If you find yourself using destructive self-talk, take a moment to step outside the situation and gain some perspective. Perhaps you are experiencing a naturally occurring low mood. Notice it and trust that it will pass soon enough. You don't need to fix anything or spend extra time reading your positive affirmation cards. If anything, have a good laugh at yourself and at this very normal part of being human.

Mental Imagery

The mind uses images for much of the information it processes. Imagery is a powerful tool for performance. The mind creates an image of a movement before initiating the movement. Think of a typical movement for your activity and describe it using words. Now describe the same movement with an image, a picture, or a demonstration and you are more likely to get the form of the movement across to someone else.

You can use imagery to practice a performance, develop self-confidence, or learn a new skill. For example, you can imagine a race from start to finish without ever going to the race site. Olympic athletes will practice an event several thousand times before setting foot at the site of the Olympics, all through imagery. We have been very successful by watching videos of World Cup and Olympic cross-country skiers and emulating the images to improve technique. One of the greatest benefits of training with athletes who are technically more proficient is that you can watch them and use that image to improve your technical skills.

Imagery techniques are best developed with an open, optimistic attitude and in a quiet setting free from distractions. Begin to develop your imagery abilities by increasing your sensory aware-ness of your activities. During training and racing focus your attention on how the activity feels, smells, tastes, sounds, and looks. This will give you a library of sensory information to create a real-life image in your mind. For example, if you are riding your bike, focus on what it feels like to ride. Imagine a miniature of yourself sitting on your shoulder and watching you ride. What would he or she see, hear, smell, and feel? Develop an image inventory from watching yourself and from being inside your body. Both kinds of images are very useful tools.

Practice imagery by finding a quiet, comfortable place to sit or lie down (fig. 11.1). Begin by gradually relaxing your body and letting go of the thoughts of the day. As you lie quietly, begin by focusing on your breathing, the easy rise and fall of your chest as you breathe. Starting with the top of your head, relax each body part by exhaling and feeling a wave of relaxation flow over the area. With each breath, move down the body, relaxing your face and neck, shoulders and upper back, arms and hands, lower back and stomach, gluteals, thighs, lower legs, and feet.

Once your entire body is relaxed and you are focused, take a moment to remind yourself of your vision, the foundation of your motivation. Then begin your mental imagery with easy images, using internal images as much as possible. Internal images are those from within your body, how you would see the activity as you do it. See yourself doing an activity with correct technique, relaxed and powerful. Initially, these imagery sessions should be short, 5 to 10 minutes. If you find yourself unable to focus or drifting into sleep, end the imagery session. End your imagery training with a final reminder of your vision. Then tell yourself to come back to the present place and time, and slowly move your hands and feet and open your eyes.

Practice your images regularly (daily) and make them more complicated and longer lasting as your imagery skills improve. You can begin to practice race images with good technique and focus, using positive statements to maximize your performance. Make the images as real as possible, with competitors, spectators, and other race day distractions. You can have several images of an upcoming event, or portion of an event. For example, you can

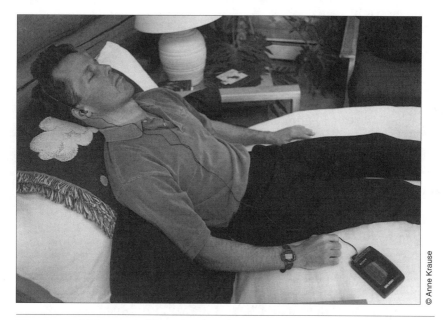

© Anne Krause

Fig. 11.1.   Make mental-imagery training part of your winning plan.

imagine a swim in a triathlon that is in smooth water, unencumbered by your competition, and you can imagine the scenario of rough chop, with many arms and legs and congestion. By practicing several potential race experiences, you will be able to develop a strategy to handle whatever comes your way on race day. You can also make an audio tape with your imagery training on it to use during your imagery, a tool we have found to be very helpful. Remember that the images need to focus on what you can control to improve your performance. With dedicated imagery practice, you will train more efficiently and will arrive at the race with the confidence of having practiced your race strategy so that you will do your best.

Focusing Skills

Elite athletes are remarkable in their ability to pay attention to what they are doing while competing or training. They have learned to associate (focus on the activity), rather than disassociate (think about other things). Thus, it seems that association techniques are an essential part of athletic performance. Focusing during exercise takes practice and an awareness of when you are not focusing appropriately. There are several questions to ask yourself while you are exercising that will help to determine if you have the right focus:

1. What am I doing right now?
2. Does what I am thinking about help me right now?
3. Is what I am thinking about something I can control?

These questions, when asked regularly, will get you in the habit of focusing your attention. If you find your focus drifting, shift your attention to positive affirmations or imagery, and then back to the activity. Start paying attention for short periods (5 to 30 seconds) during your training and gradually lengthen your period of attention as your focusing skills improve.

One way to improve focusing skills is by doing technique drills (fig. 11.2). We've described body speeds in chapter 4, so let's use that as an example. The primary goal in doing body speeds is to achieve as much speed as possible while remaining relaxed and efficient. As you do these drills, your ability to concentrate on sustaining relaxed, efficient technique will improve. By the time you are ready to race, your ability to feel relaxed and efficient will

© John Kelly

Fig. 11.2. Technique drills can also help you hone your mental sharpness for racing.

be imbedded in your muscle memory and it will be easier to maintain your focus on staying relaxed throughout the race.

Relaxation Techniques

Another common thread among accomplished athletes is that they make their activity appear to be effortless. Much of this image is due to the athlete's ability to relax during activity. As you become more skilled doing an activity, you tend to eliminate unnecessary muscular contractions, those that don't contribute to your motion. For example, a death grip on the handlebars of a bicycle does little to move the bike and much to cause fatigue in the neck, shoulders, and arms.

As with all mental techniques, you can learn relaxation with practice. A good time to increase your awareness of a relaxed state is during your imagery training. As you settle down to practice your imagery, focus on the feeling of your body relaxing. During your training and racing, do an inventory of your body by checking for and releasing tension. Focus on letting go of unnecessary tension and releasing your speed, rather than forcing speed with tense muscles. Remember that loose, relaxed muscles are powerful, quick, and efficient.

MAKE THE MOST OF YOUR DAY(S) OFF

We encourage every athlete we train to take one day off every other week, if not every week. Since recovery is such an important part of the total training process, it's wise to make the most of your days off. A day off means a day with no scheduled training, but it can include several things, such as the following:

1. Take the day totally off from any kind of training in your primary sports. If you must do some exercise, take a walk or play a sport that you love but don't do very often anymore, such as tennis, golf, or fishing (be careful not to overdo it).
2. Schedule a massage.
3. Do some mental imagery or relaxation exercises.
4. Play with your children, spouse, or friends. Do something fun and relaxing.
5. Volunteer your time and energy to help others, even if it's only for an hour.
6. Catch up in your training log entries and review the log and journal.
7. Take a nap.
8. Read a good novel.
9. Soak in a hot tub, take a sauna, or relax in a steam room.
10. Take a walk on a nature trail.

The list could go on and on. Just remember how important it is to remove yourself from the training routine and replenish your mind and body with rest.

TRAINING AND RACING AS PLAY

Every training session and race that we do is an opportunity to play. As children, play was our work, and we were very busy at our tasks. As adults, life can seem complicated and complex, with little time or consciousness about letting ourselves truly re-create through play. We've all known athletes who take themselves and their success in sports so seriously that we wonder if they have any fun at all. We believe that a lack of play in training and racing can inhibit reaching one's true athletic potential. Since it's very difficult to control the outcome of any race, you might as well focus on having as much fun as possible in training and racing.

Training and racing contain incredible opportunities for socializing with others. In a way, this is adult play. We suggest that you surround yourself with people who support what you are doing, either family, friends, and coworkers who offer moral support, or qualified coaches and people with whom you train who provide active participatory support. It's amazing what you can learn about others and about yourself through the experiences provided in sports if you just allow it to happen.

We encourage you to seek out opportunities to play as much as possible in sports. Every week, be conscious of your playfulness. Do some training in new terrain; include minicontests with your training partners such as occasionally sprinting 50 yards to a designated road sign or passing a Frisbee back and forth during a short run; combine five activities into one longer training session; stop at a playground and do some jungle gym or swinging for five minutes (fig. 11.3). Use your imagination and see just how much fun you can create.

ENJOYING THE BENEFITS OF TRAINING AND RACING

Better health, improved self-image and confidence, the mastering of a challenge, and associations with like-minded individuals are just some of the benefits of the endurance athlete's lifestyle. In the search for the perfect athletic experience you may lose sight of these benefits and forget to see the big picture. This is part of life, and a focus on only the objective outcome of races or training is a limited view at best. Periodically remind yourself of your good fortune to be able to choose to pursue athletic excellence.

Many of you are searching for your own personal limits, pushing yourselves to excel. That is a noble search and sometimes the answers lie outside everyday training and racing. Take advantage of your athletic abilities beyond your primary activities and seek new or unfamiliar territory. Sometimes there are unforeseen rewards from a new experience, such as

© Anne Krause

Fig. 11.3.   Being serious about training doesn't mean you can't have fun too!

snowshoeing through newly fallen snow, canoeing on a wilderness river, hiking in terrain that is completely different from your home turf, or discovering a new trail in your own backyard that you've run by a hundred times but never bothered to take. These can serve as a refreshing reminder of why you do what you do.

As an athlete, you are an ambassador of good health. Consider that you have a stewardship in health and fitness, so strive to get others involved so that they can experience some of the great things accomplished under human power. Be a good example, with a positive attitude and an ever present sense of adventure. Smile to people you pass and be sure to wave a "thank you" to motorists who are courteous enough to give you a lot of room as they pass by. Always say thanks to race organizers and workers, since they make it possible for you to compete at any event. Share your experiences with others and remember that sport can be a metaphor for living all aspects of our lives.

PLUSES AND MINUSES OF *SERIOUS* TRAINING

Systematic training, be it with our SERIOUS system, or with another method, can be a great asset when used effectively. It makes it fairly simple to plan, implement, and track training, thereby allowing full opportunity to assess progress and make meaningful adjustments.

It is very important to maintain the position that SERIOUS training must work in your favor, rather than you becoming "a slave" to it. Some athletes train systematically without maintaining their common sense. Once they write out the plan in black and white, they follow it exactly as planned, regardless of what their body or common sense may be telling them. It is essential that you use SERIOUS training simply as another training tool. It will rarely be perfect, but used properly, it will guide you to achieve your greatest potential in sports. Happy trails!

© John Kelly

FROM EXPERIENCE
JEFF SIMONS, PhD

As a sport psychologist to many serious athletes, one of the major motivational fallacies that I have encountered is the demand to be perfect. In fact, the more serious the athlete, the more likely he or she will express a commitment to perfection. Unfortunately, despite the virtues attributed to striving for perfection, using perfect as your performance standard can be both demoralizing and an ineffective motivator.

Perfection—complete flawlessness and exactness—is not attainable. The fact is that nothing is absolutely perfect (except in the Zen sense that everything is "perfect," *just at it IS*, flaws and all). To attain perfection in sport an athlete would need to execute every single skill flawlessly at precisely the required moment under ideal conditions and where no one or nothing interferes in any way. Perfection requires a perfect situation. (What is the chance that the conditions will be perfect at your next big event?) Relative perfection may happen but only as a miraculous coincidence of the universe. Let's get real; perfection cannot be made to happen in human performance!

Athletes often protest, "But isn't the idea of striving for perfection just a way of expressing desire to improve?" Yes, it can be. More often, though, the focus on perfection sets up unrealistic standards and expectations that virtually guarantee failure. I see it regularly in elite sport. When performance is evaluated against the standard of perfection everything else becomes a failure. Repeated failures dash enthusiasm and destroy positive forms of motivation, especially enjoyment and the desire to seek out challenges. Furthermore, "perfect" requires far too many things that are beyond anyone's control. Intuitively, we all sense that we do not control perfection. Thus, when we demand perfection we feel out of control. Once people feel loss of control, they either give up or become progressively more anxious. Beyond ruining potentially wonderful experiences, neither apathy nor anxiety lead to outstanding performance. It may seem noble, virtuous, and socially correct to demand perfection of yourself, but that mind-set creates far more trouble than excellence.

What the serious athlete needs is a mind-set that will help her or him to pursue excellence in a meaningful way. This mind-set should have all the positive connotations of striving for perfection, coupled with a healthy perspective on reality and a sense of optimism about achieving success. Instead of perfect, the best approach that I have found is for athletes to focus on optimal.

Optimal performance is about achieving the best under the conditions which occur. The optimization mind-set combines the desire for the greatest possible performance with the understanding that training and competition happen within variable and often unpredictable conditions. Unlike perfection, "optimal" makes no demands that you cannot handle. There is no need to control the uncontrollable. Furthermore, "optimal" makes no requirements on conditions. It is therefore possible to optimize whatever conditions may occur at the moment of performance.

An optimization mind-set keeps you focused on what you *can* do. It keeps you in control of your performance and gives you real chances for consistent success. Training yourself to optimize teaches you to be flexible and adaptable without losing sight of what you want to achieve. It will also provide a sense of security that you can handle whatever happens. Most importantly for many athletes, optimizing competitive situations will bring home the best results possible.

Take a look at how your goals and expectations may be affecting your training and competitive performance. Does your approach to excellence make you feel in control, optimistic, and eager for the challenge? Or does the demand to be perfect in your sport make you feel out of control, doubtful, and anxious? Remember, you do not control most of what goes on around you, but you do control how you choose to perceive the conditions and how you decide to respond. An optimization mind-set will give you the best chance to achieve what you want. And it is within your power.

Appendix A.1
Determining Your Year Hours

1. Rate your present level of fitness on a scale of 1 to 10, with 1 being totally unfit and 10 being your best fitness level ever.

   Your rating _____

2. How much aerobic exercise have you done in the last six months? Use an average number of hours per week. _____

3. Of the average number of hours per week determined in question #2, what percentage of those hours were done in each activity?

Activity/Sport	Percentage of average training hours/week
Example: Cycling	30%
1. _____	_____
2. _____	_____
3. _____	_____
4. _____	_____
5. _____	_____
6. _____	_____

4. How much time do you have available per week for training?

   _____ hours

5. Have you successfully trained more hours than your current average in past years? If, yes, how much more?

   _____ hours per week

6. Do you want to decrease, maintain, or increase the amount of training in your new program?

   Decrease ____ %   Maintain ____   Increase ____ %

7. Your planned year hours _____

Training plan for _____

Name _____

1 Year hours to train _____

1 Cycle	**2** Date	**3** Stage	**3** Emphasis	**4** % year hours	**5** Periodization % Week 1	2	3	4
1								
2								
3								
4								
5								
6								

Training plan for _____

Name _____

Year hours to train _____

Cycle	Date	**1** Stage	**2** % of hours	Speed	Endurance	Race/pace	Interval	Over-distance	Up/vertical	Strength

3 Percentage per 4-week cycle

Cycle	Date	Stage	% of hours							
1										
2										
3										
4										
5										
6										

Training plan for _____

Name _____

Projected year hours to train _____

Objective _____

1 Four-week cycle		1				2				3			
2 Training stage													
Week numbers		1 – 4				5 – 8				9 – 12			
3 Actual dates													
4 % of year hours													
5 Hours/cycle													
Week number	1	2	3	4	5	6	7	8	9	10	11	12
6 Periodization													
7 Hours/week													
8 Below: Total minutes per week of each SERIOUS component													
Speed													
Endurance													
Race/pace													
Intervals													
Overdistance													
Up/vertical													
Strength													

1 Four-week cycle	4				5				6			
2 Training stage												
Week numbers	13 – 16				17 – 20				21 – 24			
3 Actual dates												
4 % of year hours												
5 Hours/cycle												
Week number	13	14	15	16	17	18	19	20	21	22	23	24
6 Periodization												
7 Hours/week												
8 Below: Total minutes per week of each SERIOUS component												
Speed												
Endurance												
Race/pace												
Intervals												
Overdistance												
Up/vertical												
Strength												

Spreadsheet Calculations With Percentages for Each Sport

Training plan for _____

Name _____

Projected year hours to train _____

Objective _____

1 Four-week cycle			1				2				3		
2 Training stage													
Week numbers			1 – 4				5 – 8				9 – 12		
3 Actual dates													
4 % of year hours													
5 Hours/cycle													
Week number	1	2	3	4	5	6	7	8	9	10	11	12
9 Below: Multiply total minutes per week of each SERIOUS component by the designated percentage for each sport activity												
Speed[1]												
Endurance[2]												
Race/pace[3]												
Intervals[4]												
Overdistance[5]												
Up/vertical[6]												
Strength[7]												

[1] **Note.** Swimming intervals incorporate speed training.

[2] **Note.** It's OK to use EN time allotments as warm-up for intervals, up/verticals, speed, or race/pace sessions.

[3] **Note.** Combine race/pace times for 2 weeks and do this workout twice per month.

[4] **Note.** It's OK to combine bike and run interval times with up/vertical interval time to create one workout when time allotments are small.

[5] **Note.** Plan to do all three sports or a bike/run "brick" in at least one session per month.

[6] **Note.** Do these sessions in terrain that is similar to the terrain in which you will race.

[7] **Note.** Sports-specific exercises recommended whenever possible.

1 Four-week cycle			**4**				**5**				**6**		
2 Training stage													
Week numbers			13 – 16				17 – 20				21 – 24		
3 Actual dates													
4 % of year hours													
5 Hours/cycle													
Week number	13	14	15	16	17	18	19	20	21	22	23	24
9 Below: Multiply total minutes per week of each SERIOUS component by the designated percentage for each sport activity													
Speed[1]													
Endurance[2]													
Race/pace[3]													
Intervals[4]													
Overdistance[5]													
Up/vertical[6]													
Strength[7]													

Training plan for _____

Name _____

Projected year hours to train _____

Daily workouts	Base stage			Intensity stage		
	Objective	% of total	Mins	Objective	% of total	Mins
1A 1B 1C						
2A 2B 2C						
3A 3B 3C						
4A 4B 4C						
5A 5B 5C						
6A 6B 6C						
7A 7B 7C						

SP = Speed
EN = Endurance
RP = Race/pace
IN = Intervals
OD = Overdistance
UP = Up/vertical
ST = Strength

Daily workouts	Peak stage			Racing stage		
	Objective	% of total	Mins	Objective	% of total	Mins
1A						
1B						
1C						
2A						
2B						
2C						
3A						
3B						
3C						
4A						
4B						
4C						
5A						
5B						
5C						
6A						
6B						
6C						
7A						
7B						
7C						

SP = Speed
EN = Endurance
RP = Race/pace
IN = Intervals
OD = Overdistance
UP = Up/vertical
ST = Strength

Training Journal

Week Starting: _____ / _____ / _____   Week# _____

SportsAdvantage™

PERSONALIZED SPORTS FITNESS SYSTEMS

Each day before training:

☐ Review goals
☐ Schedule training—refer to plan
☐ Select today's speed item
☐ Select today's technique item
☐ Select today's mental training item
☐ Visualize today's training

Each day after training:

☐ Enter training data in log
☐ Make journal entries
☐ Acknowledge today's results
☐ Plan tomorrow's training

This week's goals _____

Day Date

1 ___

2 ___

3

4

5

6

7

© Copyright 1995 Compufit, Inc. • 372 Governor Chittenden Rd • Williston • Vermont • 05495   Tel (802)660.9660   Fax (802)660.9661

Training Log

SportsAdvantage™
PERSONALIZED SPORTS FITNESS SYSTEMS

Week Starting: ___/___/___ Week# _____

Day/date	1			2			3			4			5			6			7			Total
Workout	A	B	C	A	B	C	A	B	C	A	B	C	A	B	C	A	B	C	A	B	C	
Speed																						
Endurance																						
Race/pace																						
Intervals																						
Overdistance																						
Up/vertical																						
Strength																						
Intensity																						
Swim																						
Bike																						
Run																						

Extra warm-up/cool-down time

Stretching

Workout complete?

Monitor your stress factors daily:

Feeling during workout — Best 5, 3, Worst 1

A.M. weight +5 / 0 / -5 — Average=

A.M. pulse +5 / 0 / -5 — Average=

Sleep hours +3 / 0 / -3 — Average=

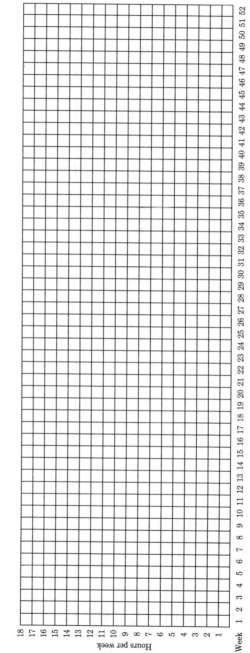

Speed
Endurance
Race/pace
Intervals

Overdistance
Up/vertical
Strength

Instructions for Appendix B Templates

The templates in appendix B are formatted differently from the worksheets in appendix A and chapter 3. Following these steps will help you use the sport-specific templates more easily.

These templates work well with a computer spreadsheet program if your computer has one. We strongly suggest that you take a few minutes to transfer the selected template to your computer spreadsheet. Adjustments and planning are much easier by spreadsheet than manually, with paper, pencil, and calculator. If you decide to do this manually however, make a few photocopies of the selected template before you begin.

First, determine the year hours you will use for the plan and enter the amount at the top of the template. (Refer to chapter 3 for information on accurately determining year hours.) Note that these templates are set up to use your total year hours, even though they are 24-week plans. We have calculated the templates accordingly.

Now determine the actual dates of each 4-week training cycle and enter them in the space provided on the template.

Next determine the total time per 4-week cycle by multiplying year hours by the percent of year hours listed for each 4-week cycle. Enter that time in the space provided on the template.

Then determine total hours per week by multiplying total time per 4-week cycle by the periodization pattern percentages for each week of the cycle. Enter the figures in the space provided on the template.

After converting hours to minutes, determine total minutes per week for each SERIOUS component by multiplying total minutes per week by the designated percentage for each SERIOUS component under each 4-week cycle. Enter these times in the spaces provided on the template.

Since multisports and some individual sports require training in more than one sport discipline, you'll need to divide the training for each SERIOUS component by the recommended percentages listed for each sport activity. These percentages were determined by analyzing typical split times form race performances. If you feel significantly strong in one sport and want to train a little more in your weaker sports, then make small adjustments to these recommendations.

Determine the best weekly pattern, or distribution of training for each week by using the examples from worksheet 3.6 and the blank form provided in appendix A.

Appendix B.1
Sprint to Olympic Distance Triathlon

1 Four-week cycle	1				2				3			
2 Training stage	BASE				BASE				INTENSITY			
Week numbers	1 – 4				5 – 8				9 – 12			
3 Actual dates												
4 % of year hours	7				8				9			
5 Hours/cycle												
Week number	1	2	3	4	5	6	7	8	9	10	11	12
6 Periodization	23	26	29	22	23	26	29	22	23	26	29	22
7 Hours/week												

8 Below: Percent per 4-week cycle for each SERIOUS component

	Cycle 1	Cycle 2	Cycle 3
Speed	0	0	5
Endurance	15	15	15
Race/pace	0	0	0
Intervals	0	5	10
Overdistance	60	55	50
Up/vertical	5	5	10
Strength	20	20	10

9 Below: Multiply total minutes per week of each SERIOUS component by the designated percentage for each sport activity

Speed
Swim @ 0%
Bike @ 50%
Run @ 50%

Endurance
Swim @ 20%
Bike @ 50%
Run @ 30%

Race/pace
Swim @ 20%
Bike @ 50%
Run @ 30%

Intervals
Swim @ 35%
Bike @ 35%
Run @ 30%

Overdistance
Swim @ 20%
Bike @ 50%
Run @ 30%

Up/vertical
Swim @ 0%
Bike @ 60%
Run @ 40%

Strength

268

1	Four-week cycle	4				5				6			
2	Training stage	INTENSITY				PEAK/RACE				RACE			
	Week numbers	13 – 16				17 – 20				21 – 24			
3	Actual dates												
4	% of year hours	9.5				8.5				8			
5	Hours/cycle												
	Week number	13	14	15	16	17	18	19	20	21	22	23	24
6	Periodization	20	30	20	30	20	30	20	30	20	30	20	30
7	Hours/week												
8	Below: Percent per 4-week cycle for each SERIOUS component												
	Speed	5				5				5			
	Endurance	15				15				10			
	Race/pace	5				10				15			
	Intervals	10				10				10			
	Overdistance	45				50				50			
	Up/vertical	10				0				0			
	Strength	10				10				10			
9	Below: Multiply total minutes per week of each SERIOUS component by the designated percentage for each sport activity												

Speed
Swim @ 0%
Bike @ 50%
Run @ 50%

Endurance
Swim @ 20%
Bike @ 50%
Run @ 30%

Race/pace
Swim @ 20%
Bike @ 50%
Run @ 30%

Intervals
Swim @ 35%
Bike @ 35%
Run @ 30%

Overdistance
Swim @ 20%
Bike @ 50%
Run @ 30%

Up/vertical
Swim @ 0%
Bike @ 60%
Run @ 40%

Strength

Appendix B.2

Half-Ironman to Ironman Distance Triathlon

1 Four-week cycle	1				2				3			
2 Training stage	BASE				BASE				INTENSITY			
Week numbers	1 – 4				5 – 8				9 – 12			
3 Actual dates												
4 % of year hours	7.5				8.5				9.5			
5 Hours/cycle												
Week number	1	2	3	4	5	6	7	8	9	10	11	12
6 Periodization	23	26	29	22	23	26	29	22	23	26	29	22
7 Hours/week												

8 Below: Percent per 4-week cycle for each SERIOUS component

Speed	0				0				0			
Endurance	15				10				10			
Race/pace	0				0				0			
Intervals	0				5				5			
Overdistance	65				60				60			
Up/vertical	0				5				10			
Strength	20				20				15			

9 Below: Multiply total minutes per week of each SERIOUS component by the designated percentage for each sport activity

Speed
Swim @ 0%
Bike @ 50%
Run @ 50%

Endurance
Swim @ 20%
Bike @ 50%
Run @ 30%

Race/pace
Swim @ 20%
Bike @ 50%
Run @ 30%

Intervals
Swim @ 35%
Bike @ 35%
Run @ 30%

Overdistance
Swim @ 20%
Bike @ 50%
Run @ 30%

Up/vertical
Swim @ 0%
Bike @ 60%
Run @ 40%

Strength

1 Four-week cycle			4			5				6			
2 Training stage			INTENSITY			PEAK/RACE				RACE			
Week numbers			13 – 16			17 – 20				21 – 24			
3 Actual dates													
4 % of year hours			10			8.5				8			
5 Hours/cycle													
Week number		13	14	15	16	17	18	19	20	21	22	23	24
6 Periodization		20	30	20	30	20	30	20	30	20	30	20	30
7 Hours/week													

8 Below: Percent per 4-week cycle for each SERIOUS component

	4	5	6
Speed	0	0	0
Endurance	10	15	15
Race/pace	5	10	15
Intervals	10	15	15
Overdistance	60	50	50
Up/vertical	5	0	0
Strength	10	10	5

9 Below: Multiply total minutes per week of each SERIOUS component by the designated percentage for each sport activity

Speed
  Swim @ 0%
  Bike @ 50%
  Run @ 50%
Endurance
  Swim @ 20%
  Bike @ 50%
  Run @ 30%
Race/pace
  Swim @ 20%
  Bike @ 50%
  Run @ 30%
Intervals
  Swim @ 35%
  Bike @ 35%
  Run @ 30%
Overdistance
  Swim @ 20%
  Bike @ 50%
  Run @ 30%
Up/vertical
  Swim @ 0%
  Bike @ 60%
  Run @ 40%
Strength

Appendix B.3
Sprint to Medium Distance Duathlon

1	Four-week cycle	1				2				3			
2	Training stage	BASE				BASE				INTENSITY			
	Week numbers	1 – 4				5 – 8				9 – 12			
3	Actual dates												
4	% of year hours	7				8				9			
5	Hours/cycle												
	Week number	1	2	3	4	5	6	7	8	9	10	11	12
6	Periodization	23	26	29	22	23	26	29	22	23	26	29	22
7	Hours/week												

8 Below: Percent per 4-week cycle for each SERIOUS component

	Cycle 1	Cycle 2	Cycle 3
Speed	0	0	5
Endurance	15	15	15
Race/pace	0	0	0
Intervals	0	5	10
Overdistance	60	55	50
Up/vertical	5	5	10
Strength	20	20	10

9 Below: Multiply total minutes per week of each SERIOUS component by the designated percentage for each sport activity

Speed Bike @ 50% Run @ 50%												
Endurance Bike @ 60% Run @ 40%												
Race/pace Bike @ 60% Run @ 40%												
Intervals Bike @ 60% Run @ 40%												
Overdistance Bike @ 60% Run @ 40%												
Up/vertical Bike @ 60% Run @ 40%												
Strength												

1 Four-week cycle	4				5				6			
2 Training stage	INTENSITY				PEAK/RACE				RACE			
Week numbers	13 – 16				17 – 20				21 – 24			
3 Actual dates												
4 % of year hours	9.5				8.5				8			
5 Hours/cycle												
Week number	13	14	15	16	17	18	19	20	21	22	23	24
6 Periodization	20	30	20	30	20	30	20	30	20	30	20	30
7 Hours/week												

8 Below: Percent per 4-week cycle for each SERIOUS component

Speed	5				5				5			
Endurance	15				15				10			
Race/pace	5				10				15			
Intervals	10				10				10			
Overdistance	45				50				50			
Up/vertical	10				0				0			
Strength	10				10				10			

9 Below: Multiply total minutes per week of each SERIOUS component by the designated percentage for each sport activity

Speed
Bike @ 50%
Run @ 50%

Endurance
Bike @ 60%
Run @ 40%

Race/pace
Bike @ 60%
Run @ 40%

Intervals
Bike @ 60%
Run @ 40%

Overdistance
Bike @ 60%
Run @ 40%

Up/vertical
Bike @ 60%
Run @ 40%

Strength

Powerman Long Course Duathlon

	Four-week cycle		1				2				3		
2	Training stage		BASE				BASE				INTENSITY		
	Week numbers		1 – 4				5 – 8				9 – 12		
3	Actual dates												
4	% of year hours		7.5				8.5				9.5		
5	Hours/cycle												
	Week number	1	2	3	4	5	6	7	8	9	10	11	12
6	Periodization	23	26	29	22	23	26	29	22	23	26	29	22
7	Hours/week												

8 Below: Percent per 4-week cycle for each SERIOUS component

Speed	0		0	0
Endurance	15		10	10
Race/pace	0		0	0
Intervals	0		5	5
Overdistance	65		60	60
Up/vertical	0		5	10
Strength	20		20	15

9 Below: Multiply total minutes per week of each SERIOUS component
by the designated percentage for each sport activity

Speed
Bike @ 50%
Run @ 50%
Endurance
Bike @ 60%
Run @ 40%
Race/pace
Bike @ 60%
Run @ 40%
Intervals
Bike @ 60%
Run @ 40%
Overdistance
Bike @ 60%
Run @ 40%
Up/vertical
Bike @ 60%
Run @ 40%
Strength

1 Four-week cycle	\multicolumn 4				5				6			
2 Training stage	INTENSITY				PEAK/RACE				RACE			
Week numbers	13 – 16				17 – 20				21 – 24			
3 Actual dates												
4 % of year hours	10				8.5				8			
5 Hours/cycle												
Week number	13	14	15	16	17	18	19	20	21	22	23	24
6 Periodization	20	30	20	30	20	30	20	30	20	30	20	30
7 Hours/week												

8 Below: Percent per 4-week cycle for each SERIOUS component

Speed	0				0				0			
Endurance	10				15				15			
Race/pace	5				10				15			
Intervals	10				15				15			
Overdistance	60				50				50			
Up/vertical	5				0				0			
Strength	10				10				5			

9 Below: Multiply total minutes per week of each SERIOUS component by the designated percentage for each sport activity

Speed
Bike @ 50%
Run @ 50%

Endurance
Bike @ 60%
Run @ 40%

Race/pace
Bike @ 60%
Run @ 40%

Intervals
Bike @ 60%
Run @ 40%

Overdistance
Bike @ 60%
Run @ 40%

Up/vertical
Bike @ 60%
Run @ 40%

Strength

Mountain Bike Cross-Country Racing

1	Four-week cycle	1				2				3					
2	Training stage	BASE				BASE				INTENSITY					
	Week numbers	1 – 4				5 – 8				9 – 12					
3	Actual dates														
4	% of year hours	7				8				9					
5	Hours/cycle														
	Week number	1	2	3	4	5	6	7	8	9	10	11	12		
6	Periodization	23	26	29	22	23	26	29	22	23	26	29	22		
7	Hours/week														

8 Below: Percent per 4-week cycle for each SERIOUS component

Speed	0	0	5
Endurance	15	15	15
Race/pace	0	0	5
Intervals	0	5	10
Overdistance	60	50	45
Up/vertical	5	10	10
Strength	20	20	10

9 Below: Multiply total minutes per week of each SERIOUS component by the designated percentage for each sport activity

Speed
On-road @ 60%
Off-road @ 40%

Endurance
On-road @ 60%
Off-road @ 40%

Race/pace
Road bike time
trials @ 0-25%
Off-road @ 75-100%

Intervals
Bike @ 60%
Run @ 40%

Overdistance
Bike @ 60%
Run @ 40%

Up/vertical
Bike @ 60%
Run @ 40%

Strength

1 Four-week cycle	4				5				6			
2 Training stage	INTENSITY				PEAK/RACE				RACE			
Week numbers	13 – 16				17 – 20				21 – 24			
3 Actual dates												
4 % of year hours	9.5				8.5				8			
5 Hours/cycle												
Week number	13	14	15	16	17	18	19	20	21	22	23	24
6 Periodization	20	30	20	30	20	30	20	30	20	30	20	30
7 Hours/week												

8 Below: Percent per 4-week cycle for each SERIOUS component

Speed	5	5	5
Endurance	10	10	10
Race/pace	10	10	15
Intervals	10	5	5
Overdistance	45	50	50
Up/vertical	10	10	10
Strength	10	10	5

9 Below: Multiply total minutes per week of each SERIOUS component by the designated percentage for each sport activity

Speed
On-road @ 60%
Off-road @ 40%

Endurance
On-road @ 60%
Off-road @ 40%

Race/pace
Road bike time
trials @ 0-25%
Off-road @ 75-100%

Intervals
Bike @ 60%
Run @ 40%

Overdistance
Bike @ 60%
Run @ 40%

Up/vertical
Bike @ 60%
Run @ 40%

Strength

Cycling—Time Trials, Criteriums, and Road Racing

1 Four-week cycle		1				2				3			
2 Training stage		BASE				BASE				INTENSITY			
Week numbers		1 – 4				5 – 8				9 – 12			
3 Actual dates													
4 % of year hours		7				8				9			
5 Hours/cycle													
Week number		1	2	3	4	5	6	7	8	9	10	11	12
6 Periodization		23	26	29	22	23	26	29	22	23	26	29	22
7 Hours/week													

8 Below: Percent per 4-week cycle for each SERIOUS component

	1	2	3
Speed	0	0	5
Endurance	15	15	15
Race/pace	0	0	5
Intervals	0	5	10
Overdistance	60	50	45
Up/vertical	5	10	10
Strength	20	20	10

9 Below: Multiply total minutes per week of each SERIOUS component by the designated percentage for each sport activity

Speed

Endurance

Race/pace

Intervals

Overdistance

Up/vertical

Strength

1 Four-week cycle	4				5				6			
2 Training stage	INTENSITY				PEAK/RACE				RACE			
Week numbers	13 – 16				17 – 20				21 – 24			
3 Actual dates												
4 % of year hours	9.5				8.5				8			
5 Hours/cycle												
Week number	13	14	15	16	17	18	19	20	21	22	23	24
6 Periodization	20	30	20	30	20	30	20	30	20	30	20	30
7 Hours/week												

8 Below: Percent per 4-week cycle for each SERIOUS component

Speed	5				5				5			
Endurance	10				10				10			
Race/pace	10				10				15			
Intervals	10				5				5			
Overdistance	45				50				50			
Up/vertical	10				10				10			
Strength	10				10				5			

9 Below: Multiply total minutes per week of each SERIOUS component by the designated percentage for each sport activity

Speed

Endurance

Race/pace

Intervals

Overdistance

Up/vertical

Strength

5 to 15 km Road Racing

1	Four-week cycle	1				2				3			
2	Training stage	BASE				BASE				INTENSITY			
	Week numbers	1 – 4				5 – 8				9 – 12			
3	Actual dates												
4	% of year hours	7				8				9			
5	Hours/cycle												
	Week number	1	2	3	4	5	6	7	8	9	10	11	12
6	Periodization	23	26	29	22	23	26	29	22	23	26	29	22
7	Hours/week												

8 Below: Percent per 4-week cycle for each SERIOUS component

Speed	0	0	5
Endurance	15	15	15
Race/pace	0	0	5
Intervals	0	10	10
Overdistance	60	50	45
Up/vertical	5	5	5
Strength	20	20	15

9 Below: Multiply total minutes per week of each SERIOUS component by the designated percentage for each sport activity

Speed

Endurance

Race/pace

Intervals

Overdistance

Up/vertical

Strength

1	Four-week cycle	4				5				6			
2	Training stage	INTENSITY				PEAK/RACE				RACE			
	Week numbers	13 – 16				17 – 20				21 – 24			
3	Actual dates												
4	% of year hours	9.5				8.5				8			
5	Hours/cycle												
	Week number	13	14	15	16	17	18	19	20	21	22	23	24
6	Periodization	20	30	20	30	20	30	20	30	20	30	20	30
7	Hours/week												

8 Below: Percent per 4-week cycle for each SERIOUS component

Speed	5				5				5			
Endurance	15				15				15			
Race/pace	5				10				15			
Intervals	10				10				10			
Overdistance	45				50				50			
Up/vertical	5				0				0			
Strength	15				10				5			

9 Below: Multiply total minutes per week of each SERIOUS component by the designated percentage for each sport activity

Speed

Endurance

Race/pace

Intervals

Overdistance

Up/vertical

Strength

Marathon Running

1 Four-week cycle		1				2				3			
2 Training stage		BASE				BASE				INTENSITY			
Week numbers		1 – 4				5 – 8				9 – 12			
3 Actual dates													
4 % of year hours		7.5				8.5				9.5			
5 Hours/cycle													
Week number	1	2	3	4	5	6	7	8	9	10	11	12
6 Periodization	23	26	29	22	23	26	29	22	23	26	29	22
7 Hours/week												

8 Below: Percent per 4-week cycle for each SERIOUS component

Speed	0	0	0
Endurance	15	15	15
Race/pace	0	0	5
Intervals	0	10	10
Overdistance	60	50	50
Up/vertical	5	5	5
Strength	20	20	15

9 Below: Multiply total minutes per week of each SERIOUS component by the designated percentage for each sport activity

Speed

Endurance

Race/pace

Intervals

Overdistance

Up/vertical

Strength

1 Four-week cycle	4				5				6			
2 Training stage	INTENSITY				PEAK/RACE				RACE			
Week numbers	13 – 16				17 – 20				21 – 24			
3 Actual dates												
4 % of year hours	10				8.5				8			
5 Hours/cycle												
Week number	13	14	15	16	17	18	19	20	21	22	23	24
6 Periodization	20	30	20	30	20	30	20	30	20	30	20	30
7 Hours/week												

8 Below: Percent per 4-week cycle for each SERIOUS component

	4	5	6
Speed	0	0	0
Endurance	15	15	15
Race/pace	5	10	15
Intervals	10	15	10
Overdistance	50	55	55
Up/vertical	5	0	0
Strength	15	5	5

9 Below: Multiply total minutes per week of each SERIOUS component by the designated percentage for each sport activity

Speed

Endurance

Race/pace

Intervals

Overdistance

Up/vertical

Strength

Appendix B.9

5 to 15 km Cross-Country Skiing Races
(can also be used for in-line skating and rowing)

1 Four-week cycle	1				2				3			
2 Training stage	BASE				BASE				INTENSITY			
Week numbers	1 – 4				5 – 8				9 – 12			
3 Actual dates												
4 % of year hours	7				8				9			
5 Hours/cycle												
Week number	1	2	3	4	5	6	7	8	9	10	11	12
6 Periodization	23	26	29	22	23	26	29	22	23	26	29	22
7 Hours/week												

8 Below: Percent per 4-week cycle for each SERIOUS component

Speed	0	0	5
Endurance	15	15	15
Race/pace	0	0	0
Intervals	0	5	5
Overdistance	60	55	50
Up/vertical	5	5	10
Strength	20	20	15

9 Below: Multiply total minutes per week of each SERIOUS component by the designated percentage for each sport activity

Speed
Classic skiing @ 35%
Freestyle skiing @ 35%
Running & other sports @ 30%

Endurance
Classic skiing @ 35%
Freestyle skiing @ 35%
Running & other sports @ 30%

Race/pace
Classic skiing @ 50%
Freestyle skiing @ 50%

Intervals
Classic skiing @ 35%
Freestyle skiing @ 35%
Running & other sports @ 30%

Overdistance
Classic skiing @ 35%
Freestyle skiing @ 35%
Running & other sports @ 30%

Up/vertical
Classic skiing @ 35%
Freestyle skiing @ 35%
Running & other sports @ 30%

Strength

1 Four-week cycle	\multicolumn 4				5				6			
2 Training stage	INTENSITY				PEAK/RACE				RACE			
Week numbers	13 – 16				17 – 20				21 – 24			
3 Actual dates												
4 % of year hours	9.5				8.5				8			
5 Hours/cycle												
Week number	13	14	15	16	17	18	19	20	21	22	23	24
6 Periodization	20	30	20	30	20	30	20	30	20	30	20	30
7 Hours/week												

8 Below: Percent per 4-week cycle for each SERIOUS component

Speed	5	5	5
Endurance	10	15	10
Race/pace	5	10	15
Intervals	10	5	10
Overdistance	45	50	50
Up/vertical	10	5	0
Strength	15	10	10

9 Below: Multiply total minutes per week of each SERIOUS component by the designated percentage for each sport activity

Speed
Classic skiing @ 35%
Freestyle skiing @ 35%
Running & other sports @ 30%

Endurance
Classic skiing @ 35%
Freestyle skiing @ 35%
Running & other sports @ 30%

Race/pace
Classic skiing @ 50%
Freestyle skiing @ 50%

Intervals
Classic skiing @ 35%
Freestyle skiing @ 35%
Running & other sports @ 30%

Overdistance
Classic skiing @ 35%
Freestyle skiing @ 35%
Running & other sports @ 30%

Up/vertical
Classic skiing @ 35%
Freestyle skiing @ 35%
Running & other sports @ 30%

Strength

15 to 50+ km Cross-Country Skiing Races

1 Four-week cycle		1				2				3			
2 Training stage		BASE				BASE				INTENSITY			
Week numbers		1 – 4				5 – 8				9 – 12			
3 Actual dates													
4 % of year hours		7.5				8.5				9.5			
5 Hours/cycle													
Week number		1	2	3	4	5	6	7	8	9	10	11	12
6 Periodization		23	26	29	22	23	26	29	22	23	26	29	22
7 Hours/week													

8 Below: Percent per 4-week cycle for each SERIOUS component

	1	2	3
Speed	0	0	5
Endurance	15	15	15
Race/pace	0	0	0
Intervals	0	5	5
Overdistance	60	55	50
Up/vertical	5	5	10
Strength	20	20	15

9 Below: Multiply total minutes per week of each SERIOUS component by the designated percentage for each sport activity

Speed
Classic skiing @ 35%
Freestyle skiing @ 35%
Running & other sports @ 30%

Endurance
Classic skiing @ 35%
Freestyle skiing @ 35%
Running & other sports @ 30%

Race/pace
Classic skiing @ 50%
Freestyle skiing @ 50%

Intervals
Classic skiing @ 35%
Freestyle skiing @ 35%
Running & other sports @ 30%

Overdistance
Classic skiing @ 35%
Freestyle skiing @ 35%
Running & other sports @ 30%

Up/vertical
Classic skiing @ 35%
Freestyle skiing @ 35%
Running & other sports @ 30%

Strength

1 Four-week cycle	4				5				6			
2 Training stage	INTENSITY				PEAK/RACE				RACE			
Week numbers	13 – 16				17 – 20				21 – 24			
3 Actual dates												
4 % of year hours	10				8.5				8			
5 Hours/cycle												
Week number	13	14	15	16	17	18	19	20	21	22	23	24
6 Periodization	20	30	20	30	20	30	20	30	20	30	20	30
7 Hours/week												

8 Below: Percent per 4-week cycle for each SERIOUS component

	4	5	6
Speed	5	5	5
Endurance	10	15	10
Race/pace	5	10	15
Intervals	10	5	10
Overdistance	50	50	50
Up/vertical	10	5	0
Strength	10	10	10

9 Below: Multiply total minutes per week of each SERIOUS component by the designated percentage for each sport activity

Speed
Classic skiing @ 35%
Freestyle skiing @ 35%
Running & other sports @ 30%

Endurance
Classic skiing @ 35%
Freestyle skiing @ 35%
Running & other sports @ 30%

Race/pace
Classic skiing @ 50%
Freestyle skiing @ 50%

Intervals
Classic skiing @ 35%
Freestyle skiing @ 35%
Running & other sports @ 30%

Overdistance
Classic skiing @ 35%
Freestyle skiing @ 35%
Running & other sports @ 30%

Up/vertical
Classic skiing @ 35%
Freestyle skiing @ 35%
Running & other sports @ 30%

Strength

Cross-Training Multisport Fitness

1	**Four-week cycle**	colspan 1			2				3					

		1	2	3
1	Four-week cycle	1	2	3
2	Training stage	BASE	BASE	INTENSITY
	Week numbers	1 – 4	5 – 8	9 – 12
3	Actual dates			
4	% of year hours	7	8	8
5	Hours/cycle			

	Week number	1	2	3	4	5	6	7	8	9	10	11	12
6	Periodization	23	26	29	22	23	26	29	22	23	26	29	22
7	Hours/week												

8 Below: Percent per 4-week cycle for each SERIOUS component

	1	2	3
Speed	0	0	0
Endurance	15	15	20
Race/pace	0	0	0
Intervals	0	5	5
Overdistance	60	55	50
Up/vertical	5	5	5
Strength	20	20	20

9 Below: Multiply total minutes per week of each SERIOUS component by the designated percentage for each sport activity

Speed
 Sport #1
 Sport #2
 Sport #3
Endurance
 Sport #1
 Sport #2
 Sport #3
Race/pace
 Sport #1
 Sport #2
 Sport #3
Intervals
 Sport #1
 Sport #2
 Sport #3
Overdistance
 Sport #1
 Sport #2
 Sport #3
Up/vertical
 Sport #1
 Sport #2
 Sport #3
Strength

1 Four-week cycle	4				5				6			
2 Training stage	INTENSITY				PEAK/RACE				RACE			
Week numbers	13 – 16				17 – 20				21 – 24			
3 Actual dates												
4 % of year hours	8				8.5				8			
5 Hours/cycle												
Week number	13	14	15	16	17	18	19	20	21	22	23	24
6 Periodization	20	30	20	30	20	30	20	30	20	30	20	30
7 Hours/week												

8 Below: Percent per 4-week cycle for each SERIOUS component

Speed	0				0				0			
Endurance	20				20				20			
Race/pace	0				0				0			
Intervals	5				10				10			
Overdistance	50				50				50			
Up/vertical	5				0				0			
Strength	20				20				20			

9 Below: Multiply total minutes per week of each SERIOUS component
by the designated percentage for each sport activity

Speed
Sport #1
Sport #2
Sport #3
Endurance
Sport #1
Sport #2
Sport #3
Race/pace
Sport #1
Sport #2
Sport #3
Intervals
Sport #1
Sport #2
Sport #3
Overdistance
Sport #1
Sport #2
Sport #3
Up/vertical
Sport #1
Sport #2
Sport #3
Strength

Appendix C

DETERMINING LACTATE THRESHOLD BY NON-INVASIVE MEANS

In chapter 2, we mentioned the concept of anaerobic threshold (AT; synonymous with lactate threshold, or LT) training, equal to level four on the heart-rate intensity scale. AT training, or threshold training, has become a very popular concept. The scientist perhaps most noted for his techniques for determining the AT is Italian physician and physiologist Francesco Conconi, who developed a method for measuring an endurance athlete's AT by non-invasive means (i.e., without taking blood samples).

As described in chapter 2, level four intensity training is intended to be synonymous with AT training. It is exercising at or slightly below the intensity that causes rubbery legs and arms; changes in ventilation from rhythmic and deep to shallow and erratic; and the subjective feeling that if you push any harder, you will probably "go under." It is very important that you learn to recognize what if feels like to be at the AT.

Using threshold training for a certain percentage of your total training volume will stimulate your body to adapt to going at hard intensities. You will increase your $\dot{V}O_2max$. Most importantly, you will increase the percentage of your $\dot{V}O_2max$ that you can effectively use before the onset of the debilitating effects of lactic acid buildup and burning. In other words, you will improve your ability to maintain a fast pace.

You may be asking, "How do I find my own AT pace or heart rate?" Subjectively, you can focus on how your legs and arms feel, the rhythm of your breathing, and your overall body feeling when doing intervals or race/pace workouts. Try to distinguish the feelings of staying within the aerobic zone and going beyond it into anaerobic exercise. Another method is to use the test Conconi, as many cyclists, skiers, and runners are doing, to determine your

AT heart rate and pace. The test Conconi will give you objective information about heart rate and pace at AT, as well as all the subjective physiological and psychological cues that indicate you are at your threshold.

THE TEST CONCONI FOR RUNNERS, SKIERS, AND TRIATHLETES

Caution: Make sure you are in good health before you try this test.

Necessary Equipment

You'll need a reliable heart-rate monitor (preferably one that uses a chest strap transmitter and wristwatch receiver, which are extremely reliable and accurate) and two assistants—one equipped with a stopwatch, a notebook, several copies of worksheet C.1, and a pencil; the second equipped with a bicycle set up with a cycle computer that reads speed in kilometers per hour (miles per hour is okay if that's all you have). Find a 200-meter indoor track with a surface smooth enough for a cyclist to ride comfortably. (Outdoor tracks may be used, but since wind is a variable, you'll have to do the test on a completely windless day.)

First, measure and mark one section of track 50 meters in length (for a 400-meter track, mark two 50-meter sections exactly 200 meters apart). Use cones or flags to mark the beginning and end of each 50-meter section so that the assistant can see them from the middle of the infield of the track.

Starting the Test

You'll be running behind the bicycling assistant around the track for each lap, so the cyclist must maintain even speed throughout each lap. Speed will be increased by a half kilometer per hour every 200 meters. After a proper 20- to 30-minute warm-up, start the test by following the cyclist at a pace that is comfortable at a heart rate intensity of level two.

After each 200-meter segment (marked by the second cone in the 50-meter section), the cyclist increases the pace by a half kilometer per hour and maintains the new pace for the entire lap. (If you are doing the test without the assistance of a cyclist pace, increase your running speed by about 5 seconds per kilometer.)

Your second assistant must time the final 50 meters of each 200-meter section so that your actual running speed in kilometers per hour can be determined. If you feel the cycle computer is accurate and that you are staying an even distance behind the bike, you can simply record the speed indicated by the cycle computer, which the cyclist can give to the recording assistant after each lap. Each time you pass the end of the marked 50 meters, call out your heart rate. Your assistant will record that figure next to the time for that 50-meter section. Continue this pattern until you feel that you have passed the AT and that your heart rate is no longer increasing as fast as your speed. You'll be running quite fast at this point.

THE TEST CONCONI FOR CYCLISTS

Necessary Equipment

As in the running test, you'll need a heart-rate monitor and an assistant. You'll also need a bike computer that measures speed and cadence. Ideally, the test is performed on a velodrome, but you can use a wind trainer to do the test indoors.

Starting the Test

After warming up for 15 to 30 minutes, start riding the first of 10 to 15 laps or intervals. Each lap should measure between 300 to 450 meters. If you are using a wind trainer, use an appropriate time for each interval (between 30 to 50 seconds per 400 meters). You need to use a moderately large gear for the duration of the test. Be sure to ride in the racing position. Maintain a constant pace during each lap. (Start at 10 mph or less if you are a beginner.) Increase your speed by 1 mph for each lap until the fatigue and burning in your legs make it impossible to continue. As you pass you assistant at the end of each lap, call out your heart rate so it can be recorded.

CALCULATING THE AT

Now come the data analysis and calculation of your AT. Calculate your running speed from the time per 50-meter section (if you

Data Sheet for Recording Heart Rate and Speed for Test Conconi

Name _____ Date _____

Loop#	Heart rate	Time (sec/50m)	Speed (kph)
1			
2			
3			
4			
5			
6			
7			
8			
9			
10			
11			
12			
13			
14			
15			
16			
17			
18			

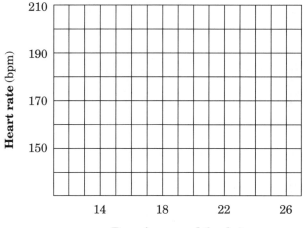

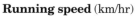

Running speed (km/hr)

cycled, you already know the speed for each lap). On the graph in worksheet C.1, plot your heart rate on the vertical axis and your speed on the horizontal axis. Theoretically, if the test went as planned, your graph should show an evenly sloping line—until the point at which your heart rate does not increase linearly relative to your speed. The speed at that point, as indicated by the "knee" in the graph, is where you reached your AT as illustrated in figure C.1. Conconi calls this point the V_d (velocity of deflection) and considers the heart rate and speed at this point to be the AT.

INTERPRETING THE AT

Now that you know your AT, what do you do with it? Every SERIOUS training plan systematically incorporates level four intensity or AT training. Each interval, uphill interval, and race/pace workout should be accomplished at 5 to 10 beats per minute below the AT heart rate. Over the course of the training plan, you should gradually increase the percentage of AT training. In theory, the AT itself will increase, occurring at a higher percentage of your $\dot{V}O_2$max, and your $\dot{V}O_2$max will also rise. Your race/pace at threshold will also improve, enabling you to cover the same distance in less time at the same intensity.

A word to the wise about the test Conconi. (I've experienced a few glitches in using this test.) First, if you're running on a track with a strong headwind on one side, your graph will look rather uneven. Second, be sure that the increase in speed with each 200 meters is systematic—that's why running behind a cyclist with a cycle computer is so helpful. If you are pacing yourself, increase your speed ever so slightly and consistently between laps. Third, be sure that your assistant starts and stops the clock precisely when you cross the marks at the beginning and end of the 50-meter section. Otherwise you may get inaccurate times. The ideal place to do this test is on an indoor track.

TESTING FREQUENCY

How often should you take the test Conconi? If logistically feasible, you can use the test every two to four weeks to check your AT during the intensity stage. If everything is going according to the theory and plan, your AT will increase gradually, and you'll be

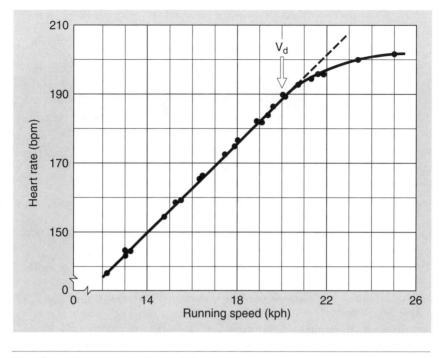

Fig. C.1. Heart rate and speed for test Conconi.

able to use each new heart rate and pace to train for intervals, uphill intervals, and race/pace. If your AT pace and heart rate decrease, it could be a sign of overtraining. Before jumping to conclusions, look at your training log to monitor all the other stress symptoms.

Although the test Conconi may be useful to many, much controversy surrounds the test and even the very notion of anaerobic threshold. Exercise physiologists are bound to continue their research and produce new arguments about this subject. Meanwhile, I encourage you to try the test Conconi—or at least tune-in to your AT feelings when you train. In any case, remember that the essential aspect of level four training is that you are training hard enough but not so hard that your exercise quickly becomes anaerobic.

Bibliography

Alter, M. (1990). *Sport stretch*. Champaign, IL: Human Kinetics.

Anderson, R. (1980). *Stretching*. Bolinas, CA: Shelter Publications.

Asmussen, E., & Boje, O. (1960). Body temperature and capacity for work. *Acta Physiologica Scandinavica*, *49*, 67.

Åstrand, P.O., & Rohdahl, K. (1977). *Textbook of work physiology*. New York: McGraw-Hill.

Barnard, R.J. (1973). Ischemic response to sudden strenuous exercise in healthy men. *Circulation, 158*, 936-942.

Bergh, U. (1981). *The physiology of cross-country ski racing*. Champaign, IL: Human Kinetics.

Bergstrom, J., Hermansen, L., Hultman, E., & Saltin, B. (1967). Diet, muscle glycogen and physical performance. *Acta Physiologica Scandinavica, 71,* 140-150.

Blom, P., Vaage, O., & Kardel, K. (1980). The effect of increasing glucose loads on the rate of glycogen resynthesis after prolonged exercise. *Acta Physiologica Scandinavica, 108*, C11.

Brick, M. (1995). *Precision multi-sport*. New York: Polar Electro Oy.

Brody, J. (1981). *Jane Brody's nutrition book*. New York: W.W. Norton.

Brody, J. (1985). *Jane Brody's good food book*. New York: W.W. Norton.

Conconi, F., Ferrari, M., Ziglio, P.G., Droghetti, P., & Codeca, L. (1982). Determination of the anaerobic threshold by a noninvasive field test in runners. *Journal of Applied Physiology, 52*, 869-873.

Costill, D.L. (1979). *A scientific approach to distance running*. Los Altos, CA: Track and Field News Press.

Costill, D.L. (1986). *Inside running: Basics of sports physiology*. Dubuque, IA: Brown & Benchmark.

Costill, D.L., & Miller, J.M. (1980). Nutrition for endurance sport: Carbohydrate and fluid balance. *International Journal of Sports Medicine, 1*, 2-14.

Costill, D.L., & Saltin, B. (1975). Muscle glycogen and electrolytes following exercise and thermal dehydration. *Metabolic adaptations to prolonged physical exercise* (pp. 352-360). Basel, Switzerland: Birkhauser Verlag.

Costill, D.L., Thomas, R., Roberts, R.A., Pascoe, D., Lambert, C., Darr, G., & Fink, W.K. (1991). Adaptations to swimming training: Influence of training volume. *Medicine and Science in Sports and Exercise, 23*(3), 371-377.

Curtis, J.D. (1989). *The mindset for winning*. La Crosse, WI: Coulee Press.

deVries, H.A. (1959). Effects of various warm up procedures on 100-yard times of competitive swimmers. *Research Quarterly, 30,* 11-20.

Duncan, D.J. (1983). *The river Why.* New York: Bantam.

Edwards, S. (1994). *The heart rate monitor book.* New York: Polar Electro Oy.

Ellsworth, N.A., Hewitt, B.F., & Haskell, W.L. (1985). Nutrient intake of elite male and female Nordic skiers. *The Physician and Sportsmedicine, 13,* 79-92.

Fink, W. (1982). Fluid intake for maximizing athletic performance. In W. Haskell (Ed.), *Nutrition and athletic performance* (p. 76). Palo Alto, CA: Bull.

Gollnick, P.D. (1985). Metabolism of substrates: Energy substrate metabolism during exercise and as modified by training. *Federation Proceedings, 44,* 353-357.

Holloszy, J., & Booth, F. (1976). Biochemical adaptations to endurance exercise in muscle. *Annual Review of Physiology, 38,* 273.

Houmard, J., & Anderson Johns, R. (1994, April). Effects of taper on swim performance. *Sports Medicine* (Auckland, New Zealand), *17,* 224-232.

Houmard, J., Johns, R., Smith, L., Wells, J., Kobe, R., & McCoggan, G. (1991). The effect of warm up on responses to intense exercise. *International Journal of Sports Medicine, 12(5),* 400-403.

Houmard, J., Scott, B., Justice, C., & Chenier, T. (1994). The effects of taper on performance in distance runners. *Medicine and Science in Sports and Exercise, 26(5),* 624-631.

Janssen, P.G. (1987). *Training, lactate, pulse rate.* Oulu, Finland: Polar Electro Oy.

Karvonen, J. (1978). *Warming up and its physiological effects.* Unpublished doctoral dissertation, University of Oulu, Finland.

Karvonen, J. (1992). Importance of warm up and cool down on exercise performance. In J. Karvonen (Ed.), *Medicine in sports training and coaching.* Dasel, Germany: Karger Publishers.

Koivisto, V., Hendler, R., & Nadel, E. (1982). Influence of physical training on the fuel-hormone response to prolonged low intensity exercise. *Metabolism, 31,* 192.

Lamb, D.R., & Murray, R. (Eds.). (1988). *Perspectives in exercise science and sports medicine: Vol. 1. Prolonged exercise.* Indianapolis, IN: Benchmark Press.

Lamb, D.R., & Williams, M.H. (Eds.). (1991). *Perspectives in exercise science and sports medicine: Vol. 4. Ergogenics—Enhancement of performance in exercise and sport.* Indianapolis, IN: Benchmark Press.

Macaraeg, P. (1983). Influence of carbohydrate electrolyte ingestion on running endurance. In E.L. Fox (Ed.), *Nutrient utilization during exercise* (pp. 91-98). Columbus, OH: Ross Laboratories.

McArdle, W.D., Katch, F.I., & Katch, V.L. (1991). *Exercise physiology: Energy, nutrition, and human performance.* Malvern, PA: Lea & Febiger.

O'Connor, F.G., Gobel, J.R., & Nirschi, R.P. (1992). Five step treatment of overuse injuries. *The Physician and Sportsmedicine, 20(10),* 120-142.

O'Connor, P.J., & Morgan, W.P. (1990). Athletic performance following rapid traversal of multiple time zones: A review. *Sports Medicine* (Auckland, New Zealand), *10(1),* 20-30.

Orlick, T. (1986). *Psyching for sport*. Champaign, IL: Leisure Press.

Pearl, B., & Moran, G.T. (1986). *Getting stronger*. Bolinas, CA: Shelter Publications.

Phaigh, R., & Perry, P. (1984). *Athletic massage*. New York: Simon and Schuster.

Phinney, D., & Carpenter, C. (1992). *Training for cycling: The ultimate guide for improved performance*. New York: Perigree.

Radcliffe, J.C., & Farentinos, R.C. (1985). *Plyometrics: Explosive power training*. Champaign, IL: Human Kinetics.

Robinson, S. (1963). Temperature regulation in exercise. *Pediatrics, 32*, 691-702.

Seaward, B. (1994). *Managing stress*. Boston: Jones & Bartlett.

Sharkey, B.J. (1984). *Training for cross-country ski racing*. Champaign, IL: Human Kinetics.

Sherman, W.M., Costill, D.L., Fink, W.J., & Miller, J.M. (1981). Effects of exercise-diet manipulation on muscle glycogen and its subsequent utilization during performance. *International Journal of Sports Medicine, 2*, 1-15.

Shevciw, T. (1986, February). Regeneration alternatives in high performance sport. *Science Periodical on Research and Technology in Sport*, 1-8.

van Mechelen, W. (1992). Running injuries: A review of the epidemiological literature. *Sports Medicine* (Auckland, New Zealand), *14(5)*, 320-335.

Wilmore, J.H. (1982). *Athletic training and physical fitness*. Boston: Allyn and Bacon.

Yessis, M. (1986, July). Recovery. *Science Periodical on Research and Technology in Sport, 2*.

Index

customization of, 199-201
Training volumes, 67, 69
Training year
  number of weeks for, 65-66
  overview of, 5-6
  planning of, 63-70
Travel, management of, 213-217

U

Uphill intervals/vertical training
  definition of, 108-109
  and intensity, 28-29
  workouts for, 123-127, 128-129

V

Vaage, O., 164
Vacations, 61
Vasa Swim Ergometer, 14
Vasa Trainer, 10, 110, 129
Vision, and achievement, 238-239
VO$_2$max
  and AT (anaerobic threshold), 28,
    105
  and endurance, 100
  and exercise stress test, 37-39
  and heart rate variations, 32-34
  and intensity, 25
  and lactic acid accumulation, 29
  and overdistance, 107-108

W

Walking, and restoration, 186
Warm-up
  checklist for, 138-139
  physiology of, 134-136
  psychology of, 136
  and year hours, 72, 74

Weekly patterns, adjustments to, 86
Weight machines, 10
Williams, M.H., 153
Work demands, 212
Worksheets
  character of four-week cycle, 74-76
  intensity levels with Karvonen
    method, 41
  percent of training components per
    four-week cycle, 77, 78
  spreadsheet training plan for year,
    77, 79, 84-85
  spreadsheet with percentages each
    sport, 80-81, 87-88
  training zones from stress test, 40
  weekly pattern of four-week cycles,
    81-83, 89-90
  for year hours, 71-74

Y

Year hours
  for ability level, 70 table 3.5
  ceiling on, 69
  definition of, 56
  determination of, 66-67
  for endurance events, 70 table 3.5
  fine-tuning volume of, 219-220
  percent recommended increase of,
    68 table 3.4
  and warm-up, 72, 74
  worksheet for, 71-74
Yessis, M., 183

Z

Ziglio, P.G., 44

About the Authors

Rob Sleamaker has trained and coached endurance athletes for almost 20 years. He earned his MS in exercise physiology from the University of Arizona in 1982. From 1983 to 1986, Rob was director of sports medicine for the U.S. Biathlon Team. He has also worked with the U.S. Cross Country Ski Team.

Since 1986 Rob has operated SportsAdvantage, which provides personalized sport and fitness training systems to individuals, as well as computer software for the sports and fitness industry. He owns VASA, Inc., a company he started in 1988 that makes the VASA trainer and a swim ergometer used internationally by leading swimmers, triathletes, surfers, and other athletes. Rob also writes frequently for major sports and fitness magazines on training for endurance sports.

Ray Browning is a seven-time Ironman Triathlon winner and the 1993 World Champion in the Mountain Man Winter Triathlon. Ray also holds an MS in kinesiology from UCLA. One of the foremost experts on cross-training, he regularly speaks to groups about the benefits and process of cross-training for fitness and sport conditioning.

Since 1988 Ray has used the SERIOUS training system to prepare for professional competitions. In 1993 he became a national-level cross-country skier. Browning is also a contributing editor for *Inside Triathlon* magazine.

304